MEDITERRANEAN
◇ COOKING ◇

OTHER BOOKS BY PAULA WOLFERT

The Cooking of South-West France
Couscous and Other Good Food from Morocco
Paula Wolfert's World of Food
The Cooking of the Eastern Mediterranean

For Nicholas Bato and Leila

MEDITERRANEAN COOKING

REVISED WITH 75 NEW RECIPES

PAULA WOLFERT

THE ECCO PRESS

THE ECCO PRESS
100 West Broad Street
Hopewell, New Jersey 08525
Published simultaneously in Canada by
Penguin Books Canada Ltd., Ontario
Printed in the United States of America

Some of the Italian and Greek recipes have previously been
published in slightly different form in the CBS International
Dining series, written and edited by the author.

The recipe for *Marmelade de pêches* is from *French Provincial
Cooking* by Elizabeth David. Copyright © 1960 by Elizabeth
David. It is reprinted by permission of Harold Ober Associates,
Incorporated.

Portions of this book have appeared in somewhat different form
in *Eating Well, Connoisseur, Cuisine, Food & Wine, Mirabella,*
the *Washington Post,* and the *New York Times.*

Designed by Joel Avirom
Design Assistant: Meghan Day Healey

FIRST EDITION

Library of Congress Cataloging-in-Publication Data

Wolfert, Paula.
    Mediterranean cooking / by Paula Wolfert. — Rev. ed.
      p.   cm.
    Includes bibliographical references and index.
    1. Cookery, Mediterranean.   I. Title.
TX725.M35W64   1994   94-8088
641.59182′2—dc20   CIP
ISBN 0-88001-402-4

94 95 96 97 98 RRD/DX 10 9 8 7 6 5 4 3 2 1

The text of this book is set in ITC Galliard

CONTENTS

INTRODUCTION TO THE REVISED EDITION

In the sixteenth century, a native of the Mediterranean, wherever he might come from, would never feel out of place in any part of the sea. To later colonial settlers their journey simply meant finding in a new place the same trees and plants, the same food on the table that they had known in their homeland; it meant living under the same sky, watching the same familiar seasons.

—Fernand Braudel

There's something special about the Mediterranean that draws people like me to want to live around it. I used to think it was the clarity of the light—luminous, strong, direct—that makes everything look sharp and intense. There was a time when I shuttled back and forth between Tangier and New York (the two poles of my existence for eighteen years), that I began to look upon it as a refuge from our North Atlantic culture, a repository of a life-style both sensual and humane.

Humanism was born around the Mediterranean, and to a diminishing extent still pervades Mediterranean lands. Architecture there is on a human scale. One lives for satisfaction and finds it in simple things. The scramble for money, status, and fame becomes irrelevant in an olive grove. After living there a while one finds oneself gentled. What better place, it seemed to me, to drop out of the rat race and seek solace in clean air, good humor, love, culture, and delicious food.

That was my Mediterranean myth, the inspiration for the original edition of this book. At that time, in the early 1970s, I was deeply concerned about the environmental degradation taking place along Mediterranean shores and the blurring of national cultures and regional cultures. I wrote, in my introduction, a kind of swan song for the Mediterranean life I was then living. My words were tinged heavily with regret.

Happily, it has turned out, I was wrong. Mediterranean cooking is, I am pleased to report, very much alive. I underestimated the pull of age-old culinary traditions and the longings of Mediterranean peoples to regain and recapture their identities. Simple authentic Mediterranean dishes are all the rage today. Anthropologists, medical scientists, and food writers study them. Better still, urban people have rediscovered and revived them.

You could always find a fine bouillabaisse in Marseilles and a superb pizza in Naples, but in Athens it was becoming difficult to find a good *avgolemono* soup, and in Spain a decent restaurant *paella* was a rarity. Now, nearly twenty years later, I find in almost every region (including those most favored by tourists) sincere attempts to revive regional traditions and wonderful, simple Mediterranean home cooking.

In Spain, there are *cotijos,* or ranches, turned into small hotels that accept paying guests who wish to experience real Andalusian life. There are *auberges de fermes* in France where you can lunch with a farmer and his family. In rural Italian villages, you will find family restaurants featuring home-style dishes, while resort hotels all over the Mediterranean frequently offer regional cooking festivals. Best of all, Mediterranean peoples have aroused their governments to save their fragile environments and to control tourism in order to preserve their region's spirit and "soul."

In preparing this new edition, I've tried to reflect this revived interest in simple country cooking, as well as all we've learned in the intervening years about good nutrition and the virtues of the "Mediterranean Diet."

Much has been written about this latter subject. A mystique has grown up around it. Even as I write, the Harvard School of Public Health, jointly with Oldways Preservation and Exchange Trust, and the World Health Organization regional office for Europe, is preparing a new "food pyramid" to demonstrate the results of numerous studies of how Mediterranean people eat.

Put very simply, the healthy Mediterranean diet relies heavily on green and yellow vegetables, grains, beans, lentils, fruits, spices, herbs, and nuts. In numerous regional Mediterranean recipes, meat is often used as a condiment—in vegetable stews, stuffed vegetables, and pilafs. Fish and seafood are frequently eaten, while red meat dishes are minimized. Olive oil is used as a cooking medium and also as a principal source of calories. Meals are often accompanied by a glass of red wine, and often a simple main dish will contain enough nourishing ingredients to constitute a meal in itself. Since most Mediterranean countries employ the tradition of first courses, or *mezze,* proper Mediterranean meals are usually well balanced.

The Mediterranean diet is not perfect. Controversies rage. And there are plenty of delicious traditional Mediterranean dishes that for reasons of health should probably not be eaten too often. This has been a spur to my revisions.

In all, I have removed approximately sixty recipes, including such savory concoctions as salt cod mousse served in puff pastry shells with poached eggs and hollandaise; a French dish of chicken, sausage, and bacon baked in a pie; chicken smothered in cheese sauce; a *bourride des pecheurs* enriched with six eggs; and other extremely rich preparations.

I have replaced these sixty with more than seventy-five new recipes representing the kind of food I personally eat today. Along with the recipes in my other books about the area, this revision represents, to my mind at least, some of the best of what the Mediterranean has to offer in terms of health as well as taste.

You will now find fewer northern and central Italian recipes, not because I no longer care for these dishes, but because with so many excellent Italian cookbooks available, their inclusion seems redundant. In their place I offer some terrific, far less-known dishes from the Italian region of Apulia, the heel of the Italian "boot."

One region previously neglected was Spain. My Catalan favorites are in *World of Food;* here I concentrate on Andalusia. Even though I knew this region for three decades, it had been years since I tasted its food at the source. I returned to rediscover its cooking along the so-called route of white pueblas, which runs through such dazzling, craggy, fortified towns as Ronda, Grazalema, Castellar de la Frontera, and Arcos de la Frontera. I ate in restaurants great and humble, and in people's homes. I worked with cooks and interviewed food writers and scholars researching the brilliant Andalusian culinary heritage. The experience was enriching, sometimes overwhelming, but by its conclusion I felt I understood the essential character of Andalusian cooking and the major historical and geographical themes that shaped it.

You will also find here new dishes from Provence and Turkey and, in fairly great quantity, Tunisia. Since there is no English-language book on Tunisian cookery and since I believe it to be a truly impressive cuisine—assertive, pungent, and often very spicy—I have tried to cover it here in some depth, offering, for example, several truly marvelous and previously unpublished couscous recipes collected on three extensive field trips.

The original Tunisians were Berbers, known for their simple good cooking. (It is believed they invented couscous.) Over the centuries numerous other culinary forces were brought to bear on this land—Phoenician, Roman, Arab, Turkish, Moorish, French—bringing recipes and techniques that melded together into a strong, vivid, colorful, and extremely tasty national cuisine.

Ever since hot red peppers were introduced to the Mediterranean, Tunisians have adored them and used them more than any other nation in the region. Fiery peppers play a role in almost every dish, usually in form of the famous *harissa* paste. And the love of heat is not confined to red peppers. In southern Tunisia, a couscous is regarded as naked without a final topping of fried green chilies.

I have reduced the number of chef's recipes, replacing them with simple, authentic family dishes, such as a simple, foolproof, and utterly delicious home method of double-marinating quail. Finally, I have dropped instructions for labor-intensive tasks such as the preparation of fresh pasta, now that excellent fresh pasta sheets are widely available. Most recipes here are easy to prepare; a few take a good deal of time. I like to make complicated dishes once in a while, when I can cook quietly without distraction, but I want a good payoff in taste and satisfaction for my efforts. I have tried to apply this test to all the recipes that might be characterized as "demanding."

Superb Mediterranean ingredients in fresh and plentiful supply are still very much in evidence in sun-drenched Mediterranean markets. Ingredients, I have always believed, are the key to Mediterranean food, and thus the organization of this book.

One can discuss Mediterranean food in terms of courses (appetizers, entrées, desserts, etc.), or in terms of national schools. But it seems more appropriate, and also more Mediterranean, to organize the dishes in terms of key flavors and tastes: the fresh aromas of wild herbs; the tang of lemons and oranges; the soft textures of dates and persimmons; the striking and often unexpected combinations of pomegranates and walnuts or lavender and olives. Eggplants, tomatoes, and peppers; chick-peas, lentils, and beans; yogurt and cheese; pasta, couscous, and figs —these are the things that Mediterranean food is all about. In the diversity of ingredients lies the unity. These ingredients constitute the bounty of the Mediterranean, the stuff of which its cuisines are built.

The Mediterranean Sea has always been a medium of cultural exchange, and its culinary glories a great result. In a long history of occupations and conquests, food ideas have crossed national boundaries and stuck when they were good. Half of the region, from the former Yugoslavia in the east to Algiers in the west, shows the strong culinary influence of the Turks. Moorish cooking impacts upon the food of southern Spain; Catalonia interacts with Languedoc and Provence; and then there is Italy, not unified until the time of Cavour, a land of regions, each with its own style of cooking, showing traces of Turkey (in Venice), North Africa (in Sicily), Spain (in Sardinia), France (in Naples), and nearly everything else. For this reason, there are still a good number of Italian recipes in this book.

In any event, I ought to confess that I have not sought to write a balanced book. I've made no attempt to give equal due to different national schools, or to present a balance between hors d'oeuvres, main courses, and desserts. My criteria have been completely different, and it might be well to list them now.

In the main, I am still interested in four things: great and famous dishes for which I can find superb recipes (my *pistou marseillaise,* for example—I've never seen a recipe for *pistou* written this way, nor eaten one nearly as good); regional and unusual dishes (so long as they are delicious) such as *tiella,* an Apulian casserole of mussels, potatoes, and tomatoes—simple to assemble, earthy and rustic in aroma, yet difficult to get right since, with so few ingredients, nothing can be compromised; dishes that illustrate contrasting or similar uses of the same materials (an endless fascination around the Mediterranean, allowing one to move about at will and probe cross-cultural connections); and delicious dishes that are not widely known.

This last task was the most difficult, since there have been so many books about Mediterranean food. But still I found wonderful things in regions not well covered in culinary literature. As an example, try the easy-to-prepare Tunisian vegetarian winter couscous, which includes all sorts of greens, including fennel, parsley, celery, and, if the cook wishes, carrot tops.

This is a personal book, a book of food that interests me, many dishes that I prepare daily for my family. I still have an old-world respect for traditional dishes, properly made with the proper ingredients, learned from Mediterranean women who prepare them. The hospitality these women offer remains one of my greatest pleasures. Around the Mediterranean, eating and sharing are indivisible.

This revised edition reflects a sampling of my taste in Mediterranean food as it can be prepared in an American kitchen. I've come to realize that it would take me five lifetimes to fully cover the Mediterranean dishes that attract me. So many fascinating recipes! So many from-the-heart home cooks! My field trips have become such an important part of my life, I can't imagine ever giving them up. I love travel, learning new languages and dialects, making contacts, hearing about recipes, then tracking them down to little villages where I meet the cook acknowledged by her peers as the one who executes the particular dish best. Recipes represent the way people live, their relation to their heritage and their land. The women who have taught me recipes have, in the process, revealed intimate aspects of their lives. To the many Mediterranean women (and men) who have helped me over the years, I want to offer again my affection and my gratitude.

Before I thank the many individuals who have assisted me along the way, I want once again to tip my hat to my favorite food writer, whom, I'm sorry to say, I never met personally but knew only through her work. I am speaking of the late Elizabeth David, author of many excellent cookbooks, whose classic *A Book of Mediterranean Food* is still for me the most inspiring of all the numerous Mediterranean cookbooks that have been written.

AND NOW FOR THANKS:

First, to my wonderful husband, Bill Bayer, who is also my best friend.

Special thanks to Simonetta Ponzone-Lanza of Brussels, and the late Mario Ruspoli of Paris. Also: Tony May, of the San Domenico Restaurant in New York; Francesca Baldeschi-Balleani; Maria Theresa Silvestri; Camillo Guerra; and Faith Willinger, who gave me so much help and advice on Italian cuisine.

For Greek recipes I want to thank: Aglaia Kremezi, Rosemary Barron, George Karamalis, Nina Vranopoulos, and Olga Thomas.

For Spanish recipes I want to thank: Elena Spencer, Ana Aranda, Sra. Soledad Gil, Marguerite Valdespino, Marisel Persilla, Rosa Grace, the Nunez de Prado family, and Loli Martinez y Fernandez.

For Turkish recipes: Ayfer Ünsal, Nevin Halici, Hakki Anli, Filiz Hösukoğlu, and Jetta Balkan.

On Tunisian food: Ahmed Laribi, Safia Hamadi, Leila El Mansour, Souad Faouzi, Mahzeria Ghaddour, Saleh and Lynn Hannachi, Jamila Hannachi, Mona Hannachi, Aziza ben Tanfous, Elias and Mona Kasri, Miriam Sebti, Najiba Chanmmakhi, Ouled-Abdessayed Khamais, Naima Touitti, and Abdelrazak Haouari.

Radoje Prica and Emilia Jovanovic taught me much about Yugoslav cooking.

Claude Thomas, Kathy Jelen, Annie Magnard, and Jacqueline Pacquant helped with French recipes, as did an old modest friend who asked me simply to call her "Tante Vivienne."

On Lebanese, Syrian, Druse, and Jordanian cooking I owe thanks to: Imam Najjar; Wahad Fakhreddine, Ammeh Fakhry, Maha Abdul Majeed, and "Madame A." of Beirut.

In Tangier many friends helped: Marie Emilie de Troostemburgh; Sarah Scoville; Kate Bouveau; the late Orford St. John; the late Madeleine van Breughel; and my constant helper in the kitchen, Fatima benLahsen Riffi.

In the United States for help in preparing this revised edition: my agent, Susan Lescher, and my editor, Susan Friedland. My warmest thanks for generous help and advice to: Arlene Wanderman, Suzanne Hamlin, Patricia Jamieson, Arthur Schwartz, Jeffrey Steingarten, Nancy Harmon Jenkins, Molly O'Neill, and Richard Sullivan. Special laurels to the team at Oldways Preservation and Exchange Trust, for encouraging me to "rethink the center of the plate."

Newtown, Connecticut
June 1994

MEDITERRANEAN
◈ COOKING ◈

GARLIC AND OIL

Once upon an afternoon in Tangier, Morocco, where I first lived in 1959, I found myself invited by a friend to taste a wild boar's head. I accepted—without a moment's hesitation!

My friend's husband had shot the boar near the mountain town of Chaouen. The carcass was hung for a few days, then soaked in a marinade. When I arrived I found my friend in the act of opening her oven door to tuck a large sprig of fresh rosemary beneath the wild pig's jaw. The head had been roasting the entire morning and the skin was already crusty and brown. As I peered in to look, the marvelous aroma of garlic hit me full in the face.

She'd prepared the head by rubbing it with salt, pepper, some chopped parsley, a half dozen cloves of garlic, and plenty of olive oil. She'd also started a sauce, simmering three heads of garlic, then pressing them through a sieve. She added some olive oil to the pulp, and then seasoned the sauce with nothing but salt and pepper.

I had never eaten a boar's head before. I found it delicious, due, I think, to the garlic sauce as well as the garlic and oil rubbed into the flesh. Matter of fact, it was the first time that I ever ate so much garlic in my life. It was then that I first understood the triumph of raw produce transformed by gastronomy.

This elixir, the blending of garlic and oil into a sauce, belongs, in the words of the American food writer Richard Olney, "to the realm of voluptuous experience." This immersion into the divine mysteries of garlic and olive oil began a quest that has lasted thirty-five years.

Pungent, heady, and earthy garlic is the essential Mediterranean flavoring and rich, clean, and fruity olive oil is the great medium for cooking. When the two are combined in a creamy suspension, something sublime is born. It is, I think, one of the great discoveries in culinary history: the amazing procedure of pounding cloves of garlic with a pinch of salt in a mortar to a thin purée, and then dribbling in olive oil, while continuing to pound or stir always in one direction for fear of collapse.

Many nations claim this invention, even the Emperor Nero took credit. It has been attributed to the ancient Athenians, too. I suspect it was invented much earlier, somewhere right in southeastern Turkey in what was once ancient Assyria at the sight of the earliest olive groves, those found along the Euphrates River.

Botanists tell us that garlic is originally from Asia. It came to the Mediterranean region via the trade and silk routes that passed through these very olive groves on to Egypt where we know it was used to help fortify the workers who built the pyramids. I can only speculate that my favorite emulsion was born there. With one of man's earliest kitchen tools—the mortar and pestle—and only two ingredients.

When describing sauces, early Roman, Greek, and Islamic writings rarely include garlic. I asked Phyllis Bober, professor of archeology at Bryn Mawr College, who told me that the earliest description of an actual emulsion of garlic and olive oil is found in the Appendix Vergiliana, Moretum, where a peasant is described making his breakfast of garlic cheese by pounding garlic, blending in soft cheese, herbs, celery, and parsley, and then stirring in olive oil. This most likely could be a forerunner to pesto, she said.

Maybe I shouldn't be so concerned with who is first in this pairing. What's important is that this discovery led to a great chain of Mediterranean creations.

The Romans brought this concept of a cheese, garlic, and olive oil emulsion to Mediterranean Spain, where the Catalans eventually created various forms of their pungent condiment, *ali-oli*. Since *ali-oli* easily separates, many Catalan cooks use an egg yolk to stabilize and also enrich it. Sometimes the egg is omitted and a little honey is used to balance the pungency of the garlic before serving the sauce with lamb, goat, or rabbit grilled over an open fire. At other times, cooked and puréed quince and apples are used as a stabilizer instead of an egg.

The great Andalusian dish, *gazpacho,* fundamental to that region's culinary identity, also has its roots in this ancient combination of garlic and olive oil. Although present-day versions could not have been made before the discovery of America and the importation of peppers and tomatoes, the first *gazpacho* is very old, as old as its ingredients—bread, garlic, oil, and vinegar. Later, with the arrival of the Moors and the expanded cultivation of the almond tree, the dish evolved into the sublime *gazpacho blanco* we know today.

The Byzantines, centered in Constantinople, used garlic lavishly, eating it raw when young and tender, or as a vegetable, roasting it in the oven, then crushing it with olive oil and salt. The Byzantines called their version *skordo.* And in medieval France, especially in the southwest, they were making a glorious pink-hued garlic and olive oil sauce that they stabilized with walnuts and called *aillade.*

Now, let us take a little tour around the contemporary Mediterranean and see this brilliant gastronomic concept in action.

Starting in the part of France called Provence, we find *aïoli,* rich in egg yolks. It has great cultural mystique when served on New Year's Eve in the center of a large presentation of fish and vegetables. All who eat the *aïoli* will have good luck throughout the coming year. Red pepper and fish entrails, crushed with garlic and olive oil, make the delicious *rouille,* which is stirred into a *bouillabaisse* to make it hardy, rich, and noble.

Moving on to the Italian Riviera, we find *agliata*—a breadcrumb-vinegar-garlic combination thickened by beating in olive oil. The Ligurians add it to vegetable soups. And, of course, we find the king of pasta sauces, *pesto,* with its luxuriant, herbal splendor, sharpened by the addition of freshly grated pecorino cheese.

Salsa verde, popular throughout Italy, is another olive oil–based sauce made with an addition of garlic, anchovies, capers, and herbs. It makes a delicious accompaniment to paper-thin slices of raw beef.

On the island of Sicily we find *salmoriglio,* a sauce of extra-virgin olive oil beaten with lemon juice, herbs, salt, and garlic.

And along the Dalmatian coast we find a strange green-tinted olive oil–garlic sauce for fish. Its special green color derives from the addition of pickled cucumbers.

Moving on to Greece, we find the modern version of the Byzantine *skordo,* made without egg yolks but thickened with mashed potatoes or soaked bread and, sometimes, crushed nuts. Now they call it *skordalia* and serve it with fried cod or stewed wild greens. Cooks in Macedonia simply dilute this garlic-oil mixture with water, which they call *tsioula,* making a simple soup for dipping bread.

In southeastern Turkey, in the olive groves surrounding the town of Kilis not far from the Euphrates, I found a regional cookbook that described a very old Anatolian soup. Cloves of garlic are fried in olive oil, then set aside. A little water is added to the oil and brought to a boil, then poured over pieces of stale bread. Meanwhile, garlic and dried mint are pounded to a pulp in a mortar and then stirred into the mixture. This they called *tirit.*

Along the Turkish coast, there is a delicious garlic and oil emulsion called *tarator*—a rich sauce thickened with mashed walnuts or hazelnuts. Some Turkish cooks, preferring a more delicate sauce, make it with almonds; still others create a resinous flavor by adding pine nuts.

In a modern Turkish cookbook, I read of many different ways one can use this sensually rich, subtly flavored sauce—with cooked favas, with zucchini, with cauliflower, with spinach stems and roots, with cooked mottled beans and scallions, with boiled potatoes, with fried eggplant, with green beans flavored with savory, with shredded lettuce, or with the addition of more oil on raw purslane.

In Syria, I found home cooks who were whipping garlic and oil into a creamy texture without any stabilizing agent at all, calling it simply *zeit bil toom,* or oil with garlic. They would add just a drop of lemon juice for sharpness and serve it along with grilled kabobs. *Zeit bil toom* doesn't hold up very long but it is a tour de force—thick as whipped cream. In Syria's northern city of Aleppo there is a fine restaurant owned by Armenians where they make a red-hued garlic-oil marinade for meats. The Wanes Restaurant in the elegant Azizie quarter serves almost all its meats bathed with this oil made red with food coloring.

In Damascus, local chick-pea houses, called *hamsani,* serve a "white" oil. An emulsion made of cold water, baking soda, garlic, and chilled olive oil that is poured over crisp pita and cooked chick-peas, the dish is made by men and served at card games. It is easy enough to whip up while someone shuffles.

In Amman, fresh coriander is pounded with garlic and mounted with oil to make a "green" oil for dipping kebabs. And in Egypt, a simple garlic-oil marinade is used for small birds such as quails that will be grilled in the open air.

In Tunisia, where food tends to be rich and spicy, there is a bowl of piquant *harissa* sauce—a pounded paste of hot pepper, ground caraway, garlic, and oil— inevitably placed on the table for dipping bread.

Algerians along the coast use a garlic-oil emulsion, called *scabetch,* to preserve fried fish.

In Morocco, olive oil is blended with garlic, cumin, paprika, fresh coriander, and parsley for a pungent marinade called *charmoula,* but don't confuse this with the creamy onion-based Tunisian one.

Having moved full circle around the Mediterranean, we arrive at the straits of Gibraltar and at the Catalan-speaking island of Minorca. Conventional wisdom has it that Richelieu brought a version of *ali-oil* from Minorca to Paris. It was the eighteenth century, the time of *haute cuisine,* and the chefs of that era were appalled by the pungency of the garlic. The chefs removed it, but retained the egg-oil concept and used the resulting sauce as an edible glue for their *pièces montées.* This mixture was called "mayonnaise," named after the city of Mahon on Minorca.

Whether or not this story is apocryphal, it has a certain charm. And it is certainly consistent with the culinary snobbery of Paris vis-à-vis other less "subtle" cuisines. But, in time, a good thing will triumph! Recently a well-known French chef exclaimed to me: "Before the combination of garlic and olive oil one should fall to one's knees in admiration!"

Superb olive oil is so basic to Mediterranean cooking (as an ingredient, flavor enhancer, and cooking medium) that I use it almost exclusively in my everyday cooking: stewing, grilling, oven roasting and pan-frying. To make a *skordalia,* the garlic sauce from Greece, I use a mildly fruity Greek oil. For a Spanish garlic and bread soup, I serve a fine extra-virgin Spanish oil in a cruet or glass bottle, to be added by each diner at the table.

Extra-virgin olive oil is especially delicious when used to cook the diminu-tively scaled foods served before a meal around the Mediterranean: Spanish *tapas;* Turkish, Greek, and Arab *mezzes;* Italian *antipasti;* North African *kemia.* Of all oils, only olive oil gives such dishes a delicious flavor and enhances the natural taste. Sometimes it is difficult to know which kind of olive oil to use. As a general rule, I deep-fry and stew with olive oil; season salads and cold dishes with extra-virgin; and use unfiltered oil for "baptizing" food after it has been cooked.

Unfiltered oil usually comes from hand-picked olives that are crushed by huge granite stones, and the oil contains tiny olive particles. This so-called flower of the oil is uniquely fragrant and delicious.

The flavor of a good olive oil is difficult to define: It can be fruity and peppery or delicate and mild, with a fresh bouquet that the so-called neutral ground nut oils cannot duplicate. Some oils have a nutty flavor or a buttery sensation on the taste buds. Others are heady and richly flavored.

Generally speaking, the central Italian region of Tuscany produces an oil that is complex with a peppery finish. The Italian Riviera produces an oil that is more subtle and delicate. Neighboring Umbria produces an earthier and less piquant oil. Southern Italian and Lebanese oil can be very strong with an even more intense olive taste. North African oil is golden, limpid, and "round," with all its flavors in harmony. French oil is light and flowery. Greek oil is fruity, strongly flavored, deep-scented, and rich. Spanish oils are also fruity and aromatic. One from Catalonia smells faintly of fresh almonds. Let your own taste be your guide. In a world of so many possibilities, there is no right choice.

The color of olive oil can vary from a pale straw hue to an emerald green, depending upon the variety of olive used and the time when the olives were picked.

For thirty-five years I'd been roaming the Mediterranean and tasting olive oils for my own pleasure. Recently I was visiting Andalusia and staying a couple of miles south of the spectacular walled town of Arcos de la Frontera, where there was a grouping of postcard-perfect, bougainvillea-covered whitewashed buildings set in an olive grove. While walking the grounds, I noticed the words *Oleum Effusem Nomen Tuum*" carved over the entrance to the courtyard. Later I asked Señora Soledad, the proprietor, what they meant. "Literally," she explained, "the words mean 'May Your Name Spread Like Oil.' You see, at one time this property was owned by the church, and even then olive oil was produced here. So they made an analogy between the way oil covers everything and spreading the word of God."

Señora Soledad paused a moment to reflect. Then she added, "That may tell you just how important olive oil is to our lives . . ."

A HEALTH NOTE ON OLIVE OIL

"Olive oil," Sicilians say, "makes all your aches and pains go away." Many people around the Mediterranean believe this and they may have a point!

Olive oil is high in monounsaturated fats. Recent studies have shown that consuming olive oil reduces the so-called bad LDL-cholesterol in your blood, while leaving the so-called good HDL-cholesterol alone, thus increasing the beneficial ratio between the two. Canola oil, on the other hand, which is higher in polyunsaturated fats than olive oil, reduces *both* the HDL and LDL in your blood, and does not widen that important ratio. While canola has the least amount of total saturated fat of any oil, it has twice as much saturated fat of dietary significance as olive oil.

Most kinds of canola oil are extracted from rapeseed with the aid of chemical solvents that must be expressed at high temperatures, whereas olive oil is made from olives that are picked, washed, pressed, and decanted. Canola oil has a shelf life of less than a year and is not very stable, whereas olive oil has a much longer shelf life, is very stable, and can be consumed without any processing.

Mediterranean peoples whose principal dietary fat is olive oil have protection against heart disease and also lower levels of breast and bowel cancers, although we don't know if it's the antioxidants in olives or the monounsaturated character of the oil—or even if the lack of saturated fat—that creates these health benefits.

Skordalia
Garlic sauce (Greece)

There is a saying in Greece: "A young bride should be able to make a *skordalia* sauce you can smell a kilometer away!"

There are many ways to make *skordalia*: with mashed potatoes or with bread and nuts. I very much like this traditional, pungent version combining almonds, garlic, olive oil, vinegar, and bread.

Skordalia should be absolutely smooth. You can make it in a wooden mortar or in a food processor.

The Greeks serve it with fried eggplant or zucchini, batter-fried salt cod, baked or poached fish, boiled beets, batter-fried mussels, or cold hard-boiled eggs.

MAKES ½ CUP, SERVING 2

> 2 small garlic cloves
> Coarse salt
> 2 thick slices stale white bread with crusts removed
> ¼ cup almonds, blanched and heated in a dry skillet to bring up flavor
> 2½ teaspoons white vinegar, or more to taste
> ¼ cup olive oil
> 1 to 2 tablespoons hot water (optional)

1. Peel the garlic, discard the green shoot, and crush with ¼ teaspoon salt in a wooden mortar until puréed.

2. Soak the bread in warm water for a few minutes and squeeze dry. Reserve ⅓ packed cup.

3. Place garlic and almonds in a food processor. With the machine on, gradually add the bread, processing until smooth. Add the vinegar alternately with the oil in a slow steady stream until the sauce is thick and smooth. Thin with water, if desired.

Taramosalata
Fish roe purée (Greece)

It is almost impossible today to find quality burnished orange fish roe, or *tarama,* even in Greece. Thus the famous roe dip, *taramosalata,* has deteriorated to the point where one often finds it gussied up with herbs and aromatics, and sometimes looking like some weird sort of strawberry cream.

The real thing, fragrant with lemon and olive oil, should be blushing orange, light and ethereal on the tongue, tasting truly of the sea. It should melt in your mouth, smell fresh, and be very light. The very best *taramosalata* I ever tasted was in Istanbul where the chef added a pinch of sugar to the mixture.

To obtain an airy *taramosalata,* use an electric beater instead of the food processor. In this version, the addition of tart drained yogurt eliminates the need for much lemon juice. The thickener of choice is crumbled bread, though some cooks used mashed potatoes, drained ricotta cheese, or a mixture of the two.

The roe of choice is gray mullet, but it is difficult to find. Most likely you will be using carp roe, which is readily available. It must be desalted, easily done under cool running water. Even with these caveats, this is an easy dish to make, delicious with thick crusty bread.

MAKES ABOUT 4 CUPS, SERVING 12

> 10 ounces carp roe *tarama*
> 2 tablespoons grated onion, rinsed and drained (see note)
> 3 tablespoons fresh lemon juice
>   Pinch of sugar
>   About 8 thick slices of stale firm white bread, crusts removed
> 1 cup milk
> 12 tablespoons extra-virgin olive oil
> 1 cup drained nonfat yogurt
>   Black olives, for garnish

1. To remove the salt, wrap the tarama in cheesecloth and set under running cold water for 5 minutes. Press out moisture, unwrap, and place in the bowl of an electric mixer. Add the onion, lemon juice, and sugar and beat on low speed until smooth.

(continued)

2. Meanwhile, soak the bread in the milk and squeeze dry; you should have 1½ cups. Gradually add the crumbled bread to the mixing bowl and continue beating, slowly adding the olive oil, as if making a mayonnaise. Beat for 10 minutes, or until the mixture is smooth and fluffy. Remove the bowl from the machine and gently fold in the yogurt. Correct the seasoning. Refrigerate for about 1 hour before serving. Decorate with black olives.

Notes: If using a food processor, process the tarama, onion, lemon juice, and sugar until smooth. With the machine running, alternately add the bread and the oil. Turn into a mixing bowl, fold in the yogurt, and correct the seasoning.

To rinse and drain onion, grate a small onion, place it in a sieve, and set under running water for an instant. Squeeze out excess moisture. Use a fork to fluff up the onions before measuring 2 tablespoons.

═══

MULLET ROE

One of the most delicious products made with mullet roe is *avgotaraho*, similar to Sicilian *bottarga* made with tuna roe. Dried and pressed roe is allowed to go hard until it turns a reddish brown. In Missolonghi, in central Greece, these hard roe "cakes" are packed in creamy wax tubes. A Christmas specialty, they are served simply in thin slices with a squirt of lemon.

If you travel to Salonika or Athens, search out a good delicatessen and purchase a pair of tubes of *avgotaraho*—its special flavor is delightful. All you have to do is break the wax and scrape off the thin membrane.

Try it on thinly sliced buttered bread with a drop of lemon juice or, even better, prepare it in the Sicilian manner by tossing thin slivers with spaghetti, sliced garlic, chopped parsley, freshly ground pepper, lemon juice, and olive oil. Sensational!

═══

Anchoïade

Anchovy oil canapés (France)

This is a modern version of an ancient traditional dish. In the classic version, anchovies that had been put up in brine were soaked, cleaned, filleted, and placed in an earthenware jar. They were covered with oil and a few drops of lemon juice or vinegar, then spiced with pepper. The jug was placed near a wood-burning stove until, after many hours, a rich thick creamy sauce was obtained. It was then spread on bread. Now there are many modern variations, including the famous one from Provence called *anchoïade de Croze,* which includes chopped figs, red peppers, and walnuts.

SERVES 4, MAKES 20 CANAPÉS

- 5 slices of stale firm white bread, trimmed, toasted, and cut into 4 squares
- 1 2-ounce can flat anchovy fillets, rinsed and drained
- ½ teaspoon finely chopped garlic
- 1 tablespoon finely chopped scallion
- 1 tablespoon finely chopped fresh parsley
- 1 teaspoon lemon juice
  Freshly ground black pepper
  Pinches of cayenne
- 3 tablespoons olive oil

1. Arrange the toasted squares side by side on a baking sheet.

2. Mash the anchovy fillets to a purée; add garlic, scallion, parsley, lemon juice, pepper, and cayenne, mixing well. Beat in the olive oil teaspoon by teaspoon. The anchovy mixture should be thick and creamy.

3. Spread a small spoonful on each bread square. Let stand 30 minutes. The bread will soak up the oil.

4. Preheat the oven to 425 degrees.

5. Set the toast in the hot oven for 10 minutes. Serve hot with drinks.

Note: This sauce can be stirred into Provençal fish soups instead of *sauce rouille* (see page 16).

Calamares en su Tinta #1

Squid in its own ink with garlic and almonds (Spain)

◘

This inky black sauced dish of squid is rich and full of garlic (seven cloves). It makes an excellent *tapa,* or can be served as a main course over rice. (See page 85 for another version with tomato sauce.)

SERVES 4 AS A MAIN COURSE, 6 AS A *TAPA*

  2 pounds squid
  ½ cup whole almonds
  2 tablespoons chopped parsley
  7 garlic cloves, peeled
  2 1-inch slices of Italian-style bread, soaked in water and squeezed dry
  ⅓ cup olive oil
  2 cups dry white wine
  1 cup water
     Salt
     Freshly ground black pepper
     Boiled rice

1. Clean the squid. Remove the sac from the head and set aside the tentacles. Peel off the outer mottled skin and discard the entrails and the thin bone. Put the ink sacs in a sieve set over a small bowl. Wash the squid, inside and out, and the tentacles under cold running water; cut into bite-size pieces.

2. Chop the almonds, then pound them in a mortar with the parsley, garlic, and bread. Fry this paste in oil for 2 to 3 minutes, stirring. Add the squid, the wine, and 1 cup water. Season with salt and pepper. Simmer, covered, for 45 minutes.

3. Crush the ink sacs and collect the ink in the bowl. Stir into the sauce, bring to a boil, season with salt and pepper, and simmer 10 minutes longer. Serve hot with boiled rice.

Gambas al Ajillo
Shrimp in garlic sauce (Spain)

This is a typical *tapas* dish, one of the many kinds of delightful hors d'oeuvres served with beer or sherry at neighborhood bars. When visiting Seville, one of the best ways to experience the wide range of this great city's gastronomy is to go *tapa* hunting, preferably in the Triana area along the banks of the Guadalquivir. Choose a bar, order a drink, and try some of the tiny special dishes offered by the house. Then move on to another bar. Most *tapas* places have their own specialties, everything from snails, shark, baby paellas, and broiled squid, to potato tortillas and miniature stews of tripe, pigs' feet, beans, or this delicious shrimp dish.

SERVES 3 TO 4

> 1 pound medium shrimp in the shell
> 2 tablespoons olive oil
> ½ onion, chopped
> ½ cup water
>   Salt
> 3 garlic cloves, peeled and crushed
> 2 tablespoons finely chopped parsley
> ¼ cup dry white wine
>   Freshly ground black pepper

1. Shell and devein the shrimp.

2. Heat the oil in a large skillet. Add the onion, water, and ¼ teaspoon salt and cook for 15 minutes, or until the water has evaporated. Allow the onions to slowly turn golden, stirring occasionally.

3. Add the garlic and half the parsley and cook 1 minute longer, stirring. Add the shrimp. Cook over brisk heat 2 minutes, or until shrimp turn pink, stirring constantly. Add the wine and season with pepper. Cook, stirring, 1 minute longer. Serve hot, sprinkled with a pinch of salt and the remaining parsley.

Sopa de Ajo
Andalusian garlic and bread soup (Spain)

The restaurant El Convento in Arcos de la Frontera serves a deeply satisfying "mush" called the Mother Superior's Garlic Soup. It looks like oatmeal but tastes so good I couldn't wait to serve it at my house. My interpretation uses whole-grain bread and a coarse white bread. Don't be put off by its homeliness—it's just too good to pass up. If in doubt, serve it by candlelight.

SERVES 6

> 2 cups cubed stale coarse-textured white bread (6 ounces)
> 2 cups cubed stale whole wheat bread (6 ounces)
> 7 teaspoons extra-virgin olive oil
> 3 small garlic cloves, minced
> 1/8 teaspoon dried red pepper flakes
> 1 large vine-ripened tomato, peeled, cored, seeded, and cut into large
>   chunks, or 2/3 cup chopped canned plum tomatoes
> 1/3 cup diced cubanelle (sweet Italian) pepper
> 6 cups chicken stock
>   Salt
>   Freshly ground black pepper

1. Using the large grating disk of a food processor, grate the bread cubes to very coarse crumbs. Set aside.

2. In an earthenware *cazuela* or a wide shallow pan, combine 1 teaspoon of the oil, garlic, hot pepper flakes, and 2 tablespoons water. Cover and cook over low heat for 10 minutes without stirring. Add tomatoes and cubanelle pepper and cook, stirring, for 2 minutes.

3. In a medium saucepan, bring the stock to a simmer. Add it to the tomato mixture, along with the bread crumbs. Cook over low heat, stirring occasionally, for 15 minutes. Remove from heat, cover, and set aside for 1 hour to allow the bread to swell and partially dissolve. Taste and adjust seasonings with salt and pepper. Ladle the soup into the bowls, drizzle the remaining 6 teaspoons olive oil over top, and serve lukewarm.

Crème à L'ail
Garlic soup (France)

In this soup, the garlic is cooked, resulting in a perfumed subtle taste. It's elegant enough for a dinner party and will convert people who are normally reticent about garlic.

Actually this is the Languedoc version of the classic *soupe à l'ail* of Provence, where they simply simmer garlic cloves and herbs in stock, then serve the mixture over toasted bread with grated cheese and sometimes a poached egg. But what makes this Languedoc version special is the liaison of oil and egg yolks instead of egg yolks and cream. It thickens the soup nicely and gives it a "southwestern touch."

When I was in Languedoc I learned to make bread croutons by brushing slices of stale bread with egg white and then setting them in the oven to toast. At first it looks as though the bread will fall apart, but the slices soon firm up and sparkle with crispness.

SERVES 4

    4 slices of stale French or Italian bread, brushed with egg white
    4 to 6 large garlic cloves, unpeeled
    2 egg yolks
    3 tablespoons olive oil
    4 to 5 cups beef or chicken stock
       Salt
       Freshly ground black pepper
       Chopped parsley

1. Toast the bread slices in a 350 degree oven until golden brown.

2. Drop the garlic cloves into boiling water and allow to cook at the boil, for 15 minutes.

3. Drain, rinse under cold running water, then peel. Mash to a purée or push through a garlic press into a mixing bowl. Beat with egg yolks and oil until thickened.

4. Bring the stock to a boil. Off heat, stir in the garlic mixture. Cook, stirring 5 minutes, until thickened. Do not allow the soup to boil. Correct the seasoning. Serve with bread slices and sprinkle with chopped parsley.

Sauce Rouille

Hot pepper and garlic sauce for Provençal
fish soups and stews (France)

Before getting into Provençal fish soups and bouillabaisse, I think it's best to begin with *rouille,* a fiery oil-based accompanying sauce. The word *rouille* means "rusty," which describes its reddish (red pimiento) coloring. *Rouille* is an excellent sauce for saffron-flavored fish soups and stews and is served occasionally, too, with *bourride.* A good *rouille* should be thick, with the consistency of a light mayonnaise. Serve it in a side dish with a very small spoon—otherwise your guests may take too much and set their mouths on fire.

MAKES ABOUT 1 CUP, SERVING 6

> 2 large garlic cloves, peeled
> 1 red bell pepper, roasted and diced
> 1 dried red pepper, soaked in warm water until soft
> 1 2-inch slice of French bread, soaked in water or fish stock and squeezed
>   dry
> 2 tablespoons olive oil
>   Salt
>   Freshly ground black pepper
> ½ cup hot fish stock

1. In a mortar, crush the garlic with the peppers and the bread until pasty.

2. Gradually work in the olive oil and blend until thick and smooth. Season with salt and pepper. Stir in the hot fish stock. Serve in a small sauceboat or bowl.

Note: To make in a food processor, use 2 tablespoons water or stock to moisten and blend the garlic, red peppers, and bread mixture before adding the oil. Then stir in the fish stock.

BOUILLABAISSE

There are marvelous *soupes aux poissons* and *soupes des pecheurs,* but true bouilla-baisse is a way of life. It is the spirit of the Mediterranean somehow captured in a deep black pot.

An assembly of from four to seven varieties of white firm-fleshed Mediterra-nean fish (at least one of which must be *rascasse*), cooked rapidly in and then served with a bouillon consisting of fish stock and olive oil flavored with saffron, fennel, parsley, garlic, onions, tomato, and salt and pepper. Some cooks add crabs, mussels, and potatoes. Inevitably, the fish and bouillon are accompanied by rounds of bread, either grilled, toasted, or fried in olive oil, and by an orange-colored sauce called *rouille,* a garlicky peppery variant of mayonnaise.

Bouillabaisse is much more than a great fish stew. In a refined version, the more varieties of rockfish—fish that graze near rock outcroppings or the rocky shore—added, the better; and in a well-made bouillabaisse one should be able to taste the distinctive character of each variety. For a purist, there are two indispens-able ingredients: frisky black *rascasse* and its larger red-hued cousin, the scorpion fish, *chapon. Rascasse* is important because of its texture and unique aromatic flavor, which carries a suggestion of the herbs and seaweed it eats off the rocks. Substitutions are futile and to import the fish by air too costly.

All fish in a bouillabaisse must be white and firm-fleshed; oily-fleshed fish are never used.

So, please make either my recipe for a *soupe de poisson "l'Aïgo-Sau"* or a *soupe de poissons "Kathy Jelen,"* and know that you are serving up a superb fish soup from Provence. If anyone should ask why you haven't given them bouillabaisse, please recite one or all of the following reasons—my own not-too-serious reasons why it's impossible to make an authentic bouillabaisse in North America.

1.

For a true bouillabaisse, people will tell you it must be made in sight of the Mediterranean and, at the very least, cooked within 100 kilometers of Marseilles. There are even purists who proclaim that the water in the soup must be taken from the fishing grounds off Cavalaire. The fact that this air and these waters are now polluted is, to the fanatic gastronome, utterly beside the point.

2.

For a true bouillabaisse, as I noted above, you need a *rascasse.* A scorpion fish is hideous and you shouldn't touch it unless its poisonous fins have been removed.

(continued)

A variant, *Helicolenus dactylopterus,* swims in North American waters, but fishermen here usually cast it back into the sea.

3.

For a true bouillabaisse, you need a base broth made from at least a hundred tiny Mediterranean rockfish. (Clam juice simply won't do.)

4.

Finally, no matter what you do there will be some silly snob who will say: "This is a rather nice fish soup, my dear—but, of course, not a true bouillabaisse."

Soupe de Poisson ''l'Aïgo-Sau''
Simple Provençal fish soup (France)

L'Aïgo Sau, an old Provençal term, refers to a fish stew somewhat similar to a bouillabaisse, but based on a single fish rather than on a medley.

SERVES 4 TO 5

- ⅓ cup olive oil
- 1 cup chopped onions
- 1 leek or 2 scallions, chopped
- ½ teaspoon finely chopped garlic
- 1 cup fresh red ripe tomatoes, peeled, seeded, and chopped
  Bouquet garni: sprigs of parsley, 1 crumbled bay leaf, fresh or dried thyme leaves, a few fennel leaves or seeds, and a piece of dried orange peel, tied together
- ¼ teaspoon pulverized saffron
  Pinch of cayenne
  Salt
- 2½ pounds fresh, white-fleshed saltwater fish, cleaned, cut into 1¼-inch chunks or slices, plus heads and trimmings
- 4 potatoes, peeled and cut into ½-inch rounds
  Freshly ground black pepper
- ½ loaf of stale French bread, cut into thin rounds, browned in olive oil, and rubbed with ½ clove of garlic (see note)
- 1 cup *sauce rouille* (page 16)

1. In a 5½-quart heavy casserole, heat the oil and cook the onions and the leek until soft but not browned. Add the garlic, tomatoes, bouquet garni, spices, and salt. Simmer, uncovered, 5 minutes, stirring frequently. Pour over 1½ quarts boiling water. Quickly bring to the boil. Add the fish heads and trimmings and cook 20 minutes.

2. Strain the cooking liquid. Pour back into the casserole and bring back to a rapid boil. Add the potatoes and the fish and cook at the boil 15 minutes, or until the fish and the potatoes are just tender. Adjust the seasoning of the soup.

3. Serve in wide soup plates with the accompanying *rouille* and the fried bread rounds.

Note: To make bread croûtes for soup, cut stale French bread into thin rounds. In a large, nonstick skillet, heat the olive oil and add the bread rounds. Sauté until golden on both sides. Rub with ½ garlic clove while still warm. Drain on paper towels.

Soupe de Poissons "Kathy Jelen"
Kathy Jelen's fish soup (France)

SERVES 6 TO 8

4 pounds assorted lean, white-fleshed fish, at least 4 kinds, such as monkfish, tilefish, sea bass, lingcod, cod, rockfish, red snapper, and halibut, skinned and cut into large serving portions; keep heads, tails, and trimmings

1 onion, stuck with 2 cloves

1 onion, quartered

2 leeks, chopped

2 small carrots, scraped and chopped

2 bay leaves, crumbled

1 fresh thyme sprig

3 parsley sprigs

3½ tablespoons tomato paste

2 garlic cloves, peeled and halved

⅓ cup dried mushrooms, soaked in water until soft

Pinch of pulverized saffron

Salt

Freshly ground pepper

1 pound (3 to 4) live crabs, blue, stone, or rock, each about 3 inches across

1½ tablespoons cornstarch (optional)

BREAD CRUMBS

1 loaf of stale French or Italian bread

4 tablespoons olive oil

2 small garlic cloves, crushed with a pinch of salt

1 cup *sauce rouille* (page 16)

1. Place the fish heads and trimmings, onions, leeks, carrots, herbs, tomato paste, garlic, mushrooms, saffron, and 2½ quarts water in a soup kettle. Add salt and pepper. Simmer, covered, for 45 minutes.

2. Meanwhile, to clean the crabs, drop them into a basin of hot water. Allow to stand 10 minutes, then drain. Pull off the tail flaps and discard the intestinal vein. Remove and discard the gills. Force the shell halves apart; remove and discard the

head and stomach. Add the crabs to the simmering fish broth or cook separately in boiling salted water. Simmer, uncovered, 5 minutes. Remove the crabs and pick out as much meat as possible. Set aside.

3. Strain the fish broth through a food mill, pressing the vegetables and fish heads to extract all their juices. Return the fish broth to the soup kettle. Bring to the boil. Slip in the firm fish. Cook over brisk heat 10 minutes. Add the tender-fleshed fish and continue to cook 10 minutes longer. Lift out the fish and remove the bones. If the soup seems too thin, thicken with cornstarch diluted in a little cold water. Bring back to the boil, stirring until thickened. Return the fish and the crabmeat to the simmering soup and allow to heat through.

4. To make garlic-flavored bread cubes for the soup, cut stale French bread into ½-inch-thick rounds. Remove the crust and cut the bread into cubes. In a large nonstick skillet, heat the olive oil and add the bread cubes. Sauté the bread until it is golden on all sides. Add the crushed garlic and sauté 30 seconds longer. Drain on paper towels and transfer to a serving bowl.

5. Serve the soup in wide soup plates. Pass a bowl of *sauce rouille* and a bowl of toasted bread cubes.

Totani Arrosto

Roast squid with garlic, tomato, and rosemary (Italy)

Here is a simple dish for summer. It is an easy and delicious way to serve medium-large squid or small cuttlefish. You must buy very fresh squid with their glistening pink-purple skins on. Ask your fishmonger to empty the pouches, but leave on the outer mottled skin. If using cuttlefish, ask him to give you the wide flat bones too. The skin or the bones will be used to keep the fish firm and straight during cooking.

Totani are a type of "flying" squid that have long tentacles, wide fins, and long, thin bodies. Their shape enables them to catapult themselves out of the water and glide through the air.

Serve with a refreshing salad of chopped tomatoes mixed with basil, tender chicory, and purslane.

(continued)

SERVES 2

   4 fresh squid or small cuttlefish (1¼ pounds total)
   2 tablespoons fruity olive oil
   1 small fresh rosemary sprig
   3 large garlic cloves, peeled and thinly sliced
     Salt
     Freshly ground white pepper
   ½ teaspoon tomato paste
     Lemon wedges

1. Preheat the oven to 475 degrees and place an oven rack as high as possible. Clean the squid or cuttlefish if the fishmonger has not done this for you. Wash and remove the tentacles and reserve. Discard the entrails, eyes, and beak. Scrape the insides of the emptied pouches with a ridged spoon. Rinse and drain dry. If using cuttlefish, save the bones and return to the pouches.

2. Arrange the squid or cuttlefish (bodies and tentacles) in a single layer in a wide shallow baking dish, preferably earthenware. Add the olive oil, rosemary, garlic, salt, and pepper. Cover with foil and bake on high rack for 10 minutes.

3. Lower heat to 400 degrees. Add the tomato paste to the cooking juices and continue to bake, uncovered, basting frequently with the pan juices, about 15 minutes, or until squid are glazed and just tender. Serve hot with lemon wedges.

Scabetch
Pickled fried fish (Algeria)

Pickled fish is found all over the Mediterranean. This recipe is based on a dish I ate in Oran and is similar to dishes found in southern France and Spain.

SERVES 6

1½ pounds small fresh fish such as smelts or sardines
    Flour seasoned with salt and freshly ground black pepper
1 cup olive oil
1 small carrot, sliced
1 small onion, sliced
4 large garlic cloves, peeled but left whole
⅔ cup white wine vinegar
¼ cup dry white wine
    Bouquet garni: imported bay leaf, thyme, parsley, and celery leaves, tied
       together
1 dried red pepper, or ¼ teaspoon cayenne
1 teaspoon salt
3 to 4 black peppercorns
    Chopped fresh parsley

1. Wash and dry the fish, roll in seasoned flour, and fry in hot oil until golden on both sides. Remove, drain carefully, and place in a deep glass or porcelain serving dish. Pour off half the frying oil.

2. Reheat the oil in a skillet and add the carrot, onion, and garlic cloves. Cook gently, stirring, until softened but not browned. Pour in the vinegar and the wine. Add the herbs, red pepper, salt, and peppercorns. Cook at the simmer for 25 minutes.

3. Pour the contents of the skillet, still hot, over the fish. Allow to cool, then refrigerate at least 36 hours before serving. Sprinkle with parsley just before serving.

Poulet au Vin d'Ail

Chicken breasts with garlic wine (France)

There are many "infused oils" around these days, but this is something different: garlic-infused white wine. It works wonderfully in this simple recipe adapted from French chef Michel Trama, imbuing a sauce for chicken breasts with a sweet nutty flavor.

SERVES 4

> ³⁄₄ cup garlic wine (see following recipe)
> 4 whole boneless chicken breasts
>   Salt
>   Freshly ground black pepper
>   Flour for dredging
> 1 tablespoon olive oil
> 2 tablespoons clarified butter
> 2 teaspoons fresh tarragon leaves, plus additional for seasoning
> ¹⁄₃ cup heavy cream

1. Make the garlic wine 1 to 2 days in advance.

2. Preheat the oven to 350 degrees.

3. Cut each breast in half and cut away fat and sinews. Remove the thin tenderloin or filet that looks like a long strip on the boned side. (These tenderloin strips should be saved in the freezer and used at some other time for a quick sauté.) Place chicken breasts between sheets of plastic wrap and flatten lightly with a rolling pin.

4. Season the chicken breasts with salt and pepper. Dredge them in flour, shaking off the excess.

5. Heat the oil and butter in a skillet. Lightly brown the chicken on both sides over high heat. Using tongs or a spatula, transfer the chicken to an ovenproof baking dish, cover with foil, and set in the oven for about 5 minutes, until chicken juices run clear.

6. Meanwhile, discard all but 1 tablespoon fat from the skillet. Add the tarragon and cook over gentle heat for 30 seconds. Deglaze with the garlic wine, then add

⅓ cup water and bring to the boil. Add the cream and reduce by boiling to a napping consistency. Adjust the seasoning with salt, pepper, and more tarragon. Place chicken on a serving dish, pour over the sauce, and serve at once.

GARLIC WINE

- 1 cup dry white wine
- 9 medium garlic cloves, unpeeled and halved
- 2 thyme sprigs
- 2 fresh tarragon sprigs
- ¼ teaspoon crushed black or white peppercorns

1. Bring wine to a boil in an enameled pan. Place remaining ingredients in a glass jar and pour in the boiling wine. Cool, cover, and refrigerate 1 to 2 days.

2. Strain through a coffee filter paper and return liquid to a clean jar. Cover and store in the refrigerator.

Poulet aux 40 Gousses d'Ail

Chicken with 40 cloves of garlic (France)

◻

This is a real garlic-lover's dish; it'll fill your whole home with its perfume.

It's famous in Provence, but my version has a southwestern touch—an accompaniment of fried fennel bulbs. For forty garlic cloves you'll need about 3 heads of garlic.

When you serve the dish, give a few cloves to each person. They can unpeel them with a fork and spread them on toasted French bread.

SERVES 4 TO 5

1   3½-pound ready-to-cook chicken
    Salt
    Freshly ground black pepper
2   bouquets garnis of Provençal herbs: bay leaf, parsley, thyme, celery
       leaves, savory, and a little rosemary
¼   cup olive oil
40   garlic cloves, unpeeled
2   tablespoons anisette or pastis
2   pounds small fennel bulbs, quartered lengthwise
    Juice of 1 lemon
    Flour
1   egg
    Bread crumbs
    Oil for frying
    Slices of French bread, ½ inch thick, toasted golden brown in the oven

1. Preheat the oven to 350 degrees.

2. Rub the chicken with salt and pepper. Stuff with one of the herb bouquets, then truss the chicken. Place in a 3-quart oval casserole, preferably earthenware. Combine oil, garlic cloves in their skins, anisette, salt, pepper, and remaining herb bouquet and dump over the bird. Cover the casserole with a tight-fitting lid. Set in the oven to bake for 1 hour 15 minutes.

3. Meanwhile, cook the fennel in boiling salted water for 20 minutes, or until barely tender. Refresh with cold running water; drain. Sprinkle with lemon juice,

salt, and pepper and roll in flour, egg, and bread crumbs. Fry in hot oil until golden brown on both sides. Drain on paper towels and keep hot until ready to serve.

4. Remove the casserole cover at table and serve directly from it. Pass a basket filled with toasted bread rounds and the fennel.

Farareej Mashwi

Broiled chicken with oil, lemon, and garlic sauce (Egypt)

SERVES 2

- 1 small chicken, quartered
- Salt
- Freshly ground black pepper
- 4 large garlic cloves, peeled and crushed
- 1/4 cup freshly squeezed lemon juice
- 3 tablespoons fruity olive oil
- 1 tablespoon chopped parsley

1. Season the chicken with salt and pepper. Combine the garlic, lemon juice, oil, and parsley in a shallow dish. Roll the chicken in the mixture to coat. Marinate for at least 1 hour.

2. Preheat the broiler. Drain the chicken, reserving the marinade. Set the broiling rack about 7 inches from the heat. Place the quarters, skin side down, on the rack and broil 10 minutes, basting often with the cooking juices and a little of the marinade. Turn the quarters over and broil the chicken 10 minutes longer. Turn and brush twice more until both sides are golden brown and crusty. Serve at once.

Pollo Tonnato

Poached chicken with tuna fish sauce (Italy)

This is a Sicilian variation on the north Italian *vitello tonnato*. The sauce is exactly the same, a tuna-enriched mayonnaise.

SERVES 8 AS A FIRST COURSE, 5 TO 6 AS A MAIN COURSE

       2 teaspoons coarse salt
       2 celery ribs, chopped
       2 small onions, sliced
       2 carrots, cut into quarters
       1 tomato
       5 black peppercorns
       4 parsley sprigs
       1 3½ to 4-pound chicken, cleaned
       2 egg yolks, at room temperature
         Salt
       1 cup olive oil, at room temperature
      ¼ cup lemon juice
       1 4-ounce can tuna fish packed in olive oil, drained
       3 flat anchovies, rinsed
       2 tablespoons capers
         Freshly ground black pepper
         Lemon quarters, sliced gherkins, and rinsed small capers for decoration

1. One or two days in advance, place the salt, celery, onions, carrots, tomato, peppercorns, and parsley in a large pot with plenty of water. Bring *almost* to the boil; slip in the chicken, partially cover, and cook at the simmer for 1 hour, or until the chicken is tender, skimming the surface often.

2. Remove the chicken, allow to cool completely, bone it, and cut into serving pieces. Reduce the cooking liquid to 1 quart. Strain and reserve ½ cup for the sauce. Save the remaining broth for some other use.

3. Beat the egg yolks with ½ teaspoon salt in a mixing bowl until thick and sticky. Add the olive oil drop by drop while beating constantly until you have a sauce the consistency of thick mayonnaise. Stir in 1 tablespoon lemon juice. Set aside.

4. Put tuna, anchovies, 1 tablespoon capers, and remaining lemon juice in the workbowl of a food processor or a blender jar; whirl until smooth. If too thick, thin with a little chicken cooking liquid. Fold into the prepared mayonnaise. Stir in the remaining capers. Taste for salt and pepper.

5. Arrange half the chicken pieces on a flat serving dish. Spread over half the sauce, cover with the remaining chicken, and then the rest of the sauce. Refrigerate. When ready to serve, decorate with lemon wedges, gherkins, and capers. Serve cool.

Ortikia Skara
Grilled quail (Greece)

In this recipe the quail are marinated in oil before grilling. Quail, like squab and other small birds, absorb oil very well, but the birds should always be fresh— never aged or hung.

SERVES 4

> 4 quail, freshly killed, cleaned, and eviscerated
> Olive oil
> 1 tablespoon dried oregano or marjoram
> 2 bay leaves, crumbled
> Salt
> Freshly ground black pepper
> 2 lemons

1. Split the quail down the back and with a cleaver flatten each one on a hard work space. Place in a large bowl, sprinkle with olive oil, oregano, bay leaves, salt, and pepper. Cover the bowl and let stand in a cool place for a few hours, turning the quail once or twice.

2. Place the quail on a grid over hot coals or under a heated broiler. Broil, basting with oil, until cooked and golden brown on both sides. Serve with lemon wedges.

Gasconnade

Leg of lamb with garlic sauce (France)

When I was in Languedoc and asking for dishes with garlic, I was overwhelmed with recipes for lamb. The combination is natural and sublime.

Note that the sauce for this *gasconnade* requires 20 to 25 garlic cloves.

SERVES 8

- 1 5-pound leg of lamb
  Salt
  Freshly ground black pepper
- 1 onion, quartered
- 1 carrot, scraped and chopped
- 1 celery rib, chopped
- 1 bay leaf, a few parsley sprigs, a little thyme
- 2 large garlic cloves, peeled and finely chopped
- 6 anchovy fillets (half a 2-ounce can), rinsed and mashed
- 3 tablespoons olive oil
- 1 tablespoon mixed fresh chopped herbs: parsley, thyme, rosemary, and savory
- 2 heads garlic (20 to 25 cloves)
- 1/2 teaspoon meat glaze (optional)

1. Preheat the oven to 425 degrees.

2. Partially bone the lamb by working a thin-bladed knife around the hip end of the leg. Loosen the flesh around the bone until you reach the joint, then twist to remove. Your butcher may do this for you. Do not remove the shank bone. Rub the cavity with pepper and very little salt.

3. Make 2 cups lamb stock with the lamb bone, trimmings, onion, carrot, celery, and bay leaf, parsley, and thyme. Simmer 1 hour.

4. While the lamb stock cooks, combine chopped garlic, anchovies, 1 1/2 tablespoons oil, and the fresh chopped herbs and rub into the cavity of the lamb. Rub the surface with the remaining oil and set in a roasting pan. Roast 15 minutes. Reduce the heat to 350 degrees and continue to roast, basting with the

pan juices, until cooked to desired doneness—12 to 14 minutes per pound for medium-rare lamb.

5. Meanwhile, drop the garlic cloves in boiling water and cook at the boil for 5 minutes. Drain, rinse under cold running water, and peel. Mash to a purée or push through a garlic press. You should have about ¼ cup puréed garlic.

6. Strain the lamb stock and reduce to 2 cups if necessary. Add the garlic purée and simmer 10 minutes.

7. Remove the lamb from the oven and let it rest 5 to 10 minutes before carving. Pour off the pan fat and discard. Add the garlic-flavored stock and cook, stirring, over high heat until reduced by half. Stir in the meat glaze and correct the seasoning. Serve the lamb sliced and pass the sauce in a sauceboat.

Confit d'Agneau

Confit *of lamb shanks with garlic croutons (France)*

This is a dish for garlic lovers. Garlic cloves, cooked with the lamb until buttery, are spread over toasted croutons and served as an accompaniment. The concept of preserved meat, or *confit,* is usually associated with legs of duck and geese simmered in duck fat, but it works very well with lamb shanks and olive oil.

SERVES 4

> ½ cup fresh orange juice
> 1 tablespoon chopped fresh parsley
> 1 to 2 teaspoons sea salt
> ¾ teaspoon freshly ground pepper
> ¼ teaspoon grated orange zest
> 1 teaspoon dried thyme
> 2 garlic cloves, peeled and sliced
> 4 small lamb shanks (about 14 ounces each), trimmed of excess fat
> 8 large garlic cloves, whole and unpeeled
> 2 cups olive oil
> 4 slices of stale French bread, cut ½ inch thick
> Sautéed fresh spinach leaves as a garnish

(continued)

1. In a shallow bowl just large enough to hold the shanks in a single layer, combine the orange juice, parsley, 1 teaspoon salt, ½ teaspoon pepper, the orange zest, thyme, and sliced garlic. Roll the shanks in the marinade and refrigerate, covered, for at least 8 hours.

2. About 3½ hours before serving time, remove meat from refrigerator. Wipe shanks clean. Preheat the oven to 300 degrees. Put the shanks and the whole garlic cloves in a 9- or 10-inch shallow glass or ceramic baking dish. Pour in the olive oil and cover with a sheet of aluminum foil. Bake in the center of the oven, turning the shanks every hour, for about 3 hours, or until very tender.

3. Brush the French bread with 2 tablespoons of the cooking oil and toast lightly in the oven about 5 minutes while the lamb is still baking. When the lamb shanks are done, remove the cooked garlic from the oil. Squeeze the creamy pulp from the skin and spread on the toasted bread. Remove the lamb shanks from the oil and nestle in the prepared spinach. Serve with the garlic croutons on the side.

Note: The oil can be strained and reused for cooking meat or vegetables. Store in the refrigerator.

Kadid

Spiced and preserved meat (Tunisia)

Here is a North African version of *confit* in which bony chunks of lamb are preserved in olive oil. The spicing and drying of the meat is similar to the treatment given to Turkish *bastourma*. The resulting flavorful pastramilike flesh is used by Tunisian cooks to give aroma, spicy flavor, and richness to an endless number of recipes, including dishes of beans and lentils, bread, couscous, and even scrambled eggs. See *Mesfouf de Jerba* (page 154).

Kadid is preserved at home. The meat, still on the bone, is cut into 1-inch-wide strips, rubbed with coarse salt and crushed garlic and left overnight to express its moisture. The next day it is wiped dry, rubbed with spices, and hung out on a line in the hot sun for several days until dry. (It is usually brought back inside each night so that damp air will not cause mold.)

Since I live in New England, I dry my strips of *kadid* on racks in a slow oven. I then simmer the chops in olive oil until a fine brown crust is formed on the surface, pack them completely in the cooking oil, top off with more olive oil, then store the meat pieces in jars in the refrigerator. Tunisian cooks insist *kadid* keeps for a year if well stored, but I have never kept it for more than a few weeks.

Shoulder lamb chops have just the right amount of bone and flesh for preserving. The preserving oil, called *dhen,* should not be discarded, since it makes an excellent fat medium for Tunisian soups and stews.

MAKES ABOUT 10 STRIPS OF *KADID*

> 1½ pounds shoulder lamb chops
> ½ cup coarse sea salt
> ½ head of garlic, cloves crushed
> 2 teaspoons dried red pepper flakes
> ½ teaspoon ground caraway
> ½ teaspoon ground coriander
> ½ tablespoon dried mint, pressed through a sieve
> 3 cups olive oil, or more as needed

1. Cut each of the chops into 3 or 4 long strips. (Use a cleaver to crack through the bones.) Rub the flesh with salt and garlic. Stack the strips in a deep bowl, cover, and refrigerate overnight.

(continued)

2. The following day, preheat the oven to 175 degrees. Dry the meat with paper towels, rub with spices and mint, and set on cake racks in the oven to dry, about 8 hours. The meat is ready when it is dry but still supple enough to bend slightly.

3. In a deep skillet or saucepan, heat olive oil to 325 degrees. Add the meat and fry until a crust forms on the flesh. Remove skillet from the heat and allow the meat and oil to cool. Divide the meat between two sterilized 1-pint mason jars. Cover with the frying oil and top off with fresh oil to completely cover the meat by 1 inch. Store in the refrigerator. As you remove pieces of *kadid,* add fresh oil to keep all the remaining pieces from being exposed to the air.

4. Soak the *kadid* in water to remove excess salt before using in a recipe, about 15 minutes.

OLIVES

All about the Mediterranean you find them—gnarled, windswept, thick, craggy, ancient trees. There was one in my garden in Tangier, a young *olivier*, perhaps no more than one hundred years old. Even among the jacarandas and fruit trees, it was the most stately, the one that looked most like it belonged.

Athena, say the Greeks, brought forth the olive tree, her gift of plenty to man. And ever since it has symbolized Mediterranean agriculture, the richness of the fruits of the earth. The olive branch has long meant peace; even now it's featured on the United Nations flag. But to me it symbolizes more—it is the sign of the Mediterranean, the sign that tells me I am in the place where man first learned how to live.

Its main bounty is oil, the great medium for cooking around the sea. But the fruit itself is eaten too, though differently in different places. Draw a line across the sole of the Italian boot, along the eastern shore of Sicily then across the water to the Tunisian–Libyan frontier. You will have cut the Mediterranean almost precisely in half, and divided opinion on the olive, too. To the east—the former Yugoslavia, Greece, Turkey, Syria, Lebanon, Egypt, and Libya—people eat the olive marinated or cured, but rarely cooked along with their food. But to the west—Italy, southern France, and Spain, and in the countries of the Maghreb— the olive is essential to cooking, appearing in every cuisine. Why? Why is it that this fruit grown about the entire sea is eaten only as a fruit in one half of the region while it is a component of dishes in the other? I have never figured it out. A great gastronomic mystery, perhaps, still waiting to be solved.

Olives can be collected when still green and unripe, then put into solutions to soak. If the farmer waits a while longer his olives will turn purple, and if he waits longer still they will become black. But even then, black and dried by the sun, they must be put in brine or oil before their bitterness goes away. All sorts of herbs are used to flavor them: bay leaves, rosemary, orange or lemon peel, fennel, oregano.

Impossible to imagine a *salade niçoise* without the famous black olives of Nice. Or a picnic in Majorca without the green Spanish ones stuffed with almonds, anchovies, or peppers from Murcia. I'll never forget a sunset on Skiathos facing the Aegean, with corn fields and olive trees surrounding the cove. I nibbled on Greek *kalamatas* and drank a chilled white St. Helena wine.

In Italy, you find them in pizzas, used in stuffings for all sorts of meats, game, and poultry, in Sicilian caponata, cooked with cauliflower or broccoli, and on spaghetti, of course, in *puttanesca* sauce. In Malta, they appear in turtle stew along with apples, chestnuts, tomatoes, raisins, capers, and nuts. I cannot conceive of Moroccan food without thinking of chicken, lemon, and olives. In Tunisia, great orchards on the coastal plain contain millions of olive trees, producing superb fruit and oil. The importance of olives is encapsulated in a delicious dish in which they are stuffed with meat, herbs, and spices, then cooked in a meat-enriched tomato sauce, and in an ancient and unusual Tunisian flat bread called *blubba,* made of barley and very ripe black olives. The olives are crushed in a traditional stone mill, water is added, and the mass is placed in a deep container. The olive oil rises to the surface, the pits sink to the bottom, and the olive flesh suspended in the middle is then removed and blended with flour to make flat bread. *Blubba* is cooked on a heated stone called a *ghannoui,* then served warm with a light dressing of fresh olive oil. In Algeria, French settlers have honored the olive by creating an olive tart. In Catalonia, olives are used as a stuffing for freshwater fish, along with mushrooms, almonds, and parsley. In Malaga, they are braised with fresh tuna; in Seville, they are roasted with loin of pork.

If you eat a steak in Toulon you may find an olive wrapped in an anchovy strip on the side of your plate. In Provence, olives will turn up in numerous daubes of beef, turkey, rabbit, or duck. And in Languedoc, they have invented something sublime, *capon à la carcassonnaise,* a capon stuffed with olives, sausage, and chicken livers, its neck stuffed separately with garlic and bread crumbs, then the whole trussed and roasted on a spit.

What more is there to say? Olives are *the* Mediterranean food, whether eaten plain as *mezzes* (appetizers) in the Levant, or in countless culinary masterpieces in Italy, France, North Africa, and Spain. What follows is a sampling, some of the best olive dishes I know. If you merely read you may sometimes think that olives are just another item on an ingredients list. But if you cook and taste, I guarantee you will know the olives are there.

NOTES ON COOKING WITH OLIVES

The taste of a dish will differ with the type of olive used, but rarely is any one type of green olive *wrong* for a dish that calls for another type of green olive, and this is true for black olives as well. The various tastes, textures, and aromas that olives provide are an almost endless source for creating new dishes or re-creating traditional ones.

I'm often asked about substituting black olives for green, or vice versa. You can do it, but keep the following points in mind: Most dishes calling for black olives use them for their weighty flavor, which goes well with other assertive flavors; green olives, on the other hand, are more subtle—they absorb flavoring and usually harmonize or blend with other ingredients.

To prepare black or green olives for cooking, choose those that have not been previously prepared with other seasonings. Rinse the olives, then taste for saltiness and bitterness.

If too salty, soak them in water to cover until palatable, then drain and rinse well.

If bitter, place in a saucepan, cover the olives with water, bring to boil, and drain. Cover with fresh water and repeat until bitterness is gone.

To pit cracked olives: Place olives in a single layer on a double thickness of kitchen toweling. Hit each olive with a mallet or heavy pestle and remove the pit. (The toweling helps cushion the blow.)

Insalata di Olive Verdi
Green olive salad (Italy)

Here's the Apulian way of marinating olives, simple and good to know because they are perfectly marinated in just two hours.

MAKES 2 CUPS

1½ cups (7 ounces) large brine-cured green olives
4 small, tender celery ribs with leaves, finely chopped
6 anchovy fillets, soaked in water for 5 minutes and drained
½ teaspoons capers, preferably salted, soaked in water for 5 minutes, and drained
½ teaspoon dried red pepper flakes
1 garlic clove, peeled and thinly sliced
1 to 2 teaspoons red wine vinegar
Olive oil

1. Rinse the olives under cold running water and drain. Gently crush each one with the side of a small cleaver. The skin and the pulp should tear but do not break the pit.

2. Finely chop together the celery, celery leaves, anchovies, and capers. In a mixing bowl, combine olives with the chopped aromatics, red pepper flakes, and garlic slices. Add vinegar and enough oil to coat. Mix well and let stand at room temperature for about 2 hours.

Yesil Zeytinli Lahmacun

Green olive and meat pies (Turkey)

Just south of the town of Gaziantep are two ancient olive-growing regions, so it isn't surprising to find various olive dishes there. Bread stuffed with olives, salads featuring olives with walnuts and pomegranates, and this splendid variation on the famous meat pies of Turkey and Syria are among them.

The olives used are green, rich in oil, and thus extremely flavorful. I use French picholine or Greek nafplion olives, soaking them in water first to remove their brine.

You can bake these pies, cool them slightly, stack them meat sides facing together, then wrap in freezer paper. They will keep up to a month in the freezer. To reheat, simply place in pairs directly on an oven rack in a preheated 425-degree oven for 5 to 10 minutes.

MAKES 16 PIES

OLIVE AND MEAT FILLING

- 5 dozen green cracked olives, preferably Greek nafplion or French picholine
- 1 pound ground lean lamb or beef
- 3/4 cup chopped green olives (about 60 olives)
- 2/3 cup grated onion
- 4 teaspoons tomato paste
- 4 teaspoons red pepper paste *(biber salcasi)* (page 94)
- 1/2 teaspoon pomegranate molasses, or to taste
- Salt to taste
- 1/2 teaspoon freshly ground black pepper
- 1 teaspoon Near East or Aleppo pepper
- A few drops of fresh lemon juice (optional)

DOUGH

- 1 package (about 2 1/2 teaspoons) active dry yeast
- 1/2 teaspoon sugar
- 1/4 cup warm water (110 to 115 degrees)
- 1 pound (about 3 3/4 cups) all-purpose flour with a high gluten content, at room temperature, plus more for kneading the dough
- 1 1/2 teaspoons fine sea salt

1$\frac{1}{8}$ cups warm water

6 tablespoons olive oil

Coarse cornmeal or bran

1. Wash the cracked olives in several waters to remove excess salt. Pit and cut into small pieces. Mix with remaining filling ingredients and blend well. Cover and refrigerate for at least 5 hours for flavors to mellow. Correct the seasoning with salt and pepper and sharpen with a little lemon juice.

2. In the bowl of a food processor, combine the yeast, sugar, and $\frac{1}{4}$ cup warm water. Pulse to blend. Cover and let stand until bubbly, about 5 minutes.

3. Add the flour and salt and pulse to combine. With the machine running, add the water and the oil and process until a soft, tacky dough forms, about 20 seconds. Turn the dough onto a lightly floured board and knead by hand for 1 to 2 minutes. Form into a ball and place it in a deep bowl; lightly brush with oil, cover bowl with plastic wrap, and let rise in a warm place until doubled in bulk, from 2 to 3 hours.

4. Return the dough to a lightly floured board and knead it again for 1 minute.

5. Punch down the prepared dough, knead for 2 minutes, then divide the dough into 16 even pieces. Flatten each piece into a thin round, cover with a floured cloth, and let rest 10 minutes.

6. Meanwhile, slowly heat a flat nonstick griddle on top of the stove. On a lightly floured work surface, roll each piece into a thin and even oval, about 7$\frac{1}{2}$ inches by 5$\frac{1}{2}$ inches. (See note.) Transfer 2 ovals to a pizza peel dusted with cornmeal or fine bran. Place about 3 tablespoons of the meat mixture on one oval; moisten fingers with cold water and spread filling evenly in a thin layer to completely cover the surface. Repeat with a second oval. Slip each onto the heated griddle and cook over medium heat for about 8 minutes, or until the bottom of each oval is cooked (regulate the heat to avoid browning). Slide each oval onto a broiler rack and broil 1 to 2 minutes. Meat should be sizzling and cooked, dough should still be supple enough to roll up. Stack in pairs with the meat inside and wrap in plastic or foil to keep warm in a 225-degree oven. Repeat with remaining breads. Serve hot or warm.

Notes: This is an easy way to thin out a round of dough: Flour a flattened round, fold in half, roll once, and unfold. Flour the round again, fold in half in the other direction, and roll again. Unfold and then roll out to a thin even round or oval.

(continued)

To hold longer, stack the ovals in pairs with the meat filling inside. The pies can be frozen, but they are at their best when freshly made. Store in plastic bags and reheat at a later time. If there is any leftover filling it can be blended with a small amount of moistened fine bulgur, shaped into patties, and grilled to be served as a snack. Serve hot or cold.

Variations

To bake the pies, preheat the oven to its highest setting. Place two heavy, well-seasoned baking sheets, preferably heavy steel, in the oven or set tiles on the racks. Slide the pies onto hot sheets or tiles. Do not close the oven door for 5 minutes. Shift the pies so that they bake evenly. Shut oven door and bake 3 to 5 minutes, until meat and dough are cooked. The dough should be pale golden on the bottom and still soft.

You can make thin breads with the same dough used for pies. Divide into golf-ball-size balls. Roll then stretch each ball until paper thin. Bake rounds on heated griddle or upside-down wok until lightly brown, about 75 seconds per side. Fold and keep in a plastic bag until dinner. Reheat and serve warm.

Pissaladière
Onion, anchovy, and olive tart (France)

There are two ways of doing this Provençal "pizza"—with tomatoes, or without. I prefer the tomato variation, but if you want to make the other, just leave the tomatoes out and increase the amount of onions. Also, if you want to serve little squares of pissaladière as an hors d'oeuvre, forget the pizza pan and use a rectangular or square baking sheet, then cut the pie with a serrated knife.

SERVES 4 TO 6

PASTRY
   1 package active dry yeast
  ½ teaspoon sugar
   2 cups all-purpose flour, sifted

1 teaspoon salt
1 tablespoon olive oil

FILLING AND TOPPING

1/4 cup strong fruity olive oil
3 large Bermuda onions, halved then thinly sliced
2 small garlic cloves, chopped
   Salt
   Freshly ground black pepper
3 to 4 tablespoons bread crumbs
2 cups fresh or canned peeled, seeded, and chopped tomatoes
2 teaspoons fresh thyme, basil, or rosemary, or 1 teaspoon dried
1/4 cup grated Parmesan or Gruyère cheese
2 2-ounce cans flat anchovy fillets, drained
12 imported pitted black olives

1. Dissolve the yeast in 2/3 cup warm sugared water and set in a warm place until bubbly.

2. Place the flour in a mixing bowl and make a well in the middle. Add salt, bubbling yeast, oil, and enough warm water to form a soft dough. Turn the dough out onto a lightly floured board and knead hard until smooth and elastic, about 10 minutes. Cover the dough loosely with a damp towel and let rise in a warm place until doubled in bulk, about 1 hour.

3. For the filling, heat half the olive oil in a 12-inch skillet, add the onions and garlic, and cook over low heat for 20 to 25 minutes, stirring often, until the onions are very soft and golden. Season with salt and pepper. Allow to cool.

4. Preheat the oven to 400 degrees. Oil a 14-inch pizza pan.

5. Punch the dough down, then roll out evenly into a 15-inch circle. Transfer to oiled pizza pan. Sprinkle the surface with bread crumbs and cover the dough to within 1 inch of its edges with the cooked onions.

6. Mix tomatoes and salt, pepper, herbs, and cheese and spread over the onions. Arrange the anchovy fillets lattice fashion on top and place an olive in each section. Dribble remaining olive oil over all. Bake 20 to 25 minutes, or until the edges of the dough are cooked and browned. Serve, hot, lukewarm, or at room temperature.

Olive Ripiene

Fried stuffed olives (Italy)

SERVES 4 TO 6

>   1 pound extra-large green olives, preferably Ascolano or Sicilian olives,
>   washed and drained
>   4 to 5 tablespoons creamy blue cheese, preferably Gorgonzola
>   6 to 8 tablespoons soft, fresh bread crumbs
>   1 egg white
>   Flour for dredging
>   Freshly ground black pepper
>   1 whole egg plus 1 egg yolk, beaten
>   1 cup or more fine dry bread crumbs
>   Olive oil for frying

1. Using a small sharp knife with a curved blade, cut diagonally into one end of an olive through to the pit. Slicing close to the pit, slowly rotate the knife at an angle to cut the flesh from pit in a long, spiral strip, as if you were peeling an orange. If the olive flesh is brittle and the pieces fall apart, they can still be used.

2. Soak the olives in a bowl of water to remove briny taste, changing water once or twice. (Sicilian olives will require 30 to 45 minutes, and Ascolano olives will require 5 minutes.)

3. Blend the cheese, soft bread crumbs, and egg white to a paste. Stuff each olive with the mixture. Fit together broken olive pieces and bind with the filling to make a sort of sandwich. Dip each filled olive into flour seasoned with pepper, then into beaten eggs, and finally dry bread crumbs. Stuffed olives can stand up to 30 minutes before frying.

4. Heat the olive oil to 350 degrees. Fry a handful of olives at a time, turning once, about 2 minutes per side, until coating is light brown. Drain on paper towels and serve hot.

Marquit Zeitoun
Ragout of stuffed olives (Tunisia)

Sometimes a dish is so haunting you can't get it out of your mind. I first tasted this highly aromatic ragout of stuffed olives some years ago at El Khalil, a family restaurant in a suburb of Tunis. It was my last meal in Tunisia on that particular trip; I went from the restaurant directly to the airport. On my flight to Rome I couldn't shake the memory of the dish—so humble, piquant, complex, offbeat, and good. From memory and taste, I worked up a recipe.

For this particular ragout, large, pulpy, flavorful olives are pitted into cork-screw shapes, then stuffed with small oval-shaped meatballs. The stuffed olives are then slowly poached in a complex multispiced tomato sauce. What is so memorable and magical, when the dish is correctly executed, is the harmony between the pungent taste of the olives, the herb flavor of the fillings, and the spiciness of the sauce. Most simple Mediterranean ragouts do not approach such finesse.

When I prepared the dish at home, everyone liked my rendition. But I wasn't sure it was as good as the version I had eaten in Tunis. Did it lack the charm of the original? Had I left out an ingredient? Was there a "trick" that might have made it better? I hoped one day to return to El Khalil and taste the original again.

Several years later my husband and I were booked on a plane with a three-hour stopover in Tunis. This was my chance. I knew that the planning had to be split-second if we were to enter the country, find a taxi, go to the restaurant, taste the ragout, and get back to the airport in time to make our flight.

I phoned the restaurant from New York. Would the proprietor promise to serve the dish that night? Madame El Mansour was flattered. She even offered to let me watch her cook it.

Tension at the airport! Only one passport control booth was open. The wait seemed interminable. Then—no taxis! It was sunset during Ramadan, and all the drivers were at home breaking the fast. No time to rent a car. What could we do? Suddenly my husband spotted a cab. "That's for us!" he yelled. He chased it and got us in and on our way. "I feel like Hemingway during the liberation of Paris, commandeering a taxi to liberate the Ritz bar," he said.

The dish was just as I remembered it. If anything, the olives were richer in flavor, their stuffing lighter and more tender, the earthy sauce even more delicious and aromatic. The restaurant too was just as marvelous and exotic. A man sitting in one corner smoked a water pipe that emitted froglike sounds. And it seemed

(continued)

there *was* a special ingredient, the Tunisian spice mixture, *tabil,* which I have since added to my recipe.

On the way back to the airport, our taxi driver (whom I had invited to eat with us, to ensure our getting back in time) had the last word. He had eaten the ragout Arab-style with his right hand. "That dish was so good," he said, "it makes you want to eat your fingers!"

The concept of stuffing olives may seem tedious, but actually it isn't. And you don't need an olive or cherry pitter; a small, sharp knife works very well.

Serve these stuffed olives surrounded by warm slices of bread. A few simple Tunisian salads served before make a good lunch.

SERVES 6

    3 dozen Sicilian-style olives (about 1½ pounds)

RAGOUT
    ¾ pound lean beef brisket or chuck
    ¼ teaspoon ground black pepper
  2½ teaspoons tabil (page 197)
    1 tablespoon olive oil
    ½ cup minced onion
    4 teaspoons tomato paste
    ½ teaspoon harissa (pages 200–201), diluted in 2 tablespoons water
      Sea salt
    1 teaspoon sweet paprika

STUFFING
    ¾ pound lean ground beef
    ½ cup coarsely chopped parsley
    ⅓ cup freshly grated Parmesan cheese
    2 eggs
      Pinch of hot paprika
    ¼ cup grated onion
  1½ teaspoons tabil (page 197)
    ½ teaspoon harissa (pages 200–201)
    ¼ teaspoon freshly ground black pepper

GARNISH
    6 New Mexican green chilies
    ¾ teaspoon fennel seeds, bruised in a mortar just before using
      Salt
    ¼ cup olive oil for shallow frying

1. Using a small knife, cut diagonally into one end of each olive through to the pit. Slicing close to the pit, slowly rotate the knife to cut the flesh from the pit in a long, spiral strip (as if you were peeling an orange). Soak in several changes of water to remove the salt. Drain well.

2. Cut the beef into tiny cubes and season with pepper and tabil. In a 12-inch nonstick skillet, heat the oil over medium-high heat. Add the meat and onion and cook, stirring, until all the moisture has evaporated and the meat has begun to brown, 3 to 4 minutes. Stir in the tomato paste and allow it to sizzle 1 minute. Then stir in the diluted harissa, pinch of salt, paprika, and 1 cup of water. Reduce the heat to low, cover, and simmer, adding about 2 tablespoons water at a time as the liquid becomes absorbed, until the meat is very tender, about 1 hour.

3. In a large mixing bowl, combine ground beef, parsley, Parmesan, eggs, hot paprika, grated onion, tabil, harissa, and ¼ teaspoon ground black pepper into a well-blended but light mixture. Use your hands, fingers extended, to gradually whip 2 tablespoons water into the mixture. Roll the stuffing into 36 balls the size of marbles. Slip a ball of stuffing into a drained olive and, with wet hands, squeeze the olive into an oval shape. Repeat with remaining olives and stuffing.

4. Add 1½ cups water to the simmering ragout. Nestle the stuffed olives in the ragout, cover with crumpled wet parchment paper and a tight-fitting lid, and simmer for 45 minutes. Turn the olives midway through cooking and add more water if the sauce appears dry. Using a slotted spoon, transfer the olives to a covered dish. Skim off any fat from the sauce and boil to reduce it to a chunky napping consistency, 1½ cups. Set aside.

5. Using a small knife, puncture each green chili pepper near the stem end. Slip a pinch of salt into the hole and let stand for at least 30 minutes. (Up to this point the dish can be made and left unrefrigerated for up to several hours in advance.)

6. Just before serving, reheat the sauce gently and glaze the stuffed olives in a hot oven. Perfume the sauce with bruised fennel seeds and correct the seasoning. Heat the olive oil in a 9-inch skillet over moderate heat. Add the peppers, cover with a spatter screen, and fry, turning once, until light brown, about 3 minutes to a side. Arrange 6 olives with lots of sauce on each of 6 plates. Garnish each with a fried pepper.

Note: Tunisians like hot spices. They also garnish their dishes with fresh chilies. This ragout is garnished with fried New Mexican green chilies, which, when prepared as described on page 96 *(felfel mokli),* lose some of their heat, won't spatter, and absorb hardly any oil during frying.

Spaghetti alla Puttanesca
Spaghetti with olive sauce (Italy)

◻

There are numerous ways of doing this famous dish. Here are three variations, all of them superb. Conventional wisdom has it that spaghetti alla puttanesca was invented by the whores of Naples as a quick and lusty fortification, and also to lure customers with a delicious aroma of olives, garlic, and anchovies simmering in rich tomato sauce. But my informants tell me otherwise. *They* say that *puttanesca* is an ideal dish for a respectable woman enjoying an illicit affair between five and seven in the afternoon. She can prepare it in advance, let it marinate while she is out on her adventure, then dash home and in five minutes serve it up to her famished spouse.

SERVES 8 TO 10

 ½ pound juicy black Greek olives, rinsed, pitted, and finely chopped
 ½ pound green olives, rinsed, pitted, and finely chopped
 1 2-ounce can anchovy fillets, rinsed and mashed
 1 tablespoon capers, rinsed and drained
 2 to 3 tablespoons chopped pickled or raw mushrooms (optional)
 2 tablespoons chopped parsley
 2 to 3 fresh basil leaves, chopped (optional)
 2 to 3 garlic cloves, finely chopped
   Freshly ground black pepper
   Extra-virgin olive oil
 2 pounds spaghetti
   Salt

1. Combine the olives, anchovies, capers, mushrooms, herbs, garlic, and pepper in mixing bowl. Pour over enough olive oil to cover. Allow to stand and marinate 2 hours, turning the ingredients often and adding more oil if necessary to keep the olive mixture completely covered.

2. Cook the pasta in boiling, salted water. Meanwhile, heat the olive mixture in a wide skillet but do not allow it to boil. Transfer the pasta when it tests *al dente* to the skillet, mix with the olives, and serve at once. Serve without grated cheese.

This variation may sound odd, but I assure you that the touch of raisins blends perfectly with everything else.

SERVES 6

> 2½ ounces black Greek olives, rinsed, pitted, and chopped
> 4 ounces green olives, rinsed, pitted, and chopped
> ½ cup yellow raisins, soaked
> ¾ cup pine nuts, chopped
> 3 anchovy fillets, rinsed and mashed
>   Cayenne
>   Extra-virgin olive oil
> 1 pound spaghetti
>   Salt

Proceed as directed above. Before serving, taste the sauce—it should be fiery.

Variation #2

This is the traditional *puttanesca,* the one you will find on the menu of a chic trattoria. It is certainly good, but I prefer the other two.

SERVES 6

> 1 cup black gaeta olives, rinsed, pitted, and chopped
> 5 anchovy fillets, rinsed and mashed
> 1 tablespoon capers, rinsed and drained
> 2 garlic cloves, finely chopped
> 1 tablespoon finely chopped parsley
>   Pinch of red pepper flakes
>   Extra-virgin olive oil
> 2 cups prepared tomato sauce, heated
> 1 pound spaghetti

1. Combine the olives, anchovy fillets, capers, garlic, parsley, and red pepper. Heat a little olive oil in a skillet and in it sauté the olive mixture 2 to 3 minutes. Add the tomato sauce and readjust the seasoning. Simmer 5 minutes.

2. Meanwhile, cook the pasta in boiling salted water. Transfer the pasta to the skillet when it tests *al dente*. Mix well and cook 30 seconds longer. Serve hot without grated cheese.

Djej bil Zeitoun Meslalla

Chicken smothered in green cracked olives (Morocco)

◪

Morocco is a country where all varieties of olives are eaten—simply cured, combined in uncooked salads, or used in complex cooked dishes. Here is one of the most famous Moroccan olive dishes, a personal favorite, too. The spicing is exotic—ginger, paprika, cumin, and saffron. This subtle nutty-flavored dish includes olives that are boiled to release some of their oil into the sauce, but it's really the lemon juice that give this dish its special twist.

I ate this first at the old palace of the Mendoub of Tangier, a rambling place with numerous salons arranged about a central court. It was extremely cold that night, so there was a charcoal brazier burning in the room. I could hear the shuffling of slippers from down the hall, and then the palace cook, a short dark woman, wizened and old, with layers of skirts tucked about her waist, appeared with a great platter full of chickens covered in olives. We ate it up, tearing apart chickens with our fingers, Moroccan style. The next day I went back and learned the recipe.

SERVES 6 TO 8

    4   pounds chicken legs and thighs
    2   large onions
    3   tablespoons olive oil
    1   tablespoon finely chopped garlic
    1   teaspoon ground ginger
    1   teaspoon freshly ground black pepper
    ½   teaspoon ground cumin
    ½   teaspoon sweet paprika
        Pinch of pulverized saffron
    ½   cup chopped parsley
    ¼   cup chopped green coriander
    3   cups water
    2   pounds Moroccan, French, or Greek green cracked olives (see note)
    ⅓   cup fresh lemon juice, or more to taste
        Salt
        Moroccan bread or whole-wheat pita

1. Trim chicken of fat. Cut up 1½ onions and pulse in a food processor (or use a hand shredder) until coarsely grated. Place grated onion into strainer and press to remove moisture. Measure ¾ cup and discard the rest. Thinly slice remaining half onion and reserve.

2. In a 5-quart casserole, blend the olive oil, garlic, ginger, pepper, cumin, paprika, and saffron to a paste. Stir in the grated onion and herbs. Continue stirring while adding the 3 cups water as if you were making mayonnaise. Add chicken, bring to a boil, reduce heat to low, and simmer, covered, for 20 minutes.

3. Meanwhile, drop olives into boiling water, simmer 1 minute, then drain.

4. Preheat the oven to 450 degrees.

5. With a slotted spoon, remove chicken from casserole and place on a baking sheet. Bake on upper shelf of oven for 15 minutes, or until meat is fully cooked and skin is lightly crisped.

6. Meanwhile, add reserved sliced onion and olives to casserole. Simmer 15 minutes. Add lemon juice to taste. Season sauce with salt, if necessary.

7. Remove chicken to a serving platter, cover completely with olives and sauce, and serve with triangles of warm bread.

Note: Not all green olives are ideal for this dish—the best are the Greek green cracked, Moroccan green cracked, and the French picholine.

Poulet à la Camarguaise

Chicken prepared in the style of the Camargue (France)

This chicken and olive dish, completely different in procedure and flavor from the more familiar chicken and olive dishes of North Africa, is from one of my favorite parts of France—the flat rough wild cowboy country of the Camargue. In the Camargue, one would accompany this dish with the delicious local rice and braised white onions.

(continued)

    1 3 to 3½-pound chicken, cut into serving pieces
       Salt
       Freshly ground black pepper
    3 tablespoons olive oil
    ½ cup diced bacon
    ½ cup chopped onion
    2 teaspoons finely chopped garlic
    ½ cup dry white wine
    1 cup fresh or canned tomato sauce
    1 cup rich chicken stock
    3 tablespoons finely chopped parsley
    1 bay leaf
    ¼ teaspoon crumbled thyme leaves, or a pinch of dried thyme
       Cayenne
       About 12 juicy black olives, rinsed and pitted
       About 12 green olives, rinsed and pitted

1. Season the chicken pieces with salt and pepper. Heat the oil in a 3½-quart heavy casserole and brown the chicken pieces on both sides. Remove the chicken and keep warm and moist.

2. Add the bacon, onion, and garlic to the pan drippings and cook, stirring, for 3 to 4 minutes. Pour in the wine, raise the heat, and cook, stirring, until most of the wine evaporates.

3. Return the chicken to the casserole and add the tomato sauce, chicken stock, half the parsley, and the herbs. Season with salt, pepper, and cayenne. Simmer, covered, 30 minutes, or until the chicken is tender. If the cooking juices are thin, raise the heat and rapidly boil down until thick.

4. Five minutes before serving, stir in the olives and correct the seasoning. Sprinkle with the remaining chopped parsley.

Sauté de Lapin à la Provençale

Sautéed rabbit with anchovies
and black olives (France)

Only very young and tender rabbits weighing about 2½ pounds should be cooked this way. The best pieces for this dish are the rump, saddle, and hindquarters.

SERVES 2 TO 3

  1 2½-pound rabbit, fresh or thawed frozen, cut into 8 pieces, liver
       reserved
  2 tablespoons Dijon mustard
  ⅓ cup olive oil
  ½ cup chopped onion
  2 garlic cloves, 1 sliced, 1 halved
  1 fresh rosemary sprig
  ½ cup dry white wine
  1 medium fresh ripe tomato, peeled, seeded, cut into ½-inch dice, or ¾
       cup coarsely chopped seeded canned tomatoes
    Pinch of sugar
1½ cups chicken broth
  1 tablespoon red wine vinegar
  1 ounce anchovy fillets, rinsed and patted dry
  6 to 9 ½-inch-thick slices of French or Italian bread
12 salt-cured black olives, pitted and coarsely chopped
    Chopped fresh parsley
    Salt
    Freshly ground black pepper

1. Wipe rabbit pieces with dampened paper toweling.

2. Whisk mustard and 1 tablespoon of the oil together in a large bowl until blended. Add rabbit pieces, turning several times to coat well. Refrigerate, covered, for at least 3 hours or overnight.

3. About 35 minutes before serving, heat 1½ tablespoons of the oil in a 12-inch skillet. Add the rabbit pieces in one layer; sauté, turning once, until golden brown

(continued)

on both sides, about 5 minutes. Add onion, sliced garlic, and rosemary; sauté until onion begins to wilt, about 2 minutes. Add wine and increase heat to high. Cook, uncovered, until wine is reduced to 2 tablespoons. Add chopped tomato, sugar, and chicken broth; heat mixture to boiling, then reduce heat to very low. Simmer gently, covered, until rabbit is just cooked through, about 10 minutes.

4. Meanwhile, heat 1 tablespoon of the oil in a small heavy skillet over medium-high heat. Add reserved liver and cook, undisturbed, 2 minutes on each side. Transfer liver, sautéing oil, and 1 additional tablespoon oil to a blender or food processor. Add vinegar and anchovy fillets; process until smooth, stopping machine and scraping down sides of container as necessary. Force mixture through a food mill to obtain a smooth sauce.

5. Brush bread slice with remaining olive oil and sauté in batches in a clean nonstick skillet until golden on each side. Rub with cut side of garlic clove; keep warm.

6. When rabbit is done, stir in liver-anchovy mixture. Add olives, parsley, and salt and pepper to taste. Cook over low heat until heated through, about 5 minutes. Transfer rabbit to a warmed serving platter. Pour some of the sauce over rabbit; pass remainder separately. Surround rabbit with croutons and serve immediately.

Palombacci alla Perugina

Wood pigeons or squabs with polenta (Italy)

◻

Traditionally *cacciagione*, the main dish of game birds, in this case wood pigeons, is brought to the table on a large serving dish accompanied by slices of toasted polenta.

Polenta—a dish made of cornmeal or semolina that has been known since the time of Caesar—is the classic accompaniment to game. To be fully appreciated it should be doused with a rich sauce of wine, vegetables, herbs, and spices. A separate vegetable dish, such as a light purée of spinach, is brought out at the same time. A mixed salad of chicory, sorrel, dandelion, romaine or escarole leaves is passed and served on separate plates.

SERVES 4

- 2 cups red Chianti wine
- 2 cups rich chicken stock
- 3/4 cup chopped carrots
- 3/4 cup chopped celery
- 3/4 cup chopped onion
- 2 whole garlic cloves, peeled
- 3 bay leaves
- 4 parsley sprigs
- 2 sage leaves, crushed
- 4 juniper berries, crushed
- 6 black peppercorns
- 1/2 tablespoon tomato paste
  Salt
- 4 1-pound squabs, drawn and trussed, plus the livers and giblets
  Flour
  Freshly ground black pepper
- 5 tablespoons olive oil
- 1 cup cornmeal
- 3/4 cup Italian black olives (preferably gaeta), rinsed and pitted
  Squeeze of lemon juice (optional)

(continued)

1. In a heavy 5-quart enameled casserole, combine the wine, chicken stock, vegetables, garlic, herbs, spices, tomato paste, and salt to taste. Bring to the boil and simmer for 1 hour.

2. Add the squab livers and giblets. Continue to cook, uncovered, over gentle heat for another hour.

3. Discard the bay leaves. Whirl the contents of the casserole in a blender, then push through a strainer. You should have about 2 cups smooth sauce. Thin with more chicken stock if too thick.

4. Dust the squabs with flour seasoned with salt and pepper. In a large casserole, heat 3 tablespoons of the olive oil over medium heat until hot. Brown the squabs in oil on all sides. Remove to a side dish, pour off the excess oil, and return the squabs to the casserole. Add the sauce. Heat to the simmer, cover tightly, and continue to cook over gentle heat for 30 minutes.

5. *To make polenta:* Slowly sprinkle the cornmeal into 4 cups simmering salted water, stirring. Reduce the heat and continue cooking, stirring constantly in one direction for 20 minutes. The polenta must be very thick and pull away from the sides of the saucepan. Pour the polenta onto a large flat plate. Allow to cool completely.

6. Add the olives to the casserole and cook, uncovered, 10 minutes more.

7. Cut the polenta with taut string into 1/4-inch-thick slices. Sauté in oil until browned on both sides or sprinkle with melted butter and grated Parmesan cheese and brown under the broiler.

8. Remove the squabs from the casserole and place them on a hot serving dish. Readjust the seasoning of the sauce. If very rich, a squeeze of lemons may be necessary. Spoon the sauce over the squab and serve at once with sautéed or toasted polenta slices.

Gigot d'Agneau, Sauce aux Olives
Leg of lamb with olive sauce in the style of Provence
(France)

This is an absolutely splendid sauce for roast lamb, one of the best ways I know to serve it. And remember, in Provence lamb is basted with hot fat, not with wine or stock.

In Languedoc there's a similar sauce served with boiled calf's head.

SERVES 6

- ½ pound lamb breast or a few lamb bones
- 3 carrots, cut up
- 3 onions, cut up
- Bouquet garni: bay leaf, parsley, thyme, and a few celery leaves, tied together
- Salt
- Freshly ground pepper
- 1 5-pound leg of lamb
- 3 garlic cloves, peeled and slivered
- Olive oil
- 1½ cups juicy black Mediterranean-type olives, rinsed, pitted, and chopped
- 1 2-ounce can anchovy fillets, rinsed and mashed
- 2 tablespoons finely chopped parsley
- 1 teaspoon finely chopped garlic
- Juice of ½ lemon
- About ¼ teaspoon cayenne

1. Prepare a lamb broth with the lamb breast or bones, carrots, onions, herbs, and 3 cups water. Season with salt and pepper. Cook, covered, 1 hour.

2. Preheat the oven to 400 degrees.

3. Make a few incisions near the lamb leg bone and insert the slivers of garlic. Rub the meat with salt, pepper, and olive oil. Place in a roasting pan and set in the oven to start browning for 15 minutes.

(continued)

4. Reduce the heat to 325 degrees and continue to roast the lamb, basting often with the lamb drippings and more oil, until the desired degree of doneness. Pink lamb registers 140 degrees on a meat thermometer, about 1 hour.

5. Remove the lamb to a heated platter and keep warm. Spoon off the excess fat in the pan and discard. Degrease and strain lamb broth. Add 1 cup broth to the pan juices. Set the pan over medium heat and stir to scrape up all the brown particles that cling to the pan. Add the remaining broth, stirring. Boil down to 2 cups. Add olives, anchovies, chopped parsley, garlic, lemon juice, and cayenne. Heat, stirring, until well combined. Correct the seasoning. Keep hot.

6. Carve the lamb and serve with the sauce in a warmed sauceboat.

Daube de Boeuf Provençale

Beef, wine, mushroom, and olive stew
as prepared in Provence (France)

This daube is so good that I include it even though it's one of the few that cannot be presented closed. We all love to break open the *daubière* before our guests and flood the dining room with the aroma of Provence. In this version, however, the olives and mushrooms are added 10 minutes before the dish is served. The loss of dining room drama is more than compensated for by olives and mushrooms, which have retained their own flavors and thus set off the blended taste of the rest of the stew.

SERVES 6

WINE MARINADE
   ½ cup sliced carrots
   ¼ cup sliced celery
   ¼ cup chopped onion
   3 tablespoons olive oil
   2 tablespoons mixed herbs: parsley, thyme, crumbled bay leaf, and
        rosemary or savory
   2 teaspoons chopped garlic
   2 cups dry red or white wine

Salt

12 black peppercorns

3 pounds grainy beef chuck, cut into 15 to 18 serving pieces, each larded with a small piece of pork fat back

2 medium onions, thinly sliced

½ cup very lean salt pork, cut into ¼-by-1-inch lardons, then blanched, rinsed, and dried

35 ounces canned tomatoes, seeded and chopped

Bouquet garni: bay leaf, parsley sprigs, thyme leaves, and a piece of dried orange peel, 2 inches by 2 inches, tied together

Flour and water paste

¼ pound fresh mushrooms, sliced

2 dozen brine-cured black olives, rinsed and pitted

2 tablespoons chopped parsley

1. The day before, make the wine marinade. In a skillet over gentle heat, soften the carrots, celery, and onion in olive oil. Add the herbs and the garlic and continue cooking, stirring, until the flavors are released. Moisten with the wine and add salt and pepper. Bring the liquid to the boil and allow to simmer 10 to 15 minutes. Remove from heat and allow to cool completely.

2. Place the beef cubes in a bowl and pour over the cooled marinade. Cover with foil and set in a cool place overnight, turning the meat once or twice.

3. Preheat the oven to 350 degrees.

4. Place the meat and the marinade in a *daubière* or heavy casserole with lid. Scatter the sliced onions over the meat; add the pork lardons, tomatoes, and the bouquet garni. Cover and, if you are using a *daubière,* seal with a thick flour and water paste. Set the daube in the oven to cook slowly for 4 to 5 hours. After 1 hour, lower oven temperature to 250 degrees.

5. Ten minutes before serving, break the flour and water seal and discard. Set the *daubière* on top of the stove over very gentle heat (to avoid breaking, place the earthenware casserole on an asbestos pad or trivet set over the flame). Add the mushrooms and the olives. Continue cooking until the mushrooms are tender. Remove the bouquet garni and skim the grease from the top of the cooking liquid. Adjust the seasoning. Sprinkle with chopped parsley. Serve with freshly cooked macaroni.

Note: Daubes are very good reheated or eaten cold.

Carne Fiambre
Stuffed beef roll (Spain)

This is an ideal dish for a summer buffet.

SERVES 6 TO 8

2½ pounds flank steak in 1 piece
Salt
Freshly ground black pepper
1 teaspoon crushed garlic
3 eggs
¼ cup olive oil
½ pound ground lean pork
⅔ cup green olives, rinsed and pitted
4 thin carrots, each about 6 inches long
3 roasted sweet red peppers, cut into long thin strips
¼ cup diced cornichons (optional)
2 to 3 tablespoons chopped parsley
Flour
1 chopped onion
2 garlic cloves, peeled and bruised
1 cup dry white wine
2 cups beef stock
1 bay leaf
1 tomato, peeled, seeded, and chopped
1 carrot, chopped

1. Butterfly the meat lengthwise using a sharp knife. Place the meat between sheets of wax paper and flatten with the side of a cleaver. Rub with salt, pepper, and crushed garlic.

2. Beat the eggs with salt and pepper until the whites and yolks are well combined. Heat 1 tablespoon olive oil in a skillet and make a firm omelet. Cool, then cut into ½-inch strips.

3. Spread the pork evenly over the meat, arrange the omelet slices, olives, carrots, sweet peppers, and cornichons on top in rows. Sprinkle with parsley and season with salt and pepper. Roll the meat into a cylinder and tie securely with string.

4. Roll the meat in flour. Heat remaining olive oil in a heavy 5½-quart casserole and brown the meat on all sides. Add chopped onion and garlic and cook until golden. Moisten with wine and stock. Add bay leaf, tomato, and chopped carrot and season with salt and pepper. Moisten a sheet of parchment paper under running water and place it crumpled over the meat. Bring the liquid to a boil, then simmer, covered, for 1½ hours.

5. To serve hot: Remove the meat and discard strings. Allow to rest 5 to 10 minutes before slicing. Strain the cooking liquid. Arrange slices overlapping on a heated long dish and moisten with some of the cooking liquid. Serve with sautéed potatoes.

6. To serve cold: Place the meat in a deep dish and pour over enough strained cooking liquid to cover the meat completely. Weight the meat. Be careful of an overflow of hot liquid. When cool, spoon off fat. Serve thinly sliced.

Mousse aux Olives Douces et au Citron
Sweet olive and lemon mousse (France)

The fresh-tasting crisp, medium-green picholine olive has just a hint of sweetness. Could this have been French chef Roger Vergé's inspiration for a similar dish served at his restaurant in Mougins?

MAKES ABOUT 3¾ CUPS, SERVING 6 TO 8

    10 ounces (2¼ cups) green olives, preferably French picholine
      1 cup plus 2 teaspoons superfine sugar
      2 cups water
      2 egg whites, at room temperature
      2 lemons
      1 envelope (¼ ounce) unflavored gelatin
      2 cups heavy cream
  1½ teaspoons Pernod

1. Rinse olives. Place between paper toweling and gently smash each one with a mallet to remove pit. Cover olives with water, bring to a boil, and drain. Repeat this procedure three more times. Taste olives. They should no longer be bitter; if

(continued)

they are, boil again and drain. Place ½ cup of the sugar and 1⅓ cups of the water in a small saucepan. Heat, stirring, until sugar dissolves. Add olives; invert a saucer over olives to keep them submerged in liquid and bring to a boil. Simmer slowly for 5 minutes. Remove from heat, cover, and let soak at least 1 day.

2. The following day, put 3 tablespoons water in a small saucepan and stir in ½ cup sugar. Place over low heat and cook until sugar dissolves. Raise the heat and bring to a boil. Boil slowly until a candy thermometer registers 240 degrees. While syrup is boiling, slowly beat egg whites with an electric beater until they froth. Raise speed to medium and beat until peaks form. Remove syrup from heat. Reduce speed and pour hot syrup in a slow steady stream onto whites, continuing to beat at low speed until whites are shiny, stiff, and cool to the touch. Set aside to cool completely.

3. Put remaining 2 tablespoons water in a small saucepan, sprinkle on gelatin, and set aside to soften for 10 minutes.

4. Drain olives, reserving syrup. Put about two thirds of the olives and ¼ cup syrup in a blender or food processor and purée. If purée is not smooth, press through a sieve. Reserve syrup and remaining olives.

5. Using a vegetable peeler, remove zest from lemons. Cut into very fine strips and blanch in boiling water for 1 minute. Drain and refresh under cold water. Simmer in the remaining sugar syrup for 5 minutes and drain. Discard syrup. Spread lemon strips on a rack to dry. Use a fork to separate any tangled strips.

6. Place saucepan of softened gelatin mixed with olive purée over low heat and warm gently, stirring until gelatin completely dissolves, 2 to 3 minutes. Let cool to room temperature, stirring every 5 minutes to keep mixture from setting.

7. In a chilled mixing bowl, whip the heavy cream and remaining 2 teaspoons sugar until just stiff enough to form soft peaks. Transfer one third of the cream to a small bowl and flavor with Pernod. Cover and refrigerate until ready to serve.

8. The whipped cream, beaten egg whites, and olive-gelatin mixture should be the same temperature before combining. Carefully fold one quarter of the whipped cream into the olive mixture to lighten. Gradually and gently fold remaining whipped cream and then egg whites into olive mixture until thoroughly blended. Carefully spoon mixture into 2-quart serving dish. Cover with plastic wrap and refrigerate until ready to serve.

9. To serve, swirl Pernod-flavored cream over mousse and decorate with remaining olives and lemon strips.

Eggplant, Tomatoes, Peppers, and Other Mediterranean Vegetables

If you come to live around the Mediterranean you will soon discover that the people here eat with the seasons. You won't find every vegetable available in the markets every month of the year, as in the stores of North America. In late summer there are piles of eggplants, zucchinis, peppers, and tomatoes and you will know it's the season for ratatouille. In fall there are mushrooms, artichokes, pumpkins, and fennel; in winter, leeks and the root vegetables, turnips and carrots; in spring, a plenitude of asparagus, radishes, and lettuce. And it is the same with the fruits: melons, peaches, and plums in summer; grapes, quince, and pears in the fall; oranges and grapefruit in winter; cherries, strawberries, and figs in the late spring.

It's a joy to eat with the seasons, to face peppers and eggplants for four or five months out of the year and discover all the good things that can be done with them. And there's the joy of anticipation, too—the wait for the next seasonal change. Little piles of artichokes appear in late fall, growing larger and larger each week while the zucchini piles decline. A new season has arrived and with it new produce. It's time for new recipes.

The seasonal approach has had a good effect on Mediterranean cooking, forcing cooks to come up with numerous uses for food that would be boring if always served the same way. The result is that Mediterranean cooks have devised a great number of imaginative uses for their produce.

I spent a summer in the early 1960s in the village of Gruz on the Dalmatian coast, and I still have a vivid memory of the market there—a great peasant market in a big public square, shaded by old plane trees. It was not like the lush markets of Cannes and Nice with their pyramids of perfectly shaped vegetables and fruits, nor the glistening supermarkets now prevalent in Palermo, which have replaced the little alley shops. It bore no resemblance either to two other favorite markets of mine: the one in Rome near the Trastevere and the Fez market of Tangier, where there is an old Riffian woman who has sold me garlic on and off for the last fifteen years. No, the market of Gruz presented amazing sight.

It was full of long wooden tables tended by craggy-faced peasant women, all wearing babushkas and holding antique scales in their hands. Donkeys and trucks poured in all morning with produce and the market did not close until dark. But what was extraordinary, aside from a certain obvious picturesqueness, was that this market offered only one seasonal item each day. I remember once when the whole place was flooded with green peppers, and every restaurant on the square served stuffed peppers and nothing else. One morning there was nothing except peaches, and then the square looked like a field of marigolds. Another time it was all red with tomatoes, and still another it was black with eggplant. On my last morning there were onions—tens of thousands—tied together into endless chains.

I've never seen anything quite like that market at Gruz—truly, it was an extraordinary place. Its rapid changes in color, its sudden shortages and surpluses, had something to do, I suppose, with fields methodically picked, and possibly with the whims of a local commissar. But its unpredictable floods of produce remain a symbol to me of all the markets of the Mediterranean, choked with the bounty of each season, telling the cook what *must* be made.

In 1982 I returned to Gruz. Alas, everything was different. I couldn't find the house where I had lived and the old market square had become a shopping mall. Worried that the break-up of Yugoslavia might have changed the landscape even more, I recently telephoned the Croatian mission to the UN. An attaché told me that it is now peaceful there and urged me to visit. Of course now there is no need.

EGGPLANT

Eggplants were brought by Arabs to the region fifteen hundred years ago from India, and ever since these purplish egg-shaped vegetables, some very small and narrow, others huge, have been a mainstay of Mediterranean cuisine. The Turks have more than fifty ways to prepare them, and the other Middle Eastern countries do nearly as well. They are good mashed, fried in oil, braised, or stuffed and baked.

The Greeks like to remove the pulp, sauté it in oil with onions, then mix it with feta cheese, eggs, parsley, salt, and pepper, restuff the shells, top them with tomato slices, sprinkle them with more oil, and bake them in the oven.

The Moroccans like to add them to couscous, and they make a big thing of the little nugget under the eggplant stem, which they slice and add to stews to impart a mushroom taste.

The Italians sometimes prepare eggplant bits like mushrooms, and in Israel they use eggplant for a dish they call "mock liver." The Italians also like to pickle them, and in southern Italy they sometimes use slices of fried eggplant instead of bread as the outer leaves of a tomato and cheese sandwich.

The Lebanese are great picklers of eggplant. They have a dish called *batinjan Makdus* consisting of partially boiled eggplants stuffed with crushed salted walnuts. They are put up in jars with olive oil, vinegar, a red pepper, and garlic cloves and left to pickle for two weeks.

In Spain there's a mixture of potatoes, ham, mushrooms, onions, white wine, and eggplant called *berenjenas duquesa*. In Provence there's an eggplant *timbale* called *papeton d'aubergines*, lightened with egg whites and served with an herbal tomato sauce. The Egyptians top fried eggplant slices with onions, seasoned tomatoes, and sugar and then bake them until brown, and the Jews of North Africa make an eggplant jam to serve with tea and toast.

Batenjal M'Charmel
Eggplant salad (Algeria)

Eggplant mixed with cumin and sharp paprika makes a delicious and handsome salad. Don't be put off by the long frying in olive oil—this is a fundamental technique of North African cooking, where a vegetable is fried until all liquid evaporates and there is only oil and vegetable left in the pan. When you turn the eggplant slices into a colander to cool, the oil will run out—but not the rich flavor.

SERVES 4 TO 6

> 2 medium eggplants (about 1 pound each)
> Salt
> Olive oil for frying
> 3 to 4 garlic cloves, peeled and crushed
> 1 tablespoon sharp paprika, or a mixture of sweet paprika and
>   2 pinches of cayenne
> 1 teaspoon ground cumin
> 2 tablespoons vinegar or lemon juice, or more taste

1. Remove three vertical strips of skin from each eggplant, leaving it striped, then cut eggplants into ½-inch-thick slices. Salt the slices and leave to drain in a colander for 30 minutes. Rinse well, squeeze gently, and pat dry with paper towels.

2. Heat about ¼ inch of oil in a skillet and fry the slices, a few at a time, over high heat until golden brown on both sides. Drain. Mash the eggplant with the garlic and spices. Fry this purée in the oil in the skillet until all liquid evaporates and there is only oil and vegetable left. Stir the purée often to avoid scorching. Drain in a colander. Season with vinegar or lemon juice to taste. Taste for salt. Serve at room temperature.

Melanzane alla Campagnola
Country-style grilled eggplant (Italy)

In this easy eggplant dish, from the Italian region of Apulia, the slices emerge crisp on the outside and creamy within—the result of soaking in salt brine before grilling. This method works beautifully, not only extracting bitter juices without oversalting, but also adding moisture, which causes the interiors to steam while the exteriors crisp when the slices are grilled near hot coals. Fresh fruity olive oil is sprinkled over the slices after grilling. Prepare at least four hours before serving.

When buying eggplant, remember to choose those that are "light in the hand" and sound hollow when tapped with the fingers.

SERVES 4 TO 5

    2 ³/₄-pound eggplants, or 1 1½-pound eggplant
       Salt
    ⅓ cup extra-virgin olive oil
    1 tablespoon chopped parsley
    1 tablespoon slivered basil leaves
    2 tablespoons slivered spearmint leaves
    2 cloves garlic, peeled and sliced
       Freshly ground black pepper
       Vinegar (optional)

1. Hull the eggplant and cut into 1-inch-thick rounds. Soak the eggplant in cold salted water (2 tablespoons salt to 1 quart water) for 30 minutes, or until the eggplant leaches brown juices.

2. Light hardwood charcoal and when there are white coals, rinse the eggplant slices, drain, and place on the grid, but not directly over the coals to avoid charring the flesh. Cover and grill the slices, turning occasionally, until golden brown and completely cooked, about 30 minutes. (The slower the cooking the creamier the centers.) Transfer the slices to a flat dish, sprinkle with olive oil, herbs, garlic, and pepper. Let the dish stand at least 4 hours, turning the slices occasionally. If desired, drizzle with a few drops of vinegar.

Charmoulit Badhinjane
Fish with eggplant and tomato sauce (Tunisia)

Here is a simple sauce for broiled or fried fish made with tomato, onion, garlic, and slices of crisp browned eggplant.

Concerning the salting of eggplant slices and the absorption of frying oil, here is a tip from Suzy Benghiat, author of *Middle Eastern Cooking* (published by Harmony Books in 1984). She writes, "instead of leaving them only ten minutes, or even two hours—which is the longest time usually recommended—leave them for at least ten hours or overnight. Then dry them with paper towels. Although they will have withered, they will recover their shape when fried and you will be astonished at how little oil they take up." A method that works well in this recipe.

If you don't want to fry the eggplant slices, you can brown them under the broiler.

SERVES 2

    1 ³⁄₄-pound eggplant
       Coarse salt
  ¹⁄₃ cup olive oil
    2 medium onions, chopped
    2 to 3 garlic cloves, peeled and sliced
    1 tablespoon tomato paste diluted in 1 cup water
  ¹⁄₂ tablespoon harissa (pages 200–201)
  ¹⁄₂ tablespoon tabil (page 197)
    2 white lean saltwater fish fillets (6 to 7 ounces each)
    1 tablespoon cider vinegar

1. Cut the eggplant into ¹⁄₂-inch rounds. Salt them and weight down with a plate in a noncorrosive colander, and leave overnight.

2. Rinse the eggplant slices, squeeze gently, and pat dry with kitchen toweling.

3. Heat the oil in a medium skillet and fry the eggplant in batches until brown on both sides. Maintain sufficient heat to seal the eggplant's surfaces, protecting it from absorbing any of the frying oil. Drain, cut into small pieces, and set aside.

4. Pour off all but 1 tablespoon of the oil from the skillet. Add the onion and 2 tablespoons water; cover and cook, stirring, over medium heat, until soft and

(continued)

golden. Add the garlic, the diluted tomato paste, the harissa, and the tabil. Cook over medium heat for 20 minutes, stirring.

5. Bake, broil, or fry the fish. Meanwhile, slip the eggplant into the sauce, add the vinegar, and correct the seasoning. Cook a few minutes to blend flavors. Pour over fish and serve.

Ćevapčići

Finely ground skewered beef (Dalmatia)

I stayed with a buxom middle-aged schoolteacher named Mrs. Jovanovic the summer I lived in Gruz, and she used to make this all the time. In the evening she'd serve *ajvar* as an accompaniment, always served, too, with a plate of chopped raw onions.

SERVES 5

 1½ pounds finely ground lean beef (ground 3 times)
  1 garlic clove, crushed
 ⅛ teaspoon grated nutmeg
 ¼ teaspoon hot Hungarian paprika, or more to taste
   Salt
   Freshly ground black pepper
  3 to 4 tablespoons club soda
   Finely chopped raw onion or rings
  2 cups *ajvar* (pages 74–75)

1. Mix meat, garlic, spices, salt, and pepper. Gradually work in the club soda. With wet hands, form the meat into 40 small sausage shapes, packing them around ten 10-inch skewers, 4 on each.

2. Broil quickly on both sides, 2 to 3 inches from a broiler flame or over hot coals, until done to taste. Serve at once with the onion and *ajvar*.

Melanzane Ripiene
Stuffed eggplant (Italy)

These aromatic and delightful eggplant halves are a specialty of Apulia and perfect for the antipasti table. Choose short and plump eggplants for this recipe.

SERVES 4

4 Italian eggplants (4 or 5 ounces each), preferably short and plump
Coarse salt

FILLING

1 teaspoon (20) small capers, rinsed and drained
8 anchovy fillets, rinsed, drained, and roughly chopped
1/4 packed cup (1 ounce) finely grated Pecorino cheese
Freshly ground black pepper
3 small garlic cloves, peeled and slivered

1 1/2 tablespoons olive oil
Pinches of Mediterranean oregano, crumbled just before using
2 teaspoons dry white wine
1 teaspoon red wine vinegar

1. Wash, drain, and hull the eggplants. Halve the eggplants lengthwise and make two or three deep slits in the flesh; do not pierce the skin. Sprinkle with salt and place cut side down in a colander. Put a heavy plate on top and let stand at least 30 minutes. Rinse thoroughly and pat dry with paper toweling.

2. In a mixing bowl, combine the capers, anchovies, cheese, and pepper and crush to make a paste, about 3 tablespoons. Divide mixture into 8 equal parts and fill the slits in the eggplant halves with garlic slivers and a portion of the paste. Reshape the eggplants.

3. In a large nonstick skillet, heat olive oil to hot but not smoking. Add the eggplant, cut side down, and reduce the heat to moderate. Cover and cook until the eggplant flesh turns golden brown, about 10 minutes. Turn each eggplant and cook, uncovered, until the flesh is tender, about 5 minutes. (Check that the flesh around the top is soft.) Place eggplant, flesh side up, on a serving plate; sprinkle with oregano, white wine, and vinegar and let stand about 20 minutes before serving.

Hünkar Beğendi
Smoky eggplant cream (Turkey)

□

The Turkish name of this smooth and delicate cream means "the sultan approved." It is a sumptuous dish of the palest, creamiest eggplant flesh blended with a mild cheese sauce, delicious with grilled kebabs, roasted meats, and poultry.

In summer, for superior flavor, grill over hardwood charcoal.

SERVES 4 TO 6 AS A SIDE DISH

2   3/4-pound eggplants
    Juice of 1 lemon
2   tablespoons butter
3   tablespoons flour
1   cup hot milk
1/2 cup grated Parmesan cheese
    Salt

1. Prick each eggplant three or four times with a toothpick; set over a high gas flame or hot coals and turn as each side becomes black and the flesh very soft. Remove the charred skin and any hard seeds while still hot. Drop into cold water mixed with the lemon juice (to keep the flesh white) and let stand at least 20 minutes.

2. Meanwhile, melt the butter in a 3-quart saucepan. Off heat, stir in the flour. Cook, stirring, until the flour turns golden in color. Whisk in the milk and continue to cook until smooth. Set over lowest heat and continue to cook, stirring occasionally, 5 to 10 minutes longer.

3. Drain the eggplant, then squeeze to remove bitter juices and excess water. Mash the eggplant with a potato masher and add to the saucepan and bring to the boil, stirring, over low heat. Stir in the cheese and adjust the seasoning with salt. Serve hot.

Baba Ghanouj

Eggplant dip with sesame seed paste (Middle East)

SERVES 4

- 1 1-pound eggplant
- 3 tablespoons tahini (sesame seed paste)
   Juice of 1 lemon
- 1 garlic clove, peeled and crushed with ½ teaspoon salt
- 3 tablespoons cold water, or more if desired
   Hot Hungarian paprika
- 2 tablespoons chopped parsley
   Olive oil

1. Prick the eggplant three or four times with a toothpick; set over a high gas flame or hot coals and turn as each side becomes black and the flesh very soft.

2. Meanwhile, put tahini, lemon juice, and crushed garlic in a food processor and blend to a smooth consistency. Add 3 tablespoons cold water to thin and lighten the mixture.

3. When the eggplant has completely collapsed, remove from the heat. When cool enough to handle, remove the charred skin and any hard seeds. Squeeze the eggplant to remove bitter juices. Mash with a wooden potato masher, then add to the tahini in the food processor; pulse once or twice to blend.

4. Put the dip in a shallow dish and garnish with paprika, parsley, and olive oil. Serve cold with pita triangles.

Ajvar

Adriatic eggplant and green pepper relish

(Dalmatia)

*A*jvar is a popular side dish, a cold chopped green pepper and eggplant relish flavored with garlic, onion, lemon juice, and fruity olive oil. It is usually pale green, but tomato pulp can be added to give it a slightly different flavor and hue.

You rarely find *ajvar* on restaurant menus, but you'll see it in nearly every home. It is one of those simple things, like Tuscan white beans and tuna fish, over which no local person makes any fuss, but which everyone eats all the time because it's so good.

Ajvar is a versatile relish, great on melba toast with drinks, superb with fish, wonderful on bread while waiting for lunch, marvelous as a snack with sliced tomatoes, firm cheese, and a glass of cold Balkan yogurt. But it goes best, I think, with the grilled skewered ground meat dish, *ćevapčići* (page 70).

I have seen black-garbed grandmothers standing over their *ajvar* pots, stirring and waiting for the moment when the strong flavors of eggplant and peppers merge. They put the relish up in jars under a layer of olive oil, then leave it to mellow in a cool place, a treasured horde that will be served throughout the year.

MAKES ABOUT 2 CUPS

- 1 pound eggplant
- 4 small, elongated, light green Italian peppers
- 1 long hot green pepper
- ½ teaspoon finely chopped garlic
- 2 tablespoons grated onion
- 2½ tablespoons lemon juice or wine vinegar
- 6 tablespoons fruity olive oil
  Salt
  Freshly ground black pepper

1. Pierce the eggplant with a fork in two or three places. To give the eggplant a good smoky flavor and still have time for other kitchen work, start the eggplant off in a preheated 375-degree oven to bake for 20 minutes, turning midway. Place the peppers (sweet and hot) on a baking sheet and set in the oven to bake for 30 minutes, turning them midway too.

2. When the eggplant has baked 20 minutes, set it over a gas flame or over hot coals and cook until it is completely soft and the skin is black and blistery. Rub off the black parched skin under cold running water, then squeeze gently to remove any bitter juices. Chop the pulp fine.

3. Remove the peppers when soft, cover with a towel, and allow to cool. Core, seed, and slip off the skins of the peppers; chop fine and mix with the eggplant. Add garlic, onion, and lemon juice. Stir in the oil a tablespoon at a time. Season with salt and pepper to taste. Chill.

TOMATO

==

It's impossible to conceive of Mediterranean food without considering the tomato, but it didn't arrive in the area until the sixteenth century when the Spanish brought it back from the New World. It was first called the "love apple" and it gradually became the region's culinary workhorse. With good reason, too, for like the eggplant it can be mashed, braised, baked, fried, stuffed, and boiled. In addition, it can be eaten raw.

I give less than a dozen tomato recipes here, but I'd write a book of tomato recipes if I could. There's a version of *tabooli* flavored with tomato juice in Turkey, and a Moroccan *tagine* that is absolutely divine. Chicken and tomatoes are simmered together and when the combination is good and thick, honey and cinnamon are added. Elizabeth David writes of a Corsican tomato dish, *pebronata,* that is served with braised beef. It's a seasoned tomato sauce with juniper berries, red wine, and fried peppers, and it shouldn't be confused with the equally famous Sicilian *peperonata,* served lukewarm or cold with meat. In Greece, they stuff small seedless tomatoes with hazelnuts, and in the Levant they use tomatoes to flavor pilaf. In fact, there are so many uses for tomatoes that one wonders what on earth Europeans did before the "love apple" arrived.

Coulis de Tomate à la Provençale

Fresh, thick tomato sauce in the style of Provence (France)

This is my personal recipe for tomato sauce—the one I used for testing all the recipes in this book. Because out-of-season tomatoes lack taste, combine a little imported tomato paste with fresh tomatoes or use canned tomatoes.

MAKES 3 CUPS

- 1 cup chopped onions
- 3 tablespoons olive oil
- 3 small garlic cloves, crushed
- 3 to 4 cups peeled, seeded, and chopped tomatoes, juices strained
- 1 bay leaf
- 1 fresh thyme sprig, or ¼ teaspoon dried thyme
- 2 cloves
- ½ teaspoon sugar
  Salt
  Freshly ground black pepper

In a heavy skillet, cook the onions in oil until soft but not browned. Add the garlic, the tomatoes, the strained tomato juices, herbs, cloves, sugar, salt, and pepper. Cook, stirring often, about 20 minutes, until thickened. Push the sauce through a food mill. Readjust the seasoning.

Note: This sauce freezes well.

TOMATO PASTE

It was only when I started work on this book that I came to fully appreciate tomato paste, the way it can create deep, rich nonacidic flavored sauces. The secret, I learned, is twofold: To use this paste only in small amounts, and to revitalize it before use.

The Tunisians understand this. They sizzle tomato paste in olive oil until it glistens, making it lively, light, and aromatic. Whenever one of my recipes calls for canned tomato paste, you will find this instruction added.

Not all tomato pastes are the same. Some, in fact, are outright nasty. I like Contadina and Pagani brands. You can make your own with crushed ripe tomatoes. Simply add salt (about 1 teaspoon per pound) and cook slowly until the tomatoes have lost most of their moisture, stirring toward the end to avoid burning. Pack paste in small dollops as described below and store in the freezer.

After opening a can of tomato paste, tear off about a dozen 12 by 12-inch sheets of plastic wrap and drop tablespoonsful of paste on each sheet. Wrap each individually into airtight packets, place the whole lot in a freezer bag, and store in the freezer. Use as needed. Frozen tomato paste will keep a long time.

Gazpacho
Cold vegetable soup (Spain)

This is the great Andalusian dish, fundamental to the Andalusian eating experience. Although contemporary versions could not have been served before the discovery of America and the importation of tomatoes and peppers to Spain, the idea is ancient. Pablo Amate, a Spanish food writer, told me "a poor peasant had appeared in Cadiz in Roman times with a dish consisting of water, oil, garlic, onion, and bread, which Julius Caesar realized would make good sustenance for his troops. Later, with the discovery of the Americas, tomatoes and other vegetables were added, until, by the eighteenth century, the word 'gazpacho' described a dish eaten by laborers from the wooden bowls in which they crushed and pounded vegetables."

Every city and village has a version. A dish that is so much a part of the Andalusian soul is naturally thought to be supremely healthy, an idea extolled by contemporary Spanish food writer Gonzalo Sol: "Each ingredient [serves] a vital function: water hydrates the body, salt retains it in the system, vinegar refreshes, oil's fat content builds up energy reserves, bread supplies carbohydrates for quick energy, and garlic provides a vitamin and mineral supplement and, more significantly, exerts a dilating effect, which promotes perspiration."

This Sevillano version of gazpacho, prepared by a young chef named Ana Aranda (who learned it from her grandmother), is simpler than most, made only of tomatoes, garlic, a little bell pepper, some soaked stale bread, fruity olive oil, and an excellent sherry wine vinegar. (Add a few anchovies for a deeper flavor.) Either way, the balance is perfect and the texture is foamy. Ana insists that water must not be added—that the tomatoes provide all the soup's liquid.

I learned when I tried to reproduce this version that no precise formula can be offered because the flavor and intensity of vegetables vary. Juicy vine-ripened tomatoes are a necessity, and the bread should be coarse and natural from a good chewy loaf. The lesson to the home cook: Make this soup at summer's end, then taste and adjust.

SERVES 4

2 slices of stale coarse-textured white bread, crusts removed

2 pounds vine-ripened tomatoes, cored, seeded, and roughly chopped

½ cup chopped red or green bell pepper

1 to 2 garlic cloves, chopped

4 to 6 anchovy fillets, rinsed and drained (optional)

1 tablespoon extra-virgin olive oil

1 teaspoon sherry wine vinegar
 Salt
 Freshly ground black pepper
 Pinch of sugar (optional)

GARNISHES

1 slice of white bread, cubed

1 teaspoon olive oil

¼ cup diced vine-ripened tomatoes

¼ cup diced red bell pepper

¼ cup diced green bell pepper

2 scallions, trimmed and finely chopped

1. Soak the bread in 1 cup water for 3 minutes. Squeeze out water. You should have about ½ cup softened bread. In a food processor, working in batches, purée bread, tomatoes, bell pepper, garlic, and anchovies, if using, until well blended and foamy. With the machine running, add oil and vinegar. If desired, strain the mixture through a sieve into a bowl. Cover and refrigerate for at least 1 hour. Then add salt and pepper to taste; the soup may need a pinch of sugar. (Recipe can be made ahead and stored, covered, in the refrigerator for up to 2 days.)

2. Preheat the oven to 350 degrees. Toss bread cubes with olive oil. Spread on a baking sheet and bake for 10 to 12 minutes, or until crisp and lightly browned. Place on a platter with the vegetable garnishes. Serve soup in chilled bowls and let each guest add garnishes.

Chorba bil Hout

Fish soup from the island of Jerba (Tunisia)

◪

I found several excellent regional dishes in a Jerbian home when I was there during Ramadan, the month of fasting from sunrise to sunset. My hostess, Maherzia Ghaddour, told me, "During this month when we break the fast, we spoil ourselves the most."

For her fast-breaking meal, she served a sharp and refreshing salad of charcoal-grilled peppers, tomatoes, and garlic, garnished with the smallest home-pickled capers (see *mechouia,* pages 88–89); *briks* (crisp pastry enclosing ground seasoned lamb and egg); and this hearty, spicy fish soup thickened with grain half the size of orzo, and drizzled at the end with good Tunisian olive oil—pure, perfumed, limpid, and delicious.

SERVES 6

- ½ pound black bass, porgy, mullet, or perch fillets
  Coarse sea salt
- 1½ pounds fish heads, frames, tails, and trimmings
- 3 tablespoons fruity olive oil
- 1 small onion, peeled and chopped
- 1½ tablespoons tomato paste
- 1½ teaspoons crushed garlic
- ¾ teaspoon hot Hungarian paprika, or more to taste
- 1½ teaspoons ground cumin
- ¼ teaspoon ground coriander
- 2 tablespoons chopped parsley
- 1 small celery sprig, chopped
- ¼ teaspoon crushed dried mint
  Freshly ground pepper
- 1 15-ounce can tomato sauce
- ⅔ cup pearl barley
  Pinch of sugar (optional)
  Juice of 1 lemon

1. Sprinkle fillets with sea salt and keep refrigerated. Wash and drain all frames, heads, and scraps.

2. In a medium soup pot, heat the olive oil and sauté the onion over low heat until lightly colored. Add the tomato paste and stir for 1 to 2 minutes, until smooth and glossy (this softens the metallic taste of canned tomato paste). Add the fish heads, frames, and trimmings and sauté until golden, about 3 minutes. Add the garlic, hot paprika, cumin, coriander, parsley, celery, mint, 1 teaspoon salt, and ½ teaspoon pepper. Sauté, stirring, until the herbs and spices become hot and fragrant. Add tomato sauce and 2 cups water and simmer 10 minutes. Remove from the heat and allow to cool.

3. Place barley in a small saucepan, add 1 quart water and ½ teaspoon salt, and bring to a boil. Cover, reduce the heat, and simmer 30 minutes, or until tender.

4. Meanwhile, strain the soup through a food mill, pressing down on all solids in order to extract as much liquid as possible. Discard the solids. Return the soup to the pot. Add the barley. If necessary, add a pinch of sugar to round out the taste. Slip in the fish fillets and poach over medium-low heat until cooked through, 5 minutes. Remove and flake the fish. Reduce the soup until it is rich and creamy. Correct the seasoning with salt, pepper, and lemon juice. Divide the flaked fish among six soup bowls, ladle over the soup, and serve hot.

Pomodori Ripieni alla Calabrese

Stuffed tomatoes in the style of Calabria (Italy)

SERVES 4

8 firm red tomatoes
Salt
¼ loaf of stale French or Italian bread
2 garlic cloves, peeled and crushed
Olive oil
1 2-ounce can anchovy fillets in oil
¼ cup pine nuts
¼ cup yellow raisins, plumped in water, then drained
2 tablespoons chopped fresh parsley
Freshly ground black pepper

1. Preheat the oven to 375 degrees.

2. Cut a slice off the top of each tomato, then scoop out the pulp and seeds and discard. Salt the shells and set them upside down to drain.

3. Thinly slice the bread, rub with garlic, and cut into ¼-inch cubes. Brown lightly in olive oil and set aside to drain on paper towels.

4. Rinse and mash the anchovies. Mix with the bread cubes, nuts, raisins, and chopped parsley. Season the mixture with pepper and very little salt. Stuff the tomatoes, cover with the tops, arrange in the baking dish, and bake 20 to 25 minutes. Serve hot or warm.

Tomates Farcis à la Provençale

Stuffed baked tomatoes (France)

The economical cook will recognize the value of using leftover beef stew to stuff red ripe tomatoes in early fall. At other times of the year, however, when tomatoes are not at their peak, I don't recommend this recipe.

To catch the delicious juices, be sure to serve the tomatoes on bread *croûtes* (rounds of stale French bread) rubbed with garlic, brushed with olive oil, and toasted in the oven.

SERVES 4

8	ripe unblemished tomatoes
	Coarse salt
	Granulated sugar
1/4	loaf of stale French bread
1/2	garlic clove
	Extra-virgin olive oil
1 1/2	cups cubed or shredded cooked beef (6 to 8 ounces) (see note)
3	tablespoons degreased and reduced meat juices (see note)
2	tablespoons chopped parsley
3	scallions, chopped
2	garlic cloves, peeled and crushed
1/3	cup bread crumbs
2	teaspoons capers, rinsed and drained
	Freshly ground black pepper
2	tablespoons butter

1. Cut a slice off the top of each tomato and set aside. Scoop out the pulp and seeds and chop the seeded pulp. Salt the shells, add a pinch of sugar, and set them upside down to drain.

2. Preheat the oven to 400 degrees.

3. Cut the bread into 8 1/2-inch rounds, rub with the garlic half, sprinkle with olive oil, and toast in the oven until golden brown.

4. In a mixing bowl, combine the beef, its reduced cooking juices, parsley, scallions, garlic cloves, 1/2 cup tomato pulp, 1/4 cup bread crumbs, and capers. Add salt and pepper to taste, blending well.

(continued)

5. Stuff the tomatoes with equal portions of the meat mixture; sprinkle with remaining bread crumbs, dot with butter, and cover with the cut-off slices of tomato. Place each tomato on a round of toasted bread. Place in a well-oiled baking dish, brush tops with oil, and bake until the tomatoes are tender, about 25 minutes. Serve warm.

Note: 1½ cups of succulent cooked and cubed beef and 3 tablespoons of savory juices can be quickly made in a pressure cooker. Place a 1¼-pound slice of beef shin along with 3 ounces blanched and cubed salt pork, 2 quartered onions, 1 whole onion stuck with a clove, 3 garlic cloves, 2 cut-up carrots, 1 quartered turnip, a small piece of orange rind, salt, pepper, parsley, bay leaf, thyme, 1 teaspoon tomato paste, and 1 cup white wine in a 4-quart pressure cooker. Cook at full pressure for 40 minutes. Cool contents. Strain, degrease juices, and reduce to 3 tablespoons. Trim the meat and cut into small cubes. Discard gristle, fat, bones, and vegetables.

Insalata Caprese
Tomato, mozzarella, and basil salad (Italy)

SERVES 4

    1 tablespoon finely chopped fresh basil leaves
    3 tablespoons olive oil
    3 red ripe tomatoes, peeled and sliced
    ½ pound fresh mozzarella cheese, thinly sliced
       Salt
       Freshly ground black pepper
       Wine vinegar

1. Marinate the basil leaves in the olive oil for 2 to 3 hours.

2. Arrange alternating slices of tomato and cheese on a long serving dish. Season with salt and pepper to taste. Spoon over the oil and chopped basil. Add just a drop of vinegar.

Calamares en su Tinta #2

Squid in its own ink with tomato sauce (Spain)

SERVES 4 TO 6

- 2 pounds large squid
- 1 cup chopped onion
- 3 tablespoons olive oil
- 1 tablespoon flour
- ½ cup dry white wine
- ½ teaspoon finely chopped garlic
- 2 tablespoons finely chopped fresh parsley
- 2 tablespoons tomato paste
- Salt
- Freshly ground black pepper

1. To clean the squid, remove and discard the head but set aside the tentacles. Discard the entrails and transparent bone but keep the ink sacs. Peel off the outer mottled skin. Wash the squid, inside and out, and wash the tentacles; cut into bite-size pieces.

2. In a skillet, cook the onion in hot oil until soft and golden. Add the squid and the tentacles and cook, stirring, 5 minutes. Sprinkle with flour and moisten with white wine. Add the garlic, parsley, and tomato paste. Simmer, covered, over gentle heat for 30 minutes.

3. Set a sieve over a bowl, crush the ink sacs in the sieve, and collect the ink. Stir into the sauce. Bring to a boil, season with salt and pepper, and allow to simmer 15 minutes. Serve with rice.

Psari Plaki

Baked fish with tomatoes and onions (Greece)

SERVES 4

4 fish steaks or fillets: halibut, bass, codfish, red snapper, or rockfish
(6 or 7 ounces each)
Lemon juice
Coarse sea salt
Freshly ground black pepper
⅓ cup olive oil
3 cups chopped onions
2 cups fresh or canned tomato sauce
⅓ cup finely chopped parsley
1 teaspoon crumbled oregano
⅛ teaspoon ground allspice or cinnamon
⅓ cup sweet red wine, such as Greek Mavrodaphne, Italian Recioto, or
port
⅓ cup finely grated bread crumbs

1. Wash the fish slices. Rub with lemon juice and rinse. Rub with salt and pepper and let stand 10 minutes. Rinse again and drain.

2. Preheat the oven to 350 degrees.

3. Heat the oil in a skillet and sauté the onions over medium heat for 5 minutes, or until soft but not browned. Add the tomato sauce, parsley, oregano, allspice, and wine. Season with salt and pepper. Cook, covered, 10 minutes.

4. Arrange the fish slices in an oiled 10-inch baking dish. Pour the sauce over the fish. Sprinkle the surface with bread crumbs and dribble over a little oil. Set on the middle rack of the oven and bake 30 minutes, or until the fish is cooked and a nice crust has formed over the sauce. Serve hot, warm, or tepid.

Keftaidakia me Saltsa

Small meatballs in tomato sauce (Greece)

SERVES 6 AS PART OF A GREEK *MEZZE*

- 1 small onion, finely chopped
- 4 tablespoons vegetable oil
- 1½ cups fresh or canned tomato sauce
- 1 tablespoon red wine vinegar
- 1 teaspoon paprika
  Freshly ground black pepper
- ½ teaspoon ground cinnamon
  Pinch of ground cloves
  Salt
- 1 pound ground beef
- 2 tablespoons grated onion
- 1 garlic clove, peeled and crushed
- ½ cup bread crumbs
- 1 teaspoon crushed mint
- ¼ teaspoon dried oregano
- 2 pinches ground allspice
- 1 egg, lightly beaten
  Flour
- 2 tablespoons butter

1. In a 1½-quart saucepan, soften the chopped onion in 2 tablespoons oil without browning. Add the tomato sauce, vinegar, paprika, ½ teaspoon black pepper, cinnamon, cloves, and salt to taste. Cook, covered, over medium heat for 20 minutes, stirring often.

2. Meanwhile, mix the ground beef with the grated onion, garlic, and bread crumbs. Add the herbs, allspice, and salt and pepper to taste. Work in the egg and blend thoroughly. With floured hands, shape into 30 1-inch balls. Fry in 2 tablespoons oil and 2 tablespoons butter until nicely browned on all sides and completely cooked. Drain on paper towels.

3. Drop the meatballs into the prepared sauce and simmer 2 to 3 minutes. Serve hot or at room temperature.

Mechouia
Mixed roasted vegetables with capers (Tunisia)

Tunisians adore this mildly hot, spicy salad of roasted peppers, tomatoes, and garlic. It accompanies couscous, salads, and slices of country-style bread. *Mechouia* is often garnished with chunks of tuna and sliced hard-cooked eggs, but I like it best embellished with tiny capers. In summer you may want to add a sprig or two of chopped purslane.

You may think that burning vegetables will ruin their flavor, but the simple char-grilling of fleshy peppers, ripe tomatoes, and fat garlic cloves creates a tasty smoky enhancement.

Peppers should be placed directly on a gas flame or over very hot hardwood charcoal so that their skins quickly blister and char. If you use this method you will obtain a wonderful smoky flavor and your peppers will not be slimy, a frequent occurrence when they are baked in the oven.

Tomatoes are broiled until their skins are blistered and charred and their flesh is cooked through. If portions of the skins become too black and hard, discard. If your tomatoes are watery they should be drained and seeded.

MAKES ABOUT 2½ CUPS, SERVING 6

- ⅔ to ¾ pound fresh smooth mildly hot chili peppers (see note)
- 1¾ pounds (4 to 5) green bell peppers
- 2 large garlic cloves, unpeeled
- ½ pound (3) red ripe tomatoes, preferably the meatier plum tomatoes
- 2 teaspoons tabil (page 197)
- ¾ teaspoon salt
- Juice of ½ lemon
- 1 to 2 tablespoons olive oil
- 1 teaspoon small capers, drained

1. Quick-char the chili and bell peppers on all sides over a high flame. If using an electric broiler, do this as close to the heat as possible. When the peppers are cool, remove stems and seeds and slip off the skins. Don't rinse under water or they will lose some of their flavor. Pulse the peppers in a food processor until finely chopped. Set aside.

2. Broil the garlic and tomatoes until softened. When the garlic is cool enough to handle, peel and crush to a purée. Seed and stem the tomatoes (if tomatoes are excessively watery, drain well). Process to a purée with the garlic.

3. In a bowl combine tomato purée, peppers, tabil, salt, and lemon juice, mixing well. Gradually beat in the olive oil. Taste and correct the seasoning. Spread out in a shallow dish, scatter the capers on top, and serve at room temperature.

Note: The mildly hot green peppers used in Tunisia appear similar to New Mexican fresh chili peppers (California Anaheims), but are closer in flavor to a poblano pepper when grilled. Since peppers vary in degree of hotness, you may have to adjust quantities. If poblanos are not available, substitute green bell peppers and one fresh jalapeño pepper.

Yesil Domates Bastisi

Green tomato gratin (Turkey)

This gratin dish from the city of Izmir takes little preparation and makes a lovely side dish for grilled fish or chicken. Use late summer green tomatoes before they ripen (or use those that are never going to get a chance). The mild acidity of green tomatoes blends perfectly with onions that have been roasted to bring out their sweetness. It all tastes wonderful with shavings of *ricotta salata*.

SERVES 6 AS A SIDE DISH

> 5 medium onions, about 1½ pounds
> 3 tablespoons olive oil
> 3 pounds green tomatoes, cut in half
> Salt
> Freshly ground pepper
> Pinch of cayenne
> 1 cup vegetable, poultry, or meat stock
> ⅓ cup thin shavings of *ricotta salata*

1. Preheat the oven to 400 degrees. Peel and chop the onions. Heat 2 tablespoons of the oil in a saucepan over moderate heat, add the onions, and stir until tender. Remove from the heat.

(continued)

2. Transfer the onions to a round, shallow baking dish. Place the tomato halves on top. Add the remaining olive oil, salt, pepper, cayenne, and stock, cover with foil, and bake in the oven until the tomatoes are tender and all the moisture has been absorbed, about 1 hour.

3. Remove the foil and crush the vegetables with a potato masher. Correct the seasoning and serve warm with thin shavings of cheese.

Mnazzalleh

Eggplant, tomatoes, and chick-peas (Middle East)

Here is a succulent Arab variation on ratatouille. Large chunks of eggplant are fried in olive oil until just golden, enrobed in a spiced tomato sauce, enriched with peeled and cracked chick-peas, then cooked until they are so soft that they collapse. The dish is then left to mellow at least 3 hours before serving.

SERVES 6

    ½ cup dried chick-peas
    4 eggplants (1½ pounds)
     Coarse salt
    ½ cup olive oil
  1½ cups sliced onions
    5 large garlic cloves
    3 ripe medium tomatoes, peeled, seeded, and chopped
    ½ cup chopped parsley
    1 teaspoon sugar
    ½ tablespoon dried mint
     Pinches of grated nutmeg or cinnamon
    2 tablespoons chopped fresh coriander

1. Soak the chick-peas in water overnight. Remove 3 vertical strips of skin from each eggplant, leaving the eggplants striped, then cut each eggplant into six chunks. Salt them and leave to drain overnight in a noncorrosive colander.

2. Drain, peel, and split the soaked chick-peas. Rinse the eggplant and squeeze dry. Slowly heat the oil in a medium skillet until hot. Add the eggplant in small

batches and fry over medium-high heat until golden brown on all sides but not fully cooked. Transfer the eggplant with a slotted spoon to a colander set over a plate to catch any excess oil.

3. Reheat the remaining oil in the skillet. Add the sliced onions and ½ cup water and cook for 20 minutes. When the water has evaporated and the onions turn golden, add the garlic, chick-peas, and tomatoes. Cook, stirring, for a minute, then add 1½ cups water. Bring to a boil, cover, and cook 20 minutes.

4. Add the eggplant to the tomato mixture, along with half the parsley, 1 teaspoon salt, sugar, mint, and nutmeg. Simmer until the eggplant is very soft, about 20 minutes. Remove from the heat and allow to cool to room temperature. Garnish with remaining parsley and the coriander and serve.

Tortilla Arcos de la Frontera
Onion, potato, and green pepper omelet (Spain)

It is true that the best food around the Mediterranean is found not in restaurants but in private homes. Spain is a formal country; for the traveler, invitations into a home do not come easily. In the last few years, however, a number of families in Andalusia have turned their ranches, palaces, hunting lodges, and manor houses into small private hotels where it is possible to eat traditional family fare.

Such a hotel is the Cortijo Fain, located a couple of miles south of the spectacular walled town of Arcos de la Frontera. The food here is not fancy. It is prepared by a local cook, not a chef, and there is no menu. One simply eats what is served. One of the dishes that I enjoyed was this tortilla.

A Spanish tortilla is a dense, moist omelet, usually made with potatoes. The cook at the Cortijo Fain adds sweet cubanelle peppers to the potatoes and serves roasted red peppers drizzled with sherry vinegar alongside. With the help of Patsy Jamieson of *Eating Well* magazine, I have adapted the original recipe to cut back on the egg yolks.

(continued)

1 tablespoon olive oil
4 all-purpose potatoes (about 1½ pounds)
2 sweet frying (cubanelle) peppers, cored, seeded, and thinly sliced
1 onion, thinly sliced
Salt
Freshly ground black pepper
3 large eggs
3 large egg whites

1. In a large nonstick skillet over medium-low heat, heat 1½ teaspoons oil. Add potatoes, peppers, and onion. Season with ½ teaspoon salt and a generous grinding of pepper. Cover and cook for 15 minutes, turning the vegetables occasionally, until potatoes are tender and lightly browned. Set aside to cool slightly. Wipe the skillet clean.

2. In a bowl, whisk the eggs, egg whites, a pinch of salt, and a generous grinding of black pepper. Add the cooled potato mixture and mix to thoroughly coat the vegetables with eggs.

3. Pour the remaining 1½ teaspoons oil into the skillet and heat over medium heat. Add the egg mixture, spreading the vegetables evenly across the skillet. Cook for 4 to 5 minutes, until the underside is browned. (It should be slightly soft in the center.) Hold a large plate over the skillet and invert the tortilla onto it. Slide the tortilla back into the skillet. Cook for 2 to 3 minutes, or until the underside is brown. The tortilla should be firm but still moist. Transfer to a serving plate and let stand a minute or two before cutting into wedges. Serve hot or at room temperature.

Ratatouille

Provençal vegetable stew (France)

Here's my recipe for the great vegetable specialty of Provence, which is echoed in almost all the Mediterranean countries. Long ago people realized that eggplant, tomatoes, and peppers made a beautiful delicious blend.

Two of the wonderful things about ratatouille are that it can be even better the second night, and that it's just as delicious cold as hot. I often spread leftover ratatouille in a gratin dish, making little indentations on the surface. When it's reheated, I break eggs into the indentations and return it to the oven until the eggs are baked.

SERVES 8 TO 10

1	pound eggplant
	Salt
3	to 5 zucchini, each about 5 inches long
2	medium green bell peppers, or 5 small elongated light-green Italian peppers
1	large onion
4	large red ripe tomatoes
6	to 8 tablespoons fruity olive oil
1	bay leaf
	Freshly ground black pepper
	Pinch of cayenne (optional)
1	teaspoon finely chopped garlic
3/4	teaspoon thyme leaves
2	tablespoons chopped fresh parsley
1	teaspoon chopped fresh basil

1. Cut the eggplant into 1-inch chunks and place in a colander. Salt them, top with a weight, and leave to drain for at least 30 minutes. Meanwhile, cut the zucchini into 1-inch chunks, salt them, and leave them to drain on paper toweling.

2. Seed, derib, and cut up the green peppers. Cut the onion into eighths. Peel, seed, and roughly chop the tomatoes.

(continued)

3. Rinse the eggplant and the zucchini in cold water; squeeze gently and pat dry with paper towels. Heat ¼ cup oil in a large skillet and lightly brown the eggplant and zucchini chunks. Transfer to a 4-quart casserole.

4. Lightly brown the green peppers in the same oil. Add to the casserole. Add the onion, tomatoes, bay leaf, and the remaining oil to the casserole. Season with salt and pepper and, if desired, cayenne. Simmer, covered, 30 minutes, stirring often. Stir in the garlic and the thyme. Cook 20 minutes more, or until thick and well blended. Serve hot or cold. Sprinkle with the fresh herbs.

Biber Salcasi
Pepper paste (Turkey)

This is a fast and easy recipe for homemade pepper paste, used to flavor pilafs, soups, bulgur salads, and stews in southeastern Turkey and northern Syria.

MAKES ABOUT ⅔ CUP

2 red bell peppers (about 1¼ pounds), cored, stemmed, and seeded
1 small hot chili pepper, cored, stemmed, and seeded
¼ teaspoon sugar
Pinch of salt
2 teaspoons olive oil

1. Purée the peppers with 2 tablespoons water, sugar, and salt in the workbowl of a food processor.

2. Transfer to a saucepan and cook over medium-high heat, stirring often, until reduced to a jamlike consistency. (It can be reduced in a microwave.) Stir in the oil. (Keeps up to a week in the refrigerator if covered with more oil. To freeze, divide into 8 parts and use when needed.)

Muhammara

Aleppo-style red pepper and walnut dip (Syria)

◘

Spicy hot pepper is tamed with ground walnuts and pomegranate molasses to make a delicious coarse dip. Pomegranate molasses (available at Middle Eastern groceries) is a reduction of ripe pomegranates and sugar to a thick, jamlike consistency. It imbues *muhammara* with a delicious sweet-and-sour flavor.

Muhammara improves and mellows if made 4 or 5 days in advance and kept tightly closed in the refrigerator.

SERVES 6

- 1½ pounds red bell peppers
- ½ cup coarsely ground shelled walnuts
- 3 tablespoons quality bread crumbs or sesame cracker crumbs
  Juice of 1 lemon, or more to taste
- 4 teaspoons pomegranate molasses (preferably Cortas brand available at Middle Eastern grocers)
- ¼ teaspoon red chili paste, or more to taste
  Salt
- ¼ teaspoon ground cumin
- 1 tablespoon olive oil

1. Roast the peppers over gas or under the broiler, turning until blackened and blistered all over. Place in a bag to soften for 10 minutes to loosen the skins. Slit the peppers open and remove the membranes, stems, and seeds. Skin and leave to drain.

2. Meanwhile, combine the walnuts and bread crumbs in a food processor and process until finely ground. Add the bell peppers, lemon juice, and pomegranate molasses and blend until creamy. Add the chili paste to taste, adjust the seasoning, and scrape into a 2-cup storage jar. Chill overnight to allow flavors to mellow.

3. When ready to serve, scrape dip into a serving dish. Decorate with ground cumin and a drizzle of olive oil.

Felfel Mokli

Fried green peppers (Tunisia)

This version of fried peppers can be made with any sort of mild hot pepper. For those who like their peppers mild, Italian frying peppers are best.

The method described in step 1 to prepare peppers for frying is a Tunisian trick. The salt extracts moisture from the peppers, which encourages steam to form and inhibits the oil from entering the incisions. The salt also flavors them deliciously. (The diner should cut away the stem and seeds.)

In southern Tunisia, a couscous is regarded as naked without a final topping of fried green chilies.

SERVES 4 TO 6

1 pound mild hot elongated green peppers (Anaheim, banana, gypsy, or
    Hungarian, or substitute Italian frying peppers)
Coarse sea salt
4 tablespoons olive oil
2 teaspoons sweet and rich-flavored vinegar
Pinch of sugar (optional)
1 clove garlic, finely sliced

1. Wash and dry the peppers. With a small knife, puncture each whole pepper near the stem end. Slip a good pinch of coarse salt into the hole and let stand at least 30 minutes.

2. In a 10-inch skillet, heat all the olive oil over moderate heat. Add half the peppers, cover, and fry, turning once, until browned on all sides, about 5 minutes.

3. Transfer the peppers to a serving dish and pour half the oil in the skillet over them. (The point is to have a tasty oil for the dressing, but not an overcooked oil.)

4. Reheat the remaining oil in the skillet, add the remaining peppers, cover and fry as directed above. Transfer the peppers to the serving dish and discard the oil in the skillet.

5. Add vinegar, sugar, and garlic to the peppers and turn them in the dressing until well coated. Cool, cover, and refrigerate overnight. Bring to room temperature before serving.

Hrous

Home-style chili paste with onion spices (Tunisia)

This delicious chili mixture, called *hrous,* is used in southern Tunisia to flavor soups, stews, and couscous. I strongly urge you to try it in the Tunisian soup with barley and fennel seeds (pages 135–36) and the couscous with meatballs (pages 158–60).

I have greatly adapted the original recipe. My version is not the same *hrous* you will taste in Gabès, a town on the edge of the Sahara known for its good cooking. But it is still one of my favorite pepper pastes.

In a typical southern Tunisian home, the cook will slice about seventy pounds of fresh onions, toss them with salt and turmeric, pack them in earthen jugs, and leave them for three months to become soft and wet. The cook will then squeeze them dry, mix them with dried peppers, tabil flavoring, small amounts of ground cloves, *ras el hanout,* ginger, and dried mint, then knead the mixture until it has the color of Bordeaux wine. The reasoning behind the three-month wait is that since onions are fresh in June while peppers aren't ready until fall, the onions, while waiting for the peppers, slightly ferment and develop a special flavor of their own. The turmeric, which is an antioxidant, keeps the onions from spoiling.

MAKES ½ CUP

- ¼ pound fresh onions, peeled and thinly sliced
  Pinch of turmeric
- 2 tablespoons coarse salt
- 7 dried New Mexico or ancho chilies
- 1 dried hot red chili pepper
- ½ teaspoon tabil (page 197) or ground coriander
- ½ teaspoon ground caraway seed
- ½ teaspoon ground black pepper
- 2 good pinches of ground cinnamon mixed with ground rosebuds
- 3 tablespoons olive oil

1. In a wide shallow bowl, mix the onions, turmeric, and salt and let stand until soft and very wet, from 1 to 3 days.

2. Place a handful of onions in cheesecloth and squeeze until they are very dry. Repeat with remaining onions.

(continued)

3. If using New Mexico chilies, stem, seed, break up, and carefully toast them in an ungreased skillet over low heat until they give off their aroma. Remove at once to avoid burning. If using anchos, cover with boiling water and let stand 30 minutes, then stem, seed, and crush the dried chili.

4. Grind chilies to a powder in a blender or food processor. Add the spices and the onions, blending well. Pack into a 1-cup dry jar, cover with oil, and tightly close. Keep refrigerated.

Peperoni Arrostiti
Grilled red peppers (Italy)

Italian cooks frequently used chopped black and green olives in pasta sauces, meat dishes, breads, and pizzas. In this dish, chopped olives are gently cooked with capers to intensify their natural earthy taste and are spread over grilled red pepper strips. Serve warm as a first course.

SERVES 4

> 4 medium red bell peppers, grilled, seeded, and peeled
> 1 teaspoon olive oil
> ½ cup gaeta olives, pitted
> 2 tablespoons small capers, drained
> ½ teaspoon chopped garlic
> Pinch of dried Mediterranean oregano
> Salt
> Freshly ground black pepper
> Balsamic vinegar

1. Cut the peppers into julienne strips. Place in a shallow dish.

2. Warm the olive oil in a skillet over moderate heat. Add the olives, capers, garlic, oregano, salt, and pepper. Stir-fry for an instant. Add a dash of vinegar and spoon over the bell peppers. Cover and let stand 5 minutes before serving.

Peperoni Arrotolati

Yellow pepper "rollmops" stuffed with
pine nuts, golden raisins, and anchovies (Italy)

Here is one of the most delightful Mediterranean stuffed vegetable dishes. It is also one of the easiest to prepare. Grilled yellow peppers are stuffed with anchovies, capers, and yellow raisins, then baked and served at room temperature. The rolled pepper quarters are small enough to pick up with the fingers and eat out of hand. Delicious either warm or at room temperature, bake the rollmops a few hours before serving.

SERVES 4

4 large yellow peppers
3 tablespoons pine nuts
3 tablespoons golden raisins, roughly chopped
3 tablespoons capers, rinsed and drained
2 ounces (8 fillets) canned anchovies, rinsed, drained, and chopped
⅔ cup soft bread crumbs
2 tablespoons grated pecorino cheese
2 tablespoons olive oil
   Salt
   Freshly ground black pepper

1. Grill the peppers over a gas flame or under the broiler, turning them until the skins are completely blackened. Wash off the blackened skin under cool running water. Stem, seed, and quarter lengthwise to make 16 rectangles. Place smooth side up on paper toweling and press down gently to remove excess moisture.

2. In the workbowl of a food processor, combine the pine nuts, raisins, capers, anchovies, bread crumbs, cheese, 1 tablespoon olive oil, salt, and pepper. Process until just blended into a rough paste. Makes about 1 packed cup.

3. A few hours before serving, preheat the oven to 425 degrees.

4. Evenly divide the stuffing and place a portion on each pepper rectangle. Roll up one slice and secure with a toothpick. Repeat with the remaining rectangles. Place on a nonstick baking sheet about ½ inch apart. Brush tops with oil. Bake until slightly crisp and spotted brown, about 20 minutes. Remove the toothpicks and serve warm or at room temperature. Do not refrigerate.

Arroz en Caldero

Rice with green or red peppers
in the style of Murcia (Spain)

SERVES 6

     3 tablespoons olive oil
     2 garlic cloves, peeled but left whole
     1 pound boneless lean pork, cut into 1-inch cubes
     1 tablespoon chopped parsley
   1/4 teaspoon pulverized saffron
       Salt
       Freshly ground black pepper
   1/2 cup chopped onion
     1 cup peeled, seeded, and chopped ripe tomatoes
     1 pound sweet red or green peppers, deribbed, seeded, and cut into long
       strips (makes 3 cups)
     2 cups short- or medium-grain rice, preferably imported Spanish rice
     1 quart boiling water or beef stock

1. Heat the oil in a 10-inch straight-sided skillet and brown the garlic and the pork on all sides. Remove the garlic cloves when soft and brown. Mash them to a purée and return to the casserole. Add the parsley and the saffron, stirring. Sprinkle with salt and pepper. Add the onion, tomatoes, peppers, and 1½ cups water. Bring to the boil. Cook, covered, over low heat for 20 minutes. Remove the cover and cook over high heat about 5 minutes, stirring, until the mixture is thick.

2. Add the rice and cook for a few minutes. Add boiling water or stock, 1½ teaspoons salt, and pepper to taste. Bring to the boil, stirring. Cook over high heat for 5 minutes, reduce heat to low and cook until rice is tender, about 17 minutes. Remove from the heat and let stand for 5 to 10 minutes before serving.

Zeytinyağli Biber Dolmasi
Cold stuffed green peppers (Turkey)

In the Balkans, eggplants, tomatoes, and peppers are often stuffed with a mixture of cheeses, then set upright in a pan and baked. All through the Balkans and the Middle East you find various vegetables stuffed with rice, pine nuts, raisins, and plenty of onions and served cold. The following peppery version is from southeastern Turkey.

SERVES 4 TO 5

- ½ cup olive oil
- 2 medium onions, peeled and grated
- 1½ teaspoons salt
- ¼ cup pine nuts
- 1 cup rice
- ¼ cup currants
- 1 scant tablespoon tomato paste
- ¾ teaspoon freshly ground pepper
- 1 teaspoon sugar
- 1 teaspoon mixed spices (¾ teaspoon ground allspice mixed with pinches of hot red pepper, crumbled Mediterranean oregano, ground cumin, and ground cinnamon)
- 2 tablespoons fresh mint leaves, shredded
- 2 tablespoons fresh lemon juice
- 10 small green bell peppers (about 2⅓ pounds)
  Lemon quarters

1. Heat half the oil in a large skillet. Add the onion, 1 teaspoon of the salt, and 1 cup water. Cook, stirring, until most of the water has evaporated, about 15 minutes. Allow the onions to turn golden, stirring occasionally. Add the pine nuts and sauté until they turn golden, about 1 minute. Add the rice and cook, stirring, 3 minutes longer. Add 1 cup hot water, currants, tomato paste, pepper, sugar, and spices. Cook over low heat until the rice is half cooked and the water is absorbed, 5 minutes. Allow to cool. Add the mint and lemon juice, tossing well.

(continued)

2. Remove the pepper tops and pull out the seeds and hard white ribs. Rinse and drain. Stuff the peppers and stand them upright in a 5-quart casserole. Heat 1½ cups water with remaining oil and add to the casserole without disturbing the peppers. Moisten a sheet of parchment paper and place it crumpled over the peppers. Bring the liquid to the boil; cover, reduce the heat, and cook 45 minutes. Turn off the heat; allow peppers to cool in the casserole without uncovering. Serve garnished with lemon quarters at room temperature or chilled as a first course or part of a buffet.

OTHER MEDITERRANEAN VEGETABLES

Zucchini, fennel, cabbage, artichokes, carrots, spinach, Swiss chard, fresh favas, and cardoons—the list of Mediterranean vegetables goes on and on. Because these appear in Mediterranean markets in quantity in their respective seasons, the Mediterranean cook has a great repertory of recipes allowing her to cook each vegetable in innumerable ways. Here is a small collection of recipes from various parts of the region, all typically Mediterranean in their ingenuity.

Les Oignons Farcis

Glazed stuffed onions (France)

In France, Spain, and Italy, stuffed dishes are likely to be the result of family cooks striving to be economical—either by stretching meager portions of meat, poultry, fish, and cheese or by using leftovers. Such cooks have devised many *plats de pauvres,* delicious farmhouse dishes that are inexpensive to make.

In this recipe, ovals of blanched onion skins and pork and mushroom stuffing work together, one adding body and the other flavor. They are cooked to a point of melting tenderness under a blanket of a creamy tomato purée.

SERVES 6 AS A FIRST COURSE

    8 medium yellow onions (about 2¼ pounds), unpeeled
        Salt
        Freshly ground black pepper
  ⅔ cup fresh tomato purée (see following recipe)
    1 tablespoon unsalted butter
    3 ounces white mushrooms, stems trimmed and caps finely chopped
    2 tablespoons plus 1 teaspoon fresh lemon juice
    1 small garlic clove, minced
  ½ pound lean ground pork
  ⅓ cup coarsely chopped flat-leaf parsley
    2 eggs, lightly beaten
    3 tablespoons freshly grated Parmesan cheese
    2 tablespoons fresh bread crumbs
    1 teaspoon fresh thyme
        Pinch of hot paprika
    3 tablespoons crème fraîche
        Pinch of cayenne

1. Make a lengthwise slit halfway through each onion from stem to root. Drop the onions into a pot of water and bring to a boil over high heat. Stir in 1 tablespoon salt and cook until the onions are very soft when pressed with a pair of tongs, 15 to 20 minutes. Drain and rinse under cold water. Discard the skin and the thick outer layer of each onion. Separate the next 3 or 4 outer layers,

(continued)

being careful not to tear them. Season with a pinch of salt and black pepper and set aside. In a food processor, purée the onion centers. Reserve 1 cup and discard the rest.

2. In a small saucepan, cook the tomato purée over high heat, stirring occasionally, until reduced to about 3 tablespoons, 8 to 10 minutes.

3. In a medium skillet, melt the butter over high heat. Add the mushrooms, 1 tablespoon of the lemon juice, salt, and black pepper. Cook until all the liquid has evaporated and the mushrooms start to brown, about 1 minute. Add the garlic and puréed onions and cook, stirring often, for 2 to 3 minutes. Add the pork and cook, crumbling the meat, for 3 minutes. Transfer the pork mixture to a bowl and let cool. Stir in the parsley, eggs, Parmesan, bread crumbs, thyme, and paprika. Season to taste with salt, black pepper, and a few drops of the remaining lemon juice.

4. Preheat the oven to 300 degrees. Butter a shallow 10-inch-round baking dish.

5. Fill each reserved onion layer with a portion of stuffing and roll up into football shapes. Arrange the onions seam side down in circles in the prepared dish.

6. In a small bowl, thin the crème fraîche with 3 tablespoons of water. Stir in a pinch of salt, the remaining lemon juice, and the tomato purée. Season with salt, pepper, and cayenne. Spread the mixture over the onions and bake for 2 to 3 hours, until meltingly tender, basting occasionally with the sauce. Serve hot or warm.

TOMATO PURÉE

Halve 3 to 4 ripe medium tomatoes or 8 plum tomatoes (about 1½ pounds) and press out the seeds. Cut the unpeeled tomatoes into small pieces. Transfer to a small nonstick saucepan and cook over moderately high heat until well reduced, about 20 minutes. Press the mixture through a sieve. You should have about ⅔ cup purée.

Gannariya Mihchiya
Stuffed artichoke bottoms (Tunisia)

Make this Tunisian dish a day in advance and refrigerate. About ten minutes before serving, bake in a hot oven until reheated and glazed.

SERVES 8 AS A SIDE DISH

  2 teaspoons olive oil
  1 clove garlic, minced
  2 tablespoons tomato paste
     Salt
     Freshly ground black pepper
     Hot Hungarian paprika
 ½ pound lean ground beef
  1 medium onion, finely chopped
 ⅔ cup coarsely chopped flat-leaf parsley
  1 teaspoon tabil (page 197)
  8 large artichokes
  1 lemon, halved
  2 tablespoons fresh lemon juice
  2 small red potatoes (6 ounces), peeled and quartered
  2 eggs, lightly beaten
 ½ cup freshly grated Parmesan cheese

1. To prepare the stuffing, heat the oil in a heavy medium-size skillet, over moderately low heat. Add half the garlic and cook for 30 seconds. Stir in the tomato paste with a wooden spoon until it begins to sizzle and shine, about 2 minutes. Gradually stir in 1½ cups water until the sauce is smooth. Bring to a boil and season with salt, black pepper, and a pinch of paprika. Simmer for 10 minutes and remove to a heavy casserole just wide enough to hold the artichokes.

2. Rinse the skillet and cook the ground beef with ½ cup of water over high heat, crumbling the meat with a fork, until almost all the liquid evaporates, about 2 minutes. Add the onion and cook until slightly softened, about 2 minutes. Stir in the parsley, tabil, and the remaining garlic. Season with salt and black pepper and cook for 30 seconds longer. Set aside to cool.

(continued)

3. Trim the artichokes by first snapping off the tough outer leaves near the base. Use a stainless steel knife to cut off the stems, then trim the crowns to within 1½ inches of the base. Use a melon baller to scoop out the hairy chokes and scrape around the inner sides to widen the cavity. Use a small knife to carefully trim the leaves, then pare any remaining hard green parts. As you work with each artichoke, rub it with the cut lemon to prevent discoloration. Put the artichoke bottoms in a bowl of water mixed with lemon juice.

4. Boil or microwave the potatoes until tender. Peel and mash with a fork. Put the potatoes, cooled meat, eggs, and Parmesan in a mixing bowl. Using one hand with fingers extended or a wooden spoon, whip the stuffing until well mixed and lightened. Season with a pinch each of salt and paprika.

5. Drain artichokes and pat dry. Stuff bottoms, shaping into well-rounded domes with wet palms. Add the artichokes to the casserole with tomato sauce and bring to a boil over high heat. Cover with a round of crumpled wet parchment or wax paper and a tight-fitting lid. Reduce the heat to low and cook until tender, about 45 minutes. Check the pan occasionally; if the sauce looks dry, add a few tablespoons water. Turn off the heat and let stand 20 minutes before removing lid.

6. Transfer the stuffed artichoke bottoms to a heatproof serving dish. Reduce cooking juices (if any) to about ⅓ cup. Strain over the artichokes. (The artichokes can be made to this point up to 1 day ahead; cover and refrigerate. Return to room temperature before proceeding.)

7. About 20 minutes before serving, preheat the oven to 500 degrees. Place the artichokes on a baking sheet and bake for about 10 minutes, until glazed. Serve at once.

Bisbas Michchi
Stuffed fennel bulbs (Tunisia)

SERVES 4

- 4 fennel bulbs
- 1 pound ground beef or lamb
- ¼ cup finely chopped parsley
- 1 teaspoon tabil (page 197)
- 2 teaspoons freshly ground black pepper
- Salt
- ¼ cup vegetable oil
- 2 eggs, lightly beaten
- 1 tablespoon grated Parmesan cheese
- 1 cup homemade or canned spicy tomato sauce

1. Wash the fennel bulbs and cut off their hard bases. Cook in boiling salted water for 15 minutes, or until they are just tender. Drain, then cut in half lengthwise.

2. Combine the meat, parsley, tabil, pepper, and salt in a mixing bowl; blend thoroughly. Fry the mixture in oil until nicely browned. Cool, then mix in the beaten eggs and cheese.

3. Preheat the oven to 400 degrees.

4. Place 4 fennel halves cut side up in a buttered, shallow baking dish; pile on the filling, top with the remaining fennel halves, spoon over the tomato sauce, and set in the oven to bake 15 to 20 minutes. Serve hot.

Marquit Khodra

Vegetable ragout (Tunisia)

Here is a dish from the town of Jendouba in the northwest corner of Tunisia. The stew is built on three layers. The first set of ingredients (meat and chick-peas flavored with tomato paste and cooked until almost tender) is topped with firm vegetables (artichokes, cardoons, and turnips), which are in turn smothered with shredded greens (spinach, parsley, and Swiss chard). The result is a nourishing, comforting, rustic vegetable stew.

SERVES 4

½ cup chick-peas, soaked overnight in water to cover
¼ cup olive oil
1 pound shoulder lamb chops, trimmed of excess fat and cut into
    ¾-inch cubes
¼ cup chopped scallions
2 tablespoons tomato paste
3 globe artichokes
¾ pound purple top turnips, pared and cut into ¾-inch chunks
1 fresh New Mexican chili, stemmed, seeded, and sliced
2 teaspoons crushed Near East or Aleppo pepper or red pepper flakes with
    seeds removed
10 ounces shredded Swiss chard leaves (about 6 packed cups)
10 ounces shredded fresh spinach leaves (about 6 packed cups)
1 cup chopped flat-leaf parsley
  Coarse sea salt
  Freshly ground black pepper
  Warm flatbread

1. Drain the chick-peas. In a small saucepan, cover the chick-peas with 2 cups cold water. Bring to a boil over high heat. Reduce the heat to medium and simmer, covered, for 10 minutes.

2. Meanwhile, in a 5-quart Dutch oven, combine the oil, lamb, and scallions and cook over medium heat, stirring often, until meat turns light brown, about 8 minutes. Add the tomato paste and stir until it glistens and coats the meat, about 2 minutes. Add the chick-peas and the cooking liquid. Cover and simmer over medium-low heat for 30 minutes.

3. Trim each artichoke by removing all the tough outer leaves; trim stem to 1 inch. Shear off the tops of the remaining green leaves, leaving about 1 inch. Use a paring knife to shave off the dark, green sections around the base. Halve each artichoke lengthwise; cut out the hairy choke, place cut side down on a work surface, and thickly slice lengthwise. Add artichokes, turnips, sliced chili, and pepper flakes to the casserole. Pile all the greens on top, sprinkle with coarse salt, cover tightly, and cook over medium-low heat for 45 minutes, stirring occasionally after 30 minutes. If necessary, add ½ cup water.

4. To serve, correct the seasoning with salt and pepper. Transfer the stew to a shallow platter or individual shallow soup bowls. Pass a basket of warm flatbread.

Hout Makli

Fresh fish with zucchini and tomato sauce (Tunisia)

This is an attractive and spicy fish dish, very popular in Tunis. Here the zucchini is fried and then added on top of the tomato sauce, so that the dish looks red with little green pinwheels scattered around. The Tunisians also make a version substituting small cubes of salted eggplant for the zucchini.

SERVES 4

>   4 fish fillets such as flounder or sole (6 or 7 ounces each)
>   Salt
>   Freshly ground black pepper
>   2 lemons
>   3 zucchini, each about 5 inches long
> ¼ cup olive oil
> ½ cup chopped onion
>   2 cups fresh or canned tomato sauce
> ½ teaspoon harissa (pages 200–201)
> ½ teaspoon finely chopped garlic
>   Oil for frying
>   Flour for dredging
>   1 egg, beaten

(continued)

1. Wash and dry the fish fillets, season with salt and pepper, and sprinkle with the juice of 1 lemon; set aside.

2. Peel the zucchini and slice into ¼-inch-thick rounds. Heat the oil in a skillet and fry the rounds until brown on both sides; drain. In the same oil, cook the onion until soft. Add the tomato sauce, harissa, garlic, salt, and pepper. Cook, uncovered, over medium-high heat, stirring, for 5 minutes. Return the zucchini to the tomato sauce and continue to cook at the simmer, uncovered, 5 minutes.

3. Meanwhile, heat enough oil to a depth of 1 inch in a deep skillet. Dip the fish fillets in flour, beaten egg, and flour and fry in oil heated to 375 degrees. Drain.

4. Add the juice of the remaining lemon to the tomato sauce, readjust the seasoning, and serve hot with the fish.

Gnawija bil Âjil

Veal stew smothered in peppers and okra (Tunisia)

In the Tunisian town of Nabeul, known for its pottery, almost every building is embellished with vivid ceramic tiles. Here I spent time with a hospitable family, the husband a bookseller, the wife a superb cook. One meal with them was as memorable as any I ate in Tunisia: platters of small chunks of veal smothered in okra; followed by a *mechoui* of roasted lamb flavored with saffron, rosemary, and garlic, surrounded by saffron-colored potatoes scented with orange flower water. We finished this amazing dinner with cups of red tea garnished with floating pine nuts; an assortment of desserts; and sweet bergamot lemons that we peeled, sniffed, and ate. "Half the pleasure of fruit is in the smelling of it," one of the guests explained.

SERVES 4 TO 6

   2 pounds boneless veal, cut into 1½ inch cubes
1½ teaspoons tabil (page 197)
    Salt
    Freshly ground black pepper
   3 tablespoons olive oil
   2 medium onions, chopped
1½ cups crushed fresh tomatoes, or 1 14-ounce can crushed tomatoes

2 green bell peppers, roasted, cleaned, and finely chopped

2 New Mexican green peppers (Anaheim) or long green peppers, roasted, cleaned, and finely chopped

1 teaspoon harissa (pages 200–201) or another homemade pepper paste, such as *biber salcasi* (page 94)

1 teaspoon sweet paprika

¾ pound small fresh okra

1. Season the veal with tabil, salt, and pepper. In a large well-seasoned skillet, brown the veal in hot oil. Add the onions to the skillet and sauté for 2 minutes. Add the tomatoes, peppers, harissa, paprika, and 1 cup water. Bring to the boil, reduce the heat, cover, and simmer for 15 minutes.

2. Meanwhile, wash the okra and trim the stems. (If okra is large, blanch in boiling water for 2 minutes and drain.) Add the okra to the skillet. (Be sure there is enough liquid to cover.) Cover the skillet and continue simmering for 20 minutes, or until meat and okra are tender and the cooking liquid has reduced to a thick gravy. Adjust the seasoning.

Ambelofássoula Tiganitá
Black-eyed pea pod fritters with skordalia *sauce (Greece)*

Cookbook author Aglaia Kremezi described this delightful recipe for bean fritters (from the beautiful island of Astypalaia) over the telephone from Greece. She learned it too late to put it into her own book, so she offered it to me for mine.

The locals, she said, make this unusual fritter with the immature pods of black-eyed peas, which are boiled, chopped, and blended with onions and mint, then gently fried and served hot or at room temperature with a *skordalia* sauce.

In Greek Macedonia, similar fritters are made with wild nettles and stewed leeks. On the Greek islands, chopped anise or chopped and well-drained tomatoes are commonly used.

I decided to substitute tough green beans when I learned from Nathalie Dupree, author of *New Southern Cooking*, that these pods are called "field snaps" in the American South, and have a similar taste.

(continued)

- ¾ pound long green beans
- 2 medium onions
- ¼ cup chopped fresh mint
- 2 eggs, lightly beaten
  Coarse sea salt
  Freshly ground black pepper
- 1 large garlic clove, crushed with ¾ teaspoon salt
- ½ cup ricotta cheese
- ⅓ to ½ cup self-rising flour (approximately)
  Olive oil
- ½ cup skordalia sauce (page 8)

1. Trim the beans. Boil them until tender. Drain well, coarsely chop, and squeeze out moisture, to make about 1½ cups. Grate the onions and squeeze out moisture.

2. In a mixing bowl, stir together beans, onion, mint, eggs, salt, pepper, garlic, and cheese; mix well. Gradually add the flour to create a batter. Do not beat.

3. Heat a film of oil in a nonstick skillet and drop batter by heaping tablespoons into hot oil. Cook over medium heat until browned on the bottom, 2 minutes. Turn over and cook 2 minutes longer. Drain on paper towels and serve hot, warm, or at room temperature. Serve with the skordalia sauce.

Fiori di Zucca Ripiene

Stuffed squash blossoms (Italy)

Here squash blossoms are stuffed with mozzarella cheese and prosciutto, then they're rolled in batter and fried. Serve them as a first course with a wedge of lemon.

Squash blossoms are available in Italian markets and greenmarkets during the summer. Use them the same day you buy them. If you grow your own from pumpkin, zucchini, or yellow squash seeds, be sure to pick them in the morning before they wilt from the heat.

 12 squash blossoms
1½ ounces top-quality prosciutto, sliced paper-thin
  2 ounces shredded mozzarella cheese (½ cup)
     Freshly ground white pepper
 ½ cup all-purpose flour
 ¼ cup cornstarch
 ½ teaspoon baking powder
     Pinch of salt (optional)
  2 cups oil for frying
 ¾ cup ice water
  1 tablespoon olive oil
  1 egg white

1. To clean the squash blossoms, dip them in a bowl of cool water, then lightly shake them dry. Using a pair of scissors, delicately cut out the pistil from inside each blossom and trim the thin green spikes and stem on the outside.

2. Trim the prosciutto of all fat; cut into a fine dice. In a bowl, mix the prosciutto and mozzarella, season with white pepper, and set aside.

3. Sift the flour, cornstarch, baking powder, and a pinch of white pepper onto a sheet of wax paper. Depending on the saltiness of the prosciutto, add the salt. (The recipe can be prepared to this point up to 4 hours ahead.)

4. About 15 minutes before serving, heat the oil in a medium skillet over moderate heat until hot but not smoking. Pour the ice water into a medium bowl and gradually stir in the flour mixture with a fork. Stir in the olive oil. Do not overmix; the batter should be slightly lumpy.

5. In a small bowl, beat the egg white until soft peaks form, then fold it into the prosciutto-mozzarella mixture. Holding the squash blossoms open by the petals, stuff the opening of each with 1 teaspoon of the filling. Dip several blossoms in the batter and immediately fry them in the hot oil, turning once, until golden and crisp, about 1 minute per side. Drain on paper towels. Coat and fry the remaining blossoms. Serve at once.

Marquit Ommalah

Pickled vegetables with spiced ground beef (Tunisia)

SERVES 3 TO 4

1 pound ground beef
3/4 teaspoon salt
1/2 teaspoon freshly ground black pepper
2 teaspoons tabil (page 197)
1 teaspoon pulverized dried mint
1 cup pickled vegetables (see note)
1 tablespoon capers
1/2 cup juicy black olives, rinsed and pitted
1/2 cup green-cracked olives, rinsed and pitted
1/4 cup chopped fresh tomato
2 tablespoons olive oil
1 teaspoon sweet paprika

1. Place the beef in a mixing bowl. Add salt, pepper, tabil, dried mint, and a few tablespoons water; blend thoroughly.

2. With wet hands, form into 16 meatballs. Place in a skillet and add the remaining ingredients plus 1 cup water. Cook, covered, over medium-low heat for 45 minutes. Serve hot.

Note: Pickled vegetables, imported from Greece, are sold in 1-pound jars in Middle Eastern markets.

CHICK-PEAS, LENTILS, AND BEANS

Chick-peas, lentils, and beans, all dried vegetables, have been cultivated around the Mediterranean since farming began. Along with onions, they are the oldest Mediterranean vegetables, but with one advantage that onions do not have—under proper conditions they can be stored a long time. High in protein, strong in nutrient value, simple to grow, store, and prepare, they are an almost perfect food.

The peoples of the Mediterranean do much with them, especially the chick-pea (garbanzo). They are a necessity for North African food, appearing in numerous couscous dishes and *tagines*.

One of the most typical of all Middle Eastern dishes is *hummus bi taheeni,* an hors d'oeuvre of mashed chick-peas and sesame paste served with olives, radishes, lemon wedges, and bread. There is a French chick-pea flour cake called *socca,* sold piping hot in the streets of Nice. Chick-peas can be used in place of favas in Egyptian *tamiya,* becoming the Israeli dish *falafel:* chick-pea fritters stuffed into Arab-style bread (*pita*).

The Italians like chick-peas, too. I've included an old Tuscan recipe for *pasta e ceci,* a thick soup of chick-peas, macaroni, and chopped pork ribs in chicken broth—a hearty winter dish. But as much as the Italians like the chick-pea, their real love is the bean. The Tuscans are known as the bean-eaters of the Mediterranean. They have a bean dish called *fagioli al fiasco*—beans cooked in a sealed bottle so that none of the flavor escapes. I've included a recipe for the famous *fagioli con tonno* (tuna with white beans) and the fancy restaurant version with Beluga caviar.

The fava bean is ever-present on the streets of Cairo, where *tamiya* is the most popular street food. If there is a fava bean equivalent of cassoulet, it is probably the Sardinian casserole *la favata,* made of favas, pork chops, homemade sausage, fennel, hot pepper, white cabbage, garlic, tomatoes, and pork fat.

Finally there are lentils, used in cooking since Roman times. In Italy, *anitra con lenticchie* is a fine presentation of braised duck with lentils. *Kushari* is an Egyptian dish of lentils and rice topped with fried onions and a spicy tomato sauce. I've included, too, a good-tasting simple Lebanese dish called *adas be sabanigh,* a hearty soup of lentils, spinach, and lemon.

Fagioli con Caviale

White beans with caviar (Italy)

This is the luxurious way of presenting white beans, served up in certain fancy Roman restaurants with Beluga caviar. It's delicious, but has always struck me as a rather expensive and decadent way to salt one's beans! Actually this dish was invented in Florence in the 1930s for a fading upper class. Then the beans were cooked with a head of garlic. The garlic was discarded before the caviar was mixed in.

SERVES 4

    2 cups dried white beans
    1 onion, stuck with 1 clove
    1 garlic clove
      Salt
    ½ teaspoon freshly ground black pepper
    1 bay leaf
    4 to 5 tablespoons extra-virgin olive oil
    1½ to 2 tablespoons fresh lemon juice
    1 2-ounce jar black caviar
      Lemon quarters

1. Pick over the beans and discard any stones. Soak in water to cover overnight. Drain and cover with fresh cold water. Add the onion, garlic, ½ teaspoon salt, black pepper, and bay leaf. Bring to the boil, lower the heat, and cook at the simmer, covered, until the beans are tender, about 1½ hours. Discard the onion, bay leaf, and garlic clove.

2. Drain the beans in a colander and place in a serving dish. Whisk the oil, lemon juice, and salt together. Correct seasoning, add to the beans, toss well, and let cool. Add the caviar, tossing well. Readjust the seasoning. Garnish with lemon quarters and serve at once.

Fagioli con Tonno

White beans with tuna (Italy)

SERVES 4 TO 6 AS A FIRST COURSE

1 8-ounce can cannellini beans, drained
¼ cup chopped scallions
¼ cup olive oil
1 to 2 tablespoons freshly squeezed lemon juice
   Salt
   Freshly ground black pepper
1 7-ounce can first-quality tuna, packed in olive oil
1 tablespoon finely chopped fresh parsley
   Pinch of crumbled Mediterranean oregano

1. Mix the beans, scallions, oil, and lemon juice. Season to taste with salt and pepper. Pile into a serving dish.

2. Break the tuna into small pieces and arrange on top of the beans. Sprinkle with herbs and serve at room temperature.

Hummus bi Taheeni

Puréed chick-peas with sesame seed paste
(Middle East)

◘

This is undoubtedly the most famous dish of the Middle East—a delicious dip, spread, hors d'oeuvre, or what have you.

In areas of the country where hard water is prevalent, dried chick-peas should be soaked in water with a pinch of baking soda. The following day the chick-peas should be well rinsed before cooking.

MAKES ABOUT 4 CUPS

- 1½ cups dried chick-peas, soaked overnight
  Coarse salt
- 3 garlic cloves, peeled
- ¾ cup sesame seed paste
- ½ cup fresh lemon juice, or more to taste
  Cayenne or hot Hungarian paprika
- 2 tablespoons chopped parsley
- 2 teaspoons olive oil

1. Place the soaked and drained chick-peas in a saucepan and cover with plenty of fresh water. Bring to a boil; skim, add ½ teaspoon salt, cover, and cook over medium heat, about 1½ hours, until the chick-peas are very soft.

2. Meanwhile, crush the garlic and salt in a mortar until a purée. Transfer to the workbowl of a food processor, add the sesame seed paste and lemon juice, and process until white and contracted. Add ½ cup cold water and process until completely smooth.

3. Drain the chick-peas, reserving the cooking liquid. Add the chick-peas to the sesame seed paste mixture and process until well blended. For a smoother texture, press the mixture through the fine blade of a food mill. Thin to desired consistency with reserved chick-pea liquid. Adjust the seasoning with more salt and lemon juice. (The *hummus* can be kept in a tightly closed jar in the refrigerator for up to a week.) Serve chilled or at room temperature with a pinch of hot paprika, parsley, and oil.

Pasta E Ceci

Pasta and chick-peas (Italy)

This is a recipe from my friend Mario Ruspoli for a robust peasant Tuscan dish. It's particularly good for lunch on a cold winter day.

SERVES 6

1	cup dried chick-peas, picked over
¼	teaspoon baking soda (optional)
	Salt to taste
1	small onion
⅓	cup olive oil
2	garlic cloves, peeled and chopped
1	cup chopped onion
12	ounces pork spareribs, cut into 1-inch squares
2	cups chicken stock
1	fresh basil sprig (optional)
1	fresh rosemary sprig or ½ teaspoon dried
	Freshly ground black pepper
1½	cups elbow macaroni
	Grated Parmesan cheese

1. Gently toss the chick-peas with the baking soda and cover with water to soak overnight.

2. Drain the chick-peas and rinse well. Place in a saucepan, cover with fresh water, and add ½ teaspoon salt, and the small onion. Bring to the boil and cook at the simmer, covered, for 1½ hours, or until the chick-peas are tender. Discard the onion.

3. Meanwhile, heat the oil in a casserole. Lightly brown the garlic, chopped onion, and pork ribs. Add the stock, herbs, and seasoning. Cover and cook 1 hour over gentle heat.

4. Push half the cooked chick-peas through a food mill or purée in an electric blender. Add the purée, the whole chick-peas, and the cooking liquid to the casserole. Bring to the boil and cook at the simmer for 15 minutes, stirring often.

5. Add 1 quart water. Taste the soup for seasoning and readjust. Bring to the boil; throw in the macaroni and cook rapidly until just tender—about 15 minutes. Serve hot and pass a bowl of grated cheese.

———

NOTES ON COOKING CHICK-PEAS
FOR SOUPS, SALADS, AND STEWS

Chick-peas (garbanzo beans) benefit from soaking overnight in plenty of water. But first I always toss them with a little baking soda, remembering to rinse the chick-peas in several waters in the morning. This yields a desirable luscious texture.

Recently I have started to cook chick-peas in salted water which does add cooking time, but the chick-peas are better seasoned and I find that I use less salt.

Cook chick-peas in a covered pot, preferably earthenware. (Enameled cast iron is a good alternative.) Or, with equal success, in much less water and without salt in a pressure cooker for about 35 minutes.

———

Harira

Chick-pea, lamb, and fresh coriander soup

(Morocco)

This soup, made with a complex spice mixture called *la kama*, is particularly savory. It is often eaten to break the fast during Ramadan. A nourishing blend of chick-peas, lamb, rice, and tomatoes, it is flavored with spices and herbs, thickened with a lightly fermented batter made with semolina flour, and accompanied by a platter of dates or honeyed cakes.

MAKES 1 GALLON, SERVING 12

  7 ounces dried chick-peas
  1/4 teaspoon baking soda (optional)
  3 tablespoons semolina flour
  1/2 cup water
  1 1/2 pounds boneless lamb from the shoulder, cut into 2-inch pieces
  3/4 cup chopped onion
  3/4 teaspoon Moroccan *la kama* (see following recipe)
    Pinch of pulverized saffron
  3/4 teaspoon salt
  1/2 cup chopped flat-leaf parsley
  3 tablespoons butter
  3/4 cup short-grain rice
  3 quarts flavorful chicken stock
  1 teaspoon freshly ground black pepper
  1 1/2 cups crushed tomatoes
  1/2 cup chopped fresh coriander leaves
  1 teaspoon sugar
    Fresh green coriander for garnish

1. Pick over the chick-peas and toss with the baking soda if desired. Soak them overnight in water to cover. In a small bowl, mix the semolina flour with the water and allow to stand at room temperature overnight.

2. Put the lamb in a deep pot and allow to brown in its own fat.

3. Drain the chick-peas and rinse well. Add them to the lamb, along with the onion, spices, salt, parsley, and water to cover. Bring to a boil and skim away the

scum. Then add 2 tablespoons of the butter (for flavor), cover the pot, and cook at the simmer for 1½ hours.

4. Meanwhile, wash the rice and drain. In a second pot, combine the chicken stock, remaining tablespoon of butter, and pepper; bring to a boil. Add the rice and boil for 20 minutes.

5. In a food processor, purée the tomatoes and coriander and add to the rice, along with sugar and the semolina flour mixture. Cook, uncovered, for 10 minutes, stirring constantly.

6. Combine the contents of the two pots and adjust the seasoning. Garnish with shredded coriander leaves.

LA KAMA
Northern Moroccan spice mixture

La kama is used to flavor soups and stews in northern Morocco.

    1 tablespoon ground ginger
    1 tablespoon ground black pepper
    1 tablespoon ground turmeric
    ½ tablespoon ground cinnamon
    1 teaspoon grated nutmeg

Combine all the ingredients.

Leb-Lebi

Chick-pea and harissa soup (Tunisia)

□

In the streets of Tunis there are numerous hole-in-the-wall soup kitchens that serve nothing but chick-pea soup. Chick-peas simmer overnight with calf's feet or marrow bones added to give heftiness and flavor. The soup is served in deep earthen bowls ladled over a good amount of stale bread cubes, then slathered with fiery harissa sauce and accented with ground cumin, lemon juice, and plenty of olive oil.

It is called in affectionate terms *leb-lebi,* which imitates the bellowing of a ram in heat, according to Tunisian philologist Ouled-Abdessayed Khamais. (In Turkey, the word refers to char-roasted chick-peas.) "When you eat *leb-lebi,*" a friend once counseled me, "bring a handkerchief because the dish is so hot with spices that the nose runs ferociously."

Stimulating as the street version is, it is further embellished with the favorite Tunisian garnish of canned tuna, capers, pickled vegetables, and hard-cooked eggs. (In private homes, a poached egg is substituted.) In this form it becomes an entire meal in itself.

SERVES 4

  1½ cups (about ½ pound) dried chick-peas, picked over
  ½ teaspoon baking soda (optional)
  1 small onion, peeled, or 1 small veal marrow bone with some meat attached, or 1 small piece of a cracked veal foot (optional)
     Coarse salt
  3 tablespoons olive oil
  3 tablespoons harissa (pages 200–201)
  1 tablespoon minced garlic
  1 tablespoon ground cumin
  3 tablespoons strained fresh lemon juice
  3 to 4 cups cubed stale peasant-style bread
  1 6-ounce can imported tuna packed in olive oil, drained and coarsely flaked
  ⅓ cup slivered pickled turnips with beets (available at Middle Eastern grocers)

½ cup thinly sliced scallions or red onion
2 tablespoons small capers, rinsed and drained
4 lemon wedges
Table harissa sauce (page 201)

1. Gently toss the chick-peas with the baking soda and cover with 1 quart water. Let stand at least 8 hours.

2. Preheat the oven to 300 degrees. Rinse the chick-peas thoroughly and place in an enameled cast-iron Dutch oven or an earthenware bowl. Add the onion or the bones and ¾ teaspoon coarse salt. Pour over 2 quarts boiling water; cover and set in the oven to simmer until tender, 2 to 3 hours.

3. Remove from the oven and discard the bones or onions. Skim and discard fat if you used the meaty bones. (Up to this point, the soup may be made 1 to 2 days in advance. Cover and refrigerate.)

4. Drain the chick-peas, reserving 4 cups liquid.

5. Put the olive oil in a straight-sided 10-inch skillet over medium heat. Add the harissa and garlic. Cook, stirring, until harissa begins to sizzle, 30 seconds. Add the chick-peas and fry for another 30 seconds. Cover with the reserved cooking liquid, bring to a boil, then reduce heat and cook gently for 5 minutes. Add the cumin and lemon juice.

6. Divide the stale bread among 4 deep soup bowls. Ladle the chick-peas and 1 cup of the cooking liquid into each of the bowls. Garnish each serving with a portion of the tuna fish, turnips, scallions, capers, and lemon wedges. Pass the table harissa sauce for those who like their food extra hot.

Variation

Serve *leb-lebi* with slices of hard-cooked eggs or poached eggs. At the end of step 5, gently break 4 eggs, 1 at a time, into barely simmering soup; cover and cook just until eggs are set, about 2½ minutes. Ladle the soup and an egg over the stale bread in each bowl; top each with the garnishes.

Garbanzos a la Catalana

Chick-peas with tomatoes, fresh sausage, and peppers (Spain)

◻

This dish, extremely popular in homes in Barcelona, normally requires a fresh sausage, which is a specialty of Catalonia. In the ingredients list I suggest some substitutes, but if you have a sausage-making machine you can make these sausages with ease. Grind ½ pound of pork with 2 to 3 ounces of pork fat, moisten the meat with a few tablespoons of white wine, salt, pepper, and pinches of cinnamon or nutmeg, powdered cloves, and crumbled thyme. Then force the seasoned meat into a casing and hang the sausage in an airy place for 24 hours. The sausage is cooked in boiling water and is eaten hot or cold.

SERVES 6

1½ cups dried chick-peas, picked over
½ teaspoon baking soda (optional)
   Salt
½ pound Catalonian sausage or fresh country-style pork sausage
5 ounces slab bacon or lean salt pork
   Oil
1 cup chopped onion
1 teaspoon finely chopped garlic
1 cup diced green bell pepper
4 large red ripe tomatoes, peeled, seeded, and chopped
   Grated nutmeg or cinnamon
¼ teaspoon ground thyme
   Freshly ground black pepper

1. Gently toss the chick-peas with the baking soda and soak overnight in water to cover. Drain, rinse well, and cook in simmering salted water, covered, about 1 hour.

2. Simmer the sausage in water for 20 minutes, or prick the bought sausages with the prongs of a fork and brown in a skillet. Drain off most of the fat and cut the sausage into 1-inch chunks; set aside.

3. Simmer the bacon or salt pork 10 minutes in water; drain and rinse well.

4. In the sausage fat or in 1 tablespoon oil, brown the bacon or salt pork, onion, garlic, and green pepper, stirring.

5. Add the tomatoes, nutmeg, thyme, salt, and pepper to taste. Cook, covered, 10 minutes. Fold in the sausage slices.

6. Preheat the oven to 375 degrees.

7. Drain the chick-peas, reserving 2 cups cooking liquid. Put the chick-peas in a 13-inch, earthenware baking dish. Spoon in the prepared tomato sauce. Moisten with the reserved cooking liquid. Season with salt and pepper to taste. Cover the dish and set in the oven to bake for 1½ hours, stirring from time to time. Serve in wide soup plates.

Morshan
Chick-peas and Swiss chard (Tunisia)

I used to joke with my husband about writing a book in which I would follow the chick-pea around the Mediterranean, using this humble pulse as a prism through which to view culinary influences and history. Here's a dish that makes the point. You will find it in old Spanish versions with cured ham as a flavoring; served with lentils in Syria; flavored with cumin in Egypt and with cinnamon in Turkey; garnished with chopped onion in Lebanon. This Tunisian version, made with tomato and chili pepper, is my favorite. It can be served as a light meal with a brine-ripened cheese (such as a creamy feta) along with pickles, bread, and a salad.

(continued)

> 3/4 pound Swiss chard leaves, stemmed, washed, and torn into large pieces
>   (see note)
> 2 large cloves garlic, peeled
> 1/2 teaspoon coarse salt
> 1 teaspoon ground coriander seeds
> 1 small dried red chili
> 2 tablespoons olive oil
> 1/2 cup minced onion
> 2 teaspoons tomato paste
> 1 cup cooked chick-peas, plus 3/4 cup cooking liquid
> 1 lemon, cut into wedges

1. Steam, parboil, or microwave the Swiss chard until tender, about 5 minutes. Set the leaves in a colander to drain, squeeze out excess moisture, and coarsely shred.

2. Crush the garlic in a mortar with the salt, coriander seed, and red chili until a thick crumbly paste forms.

3. Heat the olive oil in a 10-inch skillet and sauté the onion until pale golden. Add the garlic paste and tomato paste and stir them in the oil until sizzling. Add the Swiss chard, chick-peas, with their cooking liquid, and cook, stirring occasionally, for 10 minutes. Remove from the heat and let stand until ready to serve. (The contents of the skillet should be very moist but not soupy. If desired, stir in more of the chick-pea liquid to further loosen the mixture.) Serve warm, at room temperature, or cold with lemon wedges.

Note: Broccoli rabe, dandelion leaves, mustard greens, kale, or turnip tops can be substituted for Swiss chard. Discard any yellow or damaged leaves. Prepare as directed in step 1 and remember that cooking times will vary.

A Tunisian housewife taught me a useful kitchen trick—to soak, drain, and then freeze chick-peas and beans. This allowed her to put soups together very quickly without having to remember to soak the chick-peas or beans the night before.

Djej bil Hamus

Chicken with chick-peas (Morocco)

SERVES 4

- ½ pound dried chick-peas, or 1 can cooked chick-peas, drained
- ¼ teaspoon baking soda (optional)
- Salt
- 1 3½-pound chicken
- 4 garlic cloves, peeled
- ½ teaspoon ground ginger
- ½ teaspoon freshly ground black pepper
- Pinch of pulverized saffron
- ½ teaspoon turmeric
- 2 tablespoons finely chopped parsley
- 1 cinnamon stick
- ¼ cup finely chopped onion
- 3 tablespoons butter
- 1 small onion, thinly sliced
- 2 tablespoons black raisins (optional)

1. Pick over the chick-peas and toss them with the baking soda. Soak overnight in water to cover.

2. To purify the chicken as it is done in Morocco, rub the flesh with a paste made with 3 crushed garlic cloves and 1 tablespoon salt. (This garlic and salt rub is used to draw out blood, remove bitterness, and enhance flavor.) Rinse the chicken well, then pat dry with paper towels. In a mixing bowl, combine the ginger, pepper, remaining garlic clove, crushed, and 2 tablespoons water. Rub this mixture all over the chicken. Cover and refrigerate overnight.

3. The next day, drain the chick-peas, rinse well, place in a saucepan, cover with fresh water, add ¾ teaspoon salt, bring to the boil, and cook at the simmer, covered, for about 1 hour, or until they are tender. Drain and submerge in a bowl of cold water. Rub the chick-peas to remove their skins, which will rise to the surface. Discard them. (If using canned chick-peas, drain and skin them, then set aside.)

(continued)

4. Place chicken, any juices in the bowl, saffron, turmeric, parsley, cinnamon stick, chopped onion, and butter in a 3½-quart casserole. Add 2½ cups water and bring to a boil. Cover and cook at the simmer for 1 hour, turning the chicken frequently in the sauce. Remove the chicken and keep warm and moist.

5. Add the finely sliced onion, cooked chick-peas, and raisins, if using them, to the sauce and cook until the onions are soft and the sauce has reduced to a thick gravy. Return the chicken to the sauce to reheat. Taste the sauce for salt and add a pinch of pulverized saffron for a good yellow color.

6. To serve, place the chicken in a deep serving dish, spoon over the chick-pea sauce, and serve at once.

Mavres Elies ke Faki

Lentil and black olive dip (Greco-Egyptian)

The homely combination of slightly salty, pungent black olives and mildly bland, earthy brown lentils is unusual and delicious. Its smooth creamy texture can be attributed not only to proper cooking of the lentils (until completely tender), but also to the softening of the thick olive skins by soaking and cooking. This method allows the dark hearty flavor of black olives to be easily released into the bulky lentil mixture. In this adapted version, from the Greek community in Cairo, extra-virgin olive oil is swirled in at the last minute to deepen the flavor.

For best flavor, allow the dip to mellow overnight. It will keep up to one week under a thin layer of olive oil.

MAKES ABOUT 2 CUPS

- ¾ cup common lentils
- 1 tablespoon brandy
- 4 ounces wrinkled black olives (oil-cured)
- 1 tablespoon capers
- 2 anchovy fillets
- 2 whole cloves garlic, peeled
- ½ teaspoon dried red pepper flakes
- 1 tablespoon dried Mediterranean oregano, crushed between fingertips

1/4 teaspoon freshly ground black pepper
2 tablespoons fresh lemon juice, or more to taste
3 tablespoons extra-virgin olive oil
Cruet of extra-virgin olive oil
Toasted triangles of pita bread

1. Pick over and wash the lentils. Put them in a saucepan, cover with water, and bring them to a full boil. Reduce the heat and cook at a simmer for 20 minutes. Add the brandy and continue to cook until lentils are tender, about 10 minutes longer. (If necessary, add cold water to keep lentils covered with liquid during the cooking.) Drain, reserving 1/2 cup cooking liquid. Crush lentils and set in a large mixing bowl.

2. Meanwhile, soak the olives in warm water for 10 minutes. Drain and pit them. You should have about 1/2 cup. Rinse the capers and anchovies to remove salt. Pat dry with paper toweling and set aside.

3. In a skillet, combine the olives, garlic, 1/2 cup of the lentil cooking liquid, red pepper flakes, oregano, and black pepper. Bring to a boil and cook, uncovered, until a thick mass forms with very little moisture left in the pan, about 5 minutes. Purée the contents in a food processor with the capers, and anchovies, and lemon juice. With the machine running, add the 3 tablespoons olive oil.

4. In a large bowl, using a large wire whisk, whip the olive mixture into the lentil purée. Correct the seasoning with more salt, lemon juice, and olive oil. Cover and refrigerate overnight. Serve decorated with a sprig of fresh thyme or parsley and drizzle with olive oil. Pass a basket of toasted triangles of pita bread.

With thanks to Rosemary Barron for sharing this recipe

Adas be Sabanekh

Lentils with spinach and lemon (Lebanon)

A springtime soup of lentils, Swiss chard, and fresh coriander may be homely to look at, but it is refreshingly acidic with lemon and fragrant with fresh coriander. This soup, which I prefer lukewarm, is a typical home-style dish, virtually unobtainable in restaurants.

SERVES 6

½ pound lentils
1 cup sliced onion
¼ cup olive oil
3 garlic cloves, peeled and finely chopped
¼ cup chopped fresh coriander
10 ounces frozen spinach leaves, completely thawed and roughly chopped
2 medium waxy potatoes, peeled and sliced
Salt
Freshly ground black pepper
¼ cup freshly squeezed lemon juice, or more to taste

1. Wash and pick over the lentils. Place in a saucepan and cover with water. Bring to the boil. Cook, covered, about 20 minutes.

2. Meanwhile, brown the onion in oil in a large casserole. Stir in the garlic and coriander. Add the spinach and sauté 5 to 6 minutes, stirring frequently. Add the potatoes, lentils, and enough lentil cooking liquid to cover. Season with salt and pepper. Bring to the boil, lower the heat, and cook at the simmer for 1 hour, or until thick and soupy, about 20 minutes. Stir in the lemon juice. Serve hot, lukewarm, or cold.

Anitra con Lenticchie
Duck with lentils (Italy)

This old country dish from the southern part of Italy uses the unique tiny light-brown lentils from Umbria or Abruzzi. They provide a creamy texture and a mildly earthy flavor and are particularly recommended, but not absolutely necessary. A good substitute is the Spanish *pardena* available from Phipps Ranch in California (see Mail-Order Sources, pages 296–97).

SERVES 5 TO 6

- 9 ounces (1¼ cups) very small light-brown lentils
- 1 large duck (5½ pounds), fresh or thawed
  Salt
  Freshly ground black pepper
- 1 tablespoon olive oil
- 1 cup chopped onion
- 3 ounces prosciutto, chopped
- 1 cup dry red wine
- 2 garlic cloves, chopped
- 2 parsley sprigs
- 2 bay leaves
- 2 chopped carrots
- 2 chopped celery ribs
- ¼ cup tomato sauce
- 2 tablespoons chopped herbs (parsley mixed with basil)

1. Pick over the lentils and rinse them under running water; set aside to drain.

2. Wash and dry the whole duck and season it with salt and pepper. With the tines of a fork prick the duck skin every 1 inch. Use a small paring knife to make deep slits in thick, fatty areas. Place the duck in a wide skillet with the oil. Brown the duck all over in the expressed fat and oil. Transfer it, breast side up, to a 5- or 6-quart casserole. Brown the wings and neck bones in the skillet; add to the casserole. Pour off all but 2 tablespoons fat from skillet; reserve another 2 tablespoons for step 3. Raise the heat under the skillet; add half the onion and the prosciutto, and cook briefly until the onion turns golden. Add the wine, garlic,

(continued)

parsley, bay leaves, salt and pepper, half the carrots, and half the celery. Bring to the boil and add to the casserole. Cover the duck with a crumpled piece of wet parchment and a tight-fitting lid. Cook over medium heat for 1½ hours.

3. Meanwhile, heat the reserved duck fat in the same skillet. Lightly brown the remaining onion, carrot, and celery. Add the lentils, salt, pepper, 3 cups water, and tomato sauce. Bring to the boil, cover and simmer the lentils until tender, about 45 minutes. If necessary add more water to keep the lentils from drying out.

4. Remove the duck to a work surface. Let it stand 10 minutes. Meanwhile, strain the cooking juices, pressing down on the debris to extract all the juices. Skim off the fat, then return liquid to the casserole and reduce to a glaze. Add the glaze to the lentils and the cooking liquid and simmer, covered, for 10 minutes to blend the flavors and thicken the liquid, if necessary. Correct the seasoning; add the fresh herbs, cover, and keep warm.

5. Heat the broiler. Cut the duck into 6 serving pieces. Rub the duck skin with a dab of olive oil. Place duck under a heated broiler to reheat thoroughly and crisp the skin. Remove from the broiler and place on a warmed serving dish. Pour the lentils around the duck and serve at once.

Tbikha

Thick barley soup from Gabès (Tunisia)

At first Gabès appears to be a dry, dusty, fairly nondescript Saharan city, the same sort of dry, sun-ravished place I had visited many times in North Africa. But there was something special here. "Gardens full of bees and flowers where one can almost eat the strong intoxicating scents," wrote André Gide in *Les Nourritures terrestres.*

Gide was referring to the giant seaside oasis that adjoins the town. In the midst of parched tan nothingness I suddenly saw green, and then heard the streams fed by numerous underground springs. In the oasis, hundreds of thousands of palms protect banana, citrus, pomegranate, and apricot trees from the sun, and these fruit trees in turn shelter innumerable gardens of beans, radishes, carrots, tomatoes, onions, and henna plants. I took a horse-drawn ride through the winding lanes, passing through a half-dozen hamlets, and then wandered on foot along the intricate network of paths that twist between the gardens and along the streams.

The food of Gabès is varied, the spicing complex. Naima Touiti, a Gabès resident and one of Tunisia's leading feminists, invited me to her home to taste some regional specialties. Among them was this hearty barley and meat soup, cooked in a sealed pot, perfumed with bruised fennel seed, seasoned with tabil, an earthy spice mixture of caraway, coriander, and garlic, and enriched with a special paste of ground sun-dried peppers, spices, and fermented onions called *hrous,* which had a depth of flavor I had never encountered before.

SERVES 6

    1   cup chopped onion
 1½   tablespoons olive oil
    1   garlic clove, peeled and sliced
 1½   tablespoons tomato paste
    2   teaspoons tabil (page 197)
    1   tablespoon *hrous* (pages 97–98)
    1   pound lamb neck, cut into 1-inch chunks
        Coarse sea salt
  ⅓   cup pearl barley, rinsed
  ½   teaspoon fennel seeds
        Freshly ground black pepper

(continued)

1. Sauté the onion in the hot oil until pale golden. Add the garlic and tomato paste and stir them in oil until sizzling. Add the tabil, *hrous,* lamb, and ½ teaspoon salt. Stir until the meat is well coated with seasoning, then add 4 cups water. Bring to a boil; simmer, covered, for 2 hours, until the meat falls easily from the bones. (Can be prepared in a pressure cooker.)

2. Place barley in a small saucepan, add 3 cups water, and bring to a boil. Cover, reduce the heat, and simmer 30 minutes, or until tender. Remove from the heat and let stand until needed.

3. Remove all the bones from the soup. Skim off the fat that rises to the top. Add the barley and cooking liquid. Bruise the fennel seeds in a mortar and add to the soup. Bring to a boil, adjust the seasoning with salt and pepper, and serve at once.

Fava Puré e Cicorielle
Mashed fava beans with potatoes and chicory (Italy)

In 1993 I visited the region of Apulia, at the southern heel of the Italian boot, to observe the Mediterranean diet in action. Apulian cuisine is definitely healthy, based on vegetables, whole-grain cereals, fish, raw salads, bread, fruits, herbs, greens, and lots of golden, limpid olive oil. Such high-fiber ingredients as cauliflower, peas, lentils, and beans are as ingeniously worked into their recipes as are the popular Mediterranean medley of tomatoes, green peppers, and eggplant.

One of the most intriguing dishes I tasted was this fluffy purée of fava beans blended with potatoes, bitter greens, and aromatic olive oil of the best quality. Served warm, it was delicious, filling, and addictive. The Pugliese used wild chicory or sow thistle as the bitter green of choice, but I found that watercress or curly chicory also worked very well.

Favas are the preferred beans in this part of Italy, where a popular saying is: "Of all fresh and dried vegetables, the fava bean is queen, sovereign of all, soaked in the evening, cooked in the morning."

To save time (they don't require an overnight soaking and peeling) I use the shelled and split favas that make homemade *falafel,* available at Middle Eastern markets.

For the fluffiest texture, you will want to keep the potatoes and favas from turning watery. The Pugliese claim that if you add salt as soon as the potatoes are tender "it fixes the starch."

Serve while still warm, accompanied by roasted bell peppers dressed with olive oil, a simple tomato salad, or, in late spring, the wild onions from the botanical family Muscari.

MAKES 4 CUPS, SERVING 6

   1 cup (5 ounces) peeled and split dried mini fava beans (available at Middle Eastern grocers)
  1/3 cup extra-virgin olive oil, preferably very fruity
   2 medium Idaho or Yukon Gold potatoes (14 ounces), peeled and thickly sliced
  1/2 pound watercress, dandelion, or wild chicory
      Sea salt
      Freshly ground white pepper

(continued)

1. Rinse the dried favas and drain. Put the favas in a 4-quart saucepan, add 5 cups of water, and 1 tablespoon of the oil. Bring to a boil, reduce the heat to medium, and simmer, partially covered, for 10 minutes. Add the potatoes and cook over medium-high heat until the favas and potatoes are tender and almost all the liquid has been absorbed, about 20 minutes. Season with ¾ teaspoon salt.

2. Meanwhile, shred the greens and place in a covered saucepan with just the water that adheres to the leaves. Set over low heat, add a pinch of salt, and cook, covered, occasionally tilting the saucepan to drain off the bitter liquid that forms. When the leaves are dry, add ⅓ cup water and cook, stirring, until tender and the water has evaporated, about 5 minutes. Remove from the heat and crush to a purée (makes about ¾ cup).

3. Push the favas and potatoes through the fine blade of a food mill. (Don't use a food processor.) Or mash the favas and potatoes by hand, and beat in just enough of the cooking liquid left in the pan to make the mixture smooth and fluffy. Gradually beat in the remaining olive oil, then the crushed greens. Correct the seasoning with salt and pepper. Pile the mixture lightly on a shallow serving dish and serve while still warm. Do not reheat.

PASTA, COUSCOUS, AND OTHER MEDITERRANEAN FARINACEOUS FOODS

One of the most convincing theories of the evolution of human culture has to do with the cereal grains. Early man was a hunter. He led a nomadic life, moving about in pursuit of wild game. But when he became a farmer and began to cultivate crops he settled down and formed communities and in these communities the germ of his culture was born. The first crops were the grains, and even today, they are the stuff that links men in all the corners of the earth. Wheat, rice, corn, barley, sorghum, and rye—they are the great connecting crops of mankind.

Men have cultivated grain around the Mediterranean Sea since before recorded time. And wheat has always been and continues to be the great Mediterranean cereal crop. There is rice, too, and some of the other grains, but wheat is king, and bread the staple of Mediterranean life.

I've decided in this book not to give any recipes for breads. I've written about them in my other books. But I felt it impossible to write a book about Mediterranean food and not dwell, for a time at least, on some of the great farinaceous foods. Hence this chapter on the making of a few Italian special pastas; a Tunisian noodle; the preparation of North African couscous and briks; green wheat, bulgur, and a few pastry dishes that did not fall easily into the other chapters devoted to flavorings, but which I wanted to include all the same.

Panzarotti

Fried stuffed ravioli with tomato-cheese sauce (Italy)

This is a very good recipe for an unusual pasta dish, given to me by Tony May, owner of San Domenico restaurant in New York.

Usually, ravioli is boiled, but here it's fried in oil. And the pasta itself is different: There are no eggs in this dough—only flour, water, and oil.

MAKES ABOUT 60 RAVIOLI, ENOUGH FOR 6 AS A FIRST COURSE

    2¼ cups all-purpose flour, preferably unbleached
    ⅓ cup olive oil
        Salt
    ½ cup cooked Swiss chard or spinach
    1 tablespoon butter
    ¼ cup chopped onion
    1 cup ricotta cheese

2 egg yolks
Freshly ground black pepper
Grated nutmeg
½ cup grated Parmesan or pecorino cheese
1 egg, beaten
1 cup fresh or canned tomato sauce
3 tablespoons diced mozzarella cheese
½ teaspoon crumbled Mediterranean oregano
Cooking oil for deep-frying
Bowl of grated Parmesan cheese

1. In a large bowl, make a mound of flour and press a hollow in the center to form a well. Add oil, 2 teaspoons salt, and enough water (about ⅓ cup) to make a firm dough. Knead. Cover the dough and set aside while making the stuffing.

2. Finely chop the Swiss chard or the spinach. In a saucepan, heat the butter and cook the onion until light brown. Add the chopped greens and cook together for 1 minute over low heat, stirring. Off heat, add the ricotta, egg yolks, pepper, nutmeg, 2 tablespoons Parmesan, and a little salt, if necessary. Combine thoroughly.

3. Divide the dough into four parts. Roll one part into a thin sheet, 11 by 17 inches. Brush with beaten egg. Place ½ teaspoonful of stuffing on the dough in three evenly spaced rows, about 2 inches apart each way. Roll out the second ball of dough to the same size, brush with egg, and place over the filling, egg side down. Lightly press around each mound with your fingers. Dip a 2-inch cookie cutter into flour and cut out disks of the mounds. Press down around the edges of each ravioli to seal securely. Line up on a floured cloth and cover with another cloth. Repeat with the remaining two balls of dough.

4. Heat the tomato sauce with the mozzarella cheese, oregano, and 2 tablespoons grated Parmesan cheese. Season with black pepper and salt, if necessary. Keep hot.

5. Heat the oil in a deep fryer to 375 degrees. Slip in the ravioli, a few at a time, making sure not to crowd the fryer, and cook 5 minutes, or until brown and puffy on both sides. Serve hot with the prepared tomato sauce. Sprinkle the *panzarotti* with the remaining cheese.

Burro Rosso

Red butter sauce (Italy)

This is an Italian red butter sauce, just enough for a pound of fresh noodles such as *tagliatelle, fettuccine,* or meatless ravioli.

SERVES 4 TO 5

- ¼ pound AA sweet butter
- 1 teaspoon tomato paste
- 2 tablespoons heavy cream
- ½ teaspoon dried sage leaves, crumbled, or 6 fresh sage leaves, slivered
- ½ teaspoon sweet paprika
- Salt
- 2 tablespoons grated Parmesan cheese
- Bowl of grated Parmesan cheese

1. Melt the butter in a small saucepan. Whisk in the tomato paste and cream. Add sage, paprika, a little salt to taste, and the 2 tablespoons cheese. Stir until smooth over low heat, but do not bring to the boil.

2. To serve, pour over freshly cooked pasta, with a bowl of grated Parmesan cheese on the side.

Orecchiette Con Patate e Rucola
"Little ears" pasta with potatoes and arugula
(Italy)

In the Italian region of Apulia, a handmade rustic pasta called *orecchiette,* or "little ears," is made with a combination of hard wheat, semolina flour, and water. First the dough is rolled into thin, cordlike lengths, then cut into small pieces, which are then, with the aid of the thumb, pressed into skull cap shapes with thick edges. The solid, rugged qualities of these "little ears" are ideal for capturing small amounts of potato cubes or sauce.

You will find *orecchiette* imported from Italy at fine Italian grocers. In this recipe, the *orecchiette* are boiled along with the cubes of potatoes and shredded arugula, and then tossed with garlic and chili-flavored olive oil. This is an ideal recipe when one's garden arugula has turned tough and chewy. (One-half-inch cubes of zucchini can be substituted for arugula.) The recipe is adapted from *Le ricette della mia cucina pugliese,* by Antonietta Pepe.

SERVES 2 TO 3

> 1 medium all-purpose potato, diced to make 1 cup
> 2 packed cups roughly chopped arugula leaves and stems
>   (about 7 ounces)
>   Coarse salt
> 5 ounces (1½ cups) dried *orecchiette* (available at Italian groceries)
> 2 tablespoons extra-virgin olive oil
> 1 garlic clove, peeled and thinly sliced
> ¼ teaspoon dried red pepper flakes, or more to taste
> ¼ cup grated sheep's milk cheese such as *ricotta salata*

1. Cook the potatoes and arugula in a large quantity of boiling salted water for 5 minutes. Add the pasta and continue cooking until tender, 8 to 10 minutes.

2. Meanwhile, put the oil, garlic, and red pepper flakes in a small saucepan and cook over low heat until the garlic turns a light golden brown, about 1 minute. Remove from heat. Add to the drained potatoes, arugula, and pasta. Toss and serve at once with a sprinkling of grated cheese.

Hlalems bil Lham

Creamy vegetable soup with noodles (Tunisia)

▣

One evening, during the Ramadan fast, I was visiting with a family in the town of Nabeul. They broke the fast with this delectable rough and hearty soup—a rich blend of beans, vegetables, a touch of hot pepper, and a handful of *hlalems,* lightly fermented dried noodles formed between the thumb and forefinger from pellets of semolina dough. These noodles, unlike ordinary pasta, add a slightly sour and nutty flavor that is much beloved. It is easy to make the dough with a food processor.

SERVES 4 TO 5

> ½ cup dried chick-peas
> ½ cup dried fava beans (optional)
> 1½ pounds lamb neck, cut up for stew or soup
> Sea salt
> Freshly ground black pepper
> 1 small onion, quartered
> 2 tablespoons olive oil
> ½ cup minced scallions
> 1 garlic clove
> 1½ tablespoons tomato paste
> 2 cups shredded spinach leaves (4 ounces)
> ½ cup chopped celery
> ⅓ cup chopped flat-leaf parsley
> 2 large artichokes, quartered and trimmed
> 1 carrot, pared and diced
> ½ teaspoon hot Hungarian paprika, or more to taste
> 1 cup dried *hlalems* (see following recipe)
> 2 long green chilies, stemmed, halved, seeded, and lightly salted
> 1 cup fresh or frozen baby peas
> 3 tablespoons shredded fresh coriander leaves

1. One day in advance, wash, pick over, and soak the chick-peas and favas, if using, in water to cover.

2. The following day, season the lamb with salt and pepper; set aside. Drain the chick-peas and favas, if using. Place them with the quartered onion in a saucepan.

Add 4 to 6 cups cold water and bring to a boil. Cook, covered, at a slow boil for 10 minutes, skimming often.

3. Meanwhile, heat the oil in a 5-quart casserole over medium heat. Add the lamb cubes and brown quickly on all sides. Add the scallions and garlic clove and cook for 2 minutes, or until the scallions soften. Stir in the tomato paste and allow it to sizzle and become glossy. Add the shredded spinach, celery, parsley, artichoke quarters, carrot, ½ teaspoon black pepper, and hot paprika. Stir to wilt and coat the vegetables with the oil, about 5 minutes. Add the chick-peas and favas and the cooking liquid to the casserole. Return to the boil over high heat, then reduce to low. Cover and simmer for 1½ hours. (The recipe can be made several hours ahead of time to this point.) Discard the quartered onion.

4. Forty minutes before serving, skim off excess fat and discard. Add enough water to the soup to make 2 quarts. Bring to the boil over high heat. Add 1½ teaspoons of salt, the prepared *hlalems,* and the green chilies and cook, partially covered, for 30 minutes, or until the *hlalems* are tender and plump. Add the peas and cook a few minutes longer. Correct the seasoning with salt, black pepper, and paprika. Sprinkle with fresh coriander and serve hot.

Note: In a pinch, you can substitute imported *cavatelli,* little hollowed out shapes, for the *hlalems,* but the soup will lack some of its charm.

HLALEMS
Noodle pasta (Tunisia)

MAKES 3 CUPS

10 ounces (2½ cups) fine semolina flour
1 cup warm water
1 teaspoon active dry yeast
½ teaspoon sea salt
1 teaspoon olive oil

1. In a bowl, preferably made of wood or earthenware, make a mound of flour and press a hollow in the center to form a well. Add the water and sprinkle with yeast. Stir to make a firm dough. Knead in the salt and continue to work the dough by hand (or in a food processor) until smooth. Brush with oil, cover with a kitchen towel, and set aside for 2 hours to rise.

2. Punch down the dough, then divide into twelve parts. Keep all but one part covered with a kitchen towel. Pinch off pieces approximately ⅛ teaspoon each. Roll between fingertips to achieve a 1-inch tapered noodle. Leave to dry, uncovered, on a flat fine sieve or dry kitchen towel for 1 day. Store dry *hlalems* in an airtight jar in the cupboard.

Note: A wooden, earthenware, or plastic bowl makes a warm support for the yeasty dough; avoid metal bowls, which are too cold.

Pasta con Mollica di Pane
Pasta with bread crumbs (Italy)

This is a real peasant pasta dish from Sicily.

SERVES 4

- 1½ teaspoons finely chopped garlic
- ¼ cup olive oil
- 2 2-ounce cans anchovies, rinsed and drained
- 1½ cups fresh or canned tomato purée (not tomato paste)
- ⅓ cup finely chopped parsley
  Freshly ground black pepper
- ½ teaspoon crumbled Mediterranean oregano
- ¾ pound spaghetti
  Salt
- ⅓ cup fresh white bread crumbs, toasted in the oven with a few drops of olive oil

1. Gently cook the garlic in olive oil until golden. Add the anchovies and mash to a purée with the back of a wooden spoon. Cook 1 minute. Stir in the tomato purée and parsley and simmer, uncovered, for 2 to 3 minutes. Season with pepper to taste. Add the oregano.

2. Cook the spaghetti in boiling salted water until tender. Drain. Toss with the hot sauce and sprinkle with the bread crumbs. Serve at once.

COUSCOUS

Say North Africa to a food lover and he'll think couscous. In Morocco, Algeria, and Tunisia, it is by far the most famous and popular food. It is simple, it is soothing, and it is delicious.

Take a container with a perforated bottom, fill it with a thousand tiny pellets of granules, and place it above a bubbling stew, and *voila!* The vapors from the stew will both swell the granules and flavor them. Eat the pellets and the stew together, and the result is happiness.

But there are two confusions to clear up. First, couscous is the name for both the finished dish and the granule that is the basis for the dish. Second, some people think that couscous is a grain. And it certainly is if you use barley kernels, green wheat, or green barley shoots to make a dish of couscous. But if you used fine semolina flour and coarse semolina mixed with water, rolled it into little lumps, then pressed the lumps through a sieve to form minute and uniform balls, it would be more akin to a pasta. These tiny balls are rolled around on another sieve to remove excess flour, then steamed and eaten right away, or steamed, dried, and stored. In dried form they are the couscous "grains" you buy at the store.

I have written extensively about them in my Moroccan cookbook, *Couscous and Other Good Food from Morocco,* and I refer interested readers there. In that book I also offer everything from the simplest Berber couscous tossed with fresh favas and downed with buttermilk, to lavish palace versions in which pigeons, nestled in the grain, are stuffed with different fillings.

Making couscous by hand is a tradition handed down from mother to daughter in North Africa, and where the average family eats couscous about twice a week, it is a vital staple. But since making it by hand takes time and many North African women work, the old method is rapidly falling out of favor.

Recently, I had a chance to visit the world's largest and most modern couscous factory, located in Sfax, the second city of Tunisia, and a major port. The manager took me on a tour. I didn't know quite what to expect, perhaps a thousand women in neat factory rows making couscous all at once. Instead, I found a completely automated plant run by men, an almost nightmare maze of broilers, vats, and chutes that turn out tons of couscous a week.

Tunisian couscous is not well known here, but as I discovered it can be very good. Chili peppers sound the predominant note. One of my favorites is a red and green specialty called *kuski ffawwar*. It combines dill and fennel tops with celery leaves and powerful flavorers like red pepper, scallions, coriander, caraway, and garlic.

A delicious nut, date, and custard dessert uses a fine-grain couscous known as *mesfouf,* which, when steaming, swells to the size of the medium couscous available in stores. The special texture and lightness of small-grain couscous make it an ideal substance for desserts.

There is also a large couscous known as *mhammas.* Pellets about the size of Italian *acine de pepe* are rubbed in olive oil, steamed for a full hour, then dumped into a sauce so that they continue cooking until they become soft. Their silky and almost sodden texture is much appreciated in many southern parts of Tunisia.

I found any number of delicious fish couscous recipes in Tunisia, too. A particularly appetizing one is prepared on the island of Jerba in a three-tiered steamer. Slices of bluefish, embedded in a mixture of chopped mint, parsley, Swiss chard, and fennel leaves, are steamed over a cinnamon-and-cumin-scented broth. The couscous, steaming in solitary splendor on top, absorbs the aromas from the two tiers below. In southern Tunisia, dried fish, octopus, and bits of pungent lamb jerky, called *kadid* (which is spiced, dried, and preserved in oil), are often used, with cubes of apricots mixed in to punctuate the salty flavors.

The most popular home-style couscous on Jerba uses red pepper, coriander, tomatoes, fresh green chilies, lamb, olive oil, and *kadid.* Dried baby sardines, called *ouzef,* add a distinctive fishy flavor that acts as a taste stimulant and catalyst. You can eliminate it if necessary, but not the lamb jerky, which gives the dish its unique flavor and a mildly crunchy texture.

Many modern Tunisian couscous dishes are hot and spicy, with lots of fiery harissa, ground coriander, cumin, and garlic. Older ones, which tend to taste both mellow and exotic, are often made with quince, raisins, and a curious blend of dried rosebuds, black pepper, and ground cinnamon. Lately it has become popular to mix the two.

Tunisians tend to steam their couscous covered, while Moroccans and Algerians do not. As a result, the Tunisian version is more tender and moist; the Moroccan and Algerian, a little fluffier and lighter.

Tunisian couscous is also presented differently. Tunisian cooks moisten their steamed grains with lots of broth and often mix the ingredients into the grains so that the dish comes to the table like a pilaf or paella. Moroccan and Algerian cooks prefer to moisten the grains lightly, with thin broth, then make a well in the center for the remaining broth and vegetables. Restaurants usually serve the various ingredients separately so that each diner can take what he likes, but in the home, couscous, like most North African food, is traditionally presented in one large bowl or platter.

The popularity of couscous just grows and grows. Many countries have come up with native versions of the north African original. There is *keskes* in Senegal, *cuscuz* in Brazil, *kouscous* in northern Greece and Turkey, and even *cuscusu* in Sicily, for which the sauce is the local fish soup. (See the *Ghiotta di pesci* in my *World of Food* for a version thickened with toasted almonds.) In Lebanon and Jordan, they make a couscous of large round semolina pellets cooked with onions and chicken and call it *mahgrabia,* which means "from the Mahgreb," the collective noun for Morocco, Algeria, and Tunisia.

Here are master instructions for the traditional handling of couscous. Follow them as indicated in the recipes that follow or your own favorite recipe.

The first and most important is: steam it. Steaming couscous is not difficult, but it is necessary, no matter what the instructions on the package say. The grains of a good couscous must be light, separate, tender, and fluffy, and steaming is the only way to achieve these qualities. I have tried various so-called "instant" brands, followed instructions, and found the results indigestible if eaten in any quantity. Couscous has an ability to expand to many times its original size. One pound (2½ cups) of processed couscous, "precooked" at the factory, can expand with proper steaming to twelve cups. If you don't steam it properly, beware: It will just go right on expanding in your stomach.

But to begin at the beginning . . .

1.

Place the couscous in a fine sieve and set under cool running water until completely wet. Dump into a bowl and allow the couscous to swell for 5 minutes, then break up the lumps.

2.

Fill the bottom part of your couscous pot with water or broth and bring the liquid to a boil. If you don't own a *couscousier,* a deep kettle and a snug fitting vegetable steamer or colander will do. If the latter doesn't fit perfectly, use padding. Dampen a cheesecloth, twist it into a strip the length of the circumference of the kettle top, and tuck it between the two parts, to make sure the steam rises only through the perforated holes. Lightly oil the inside of the steamer, but don't line those holes with cheesecloth. The rising steam will not allow the couscous, no matter how small, to fall through. Don't let the perforated top touch the boiling liquid below either.

3.

With the perforated top in place, pile the moistened couscous in it when liquid is boiling. If directions call for covering, cover tightly and steam 30 to 40 minutes.

4.

Optional second steaming: Midway in the cooking, place the couscous in a large shallow pan and spread it out with a long fork. Sprinkle some salt and cold water (1 cup per pound of couscous) over the grains. Separate and break up lumps by lifting and stirring gently. Oil your hands lightly and gently rework the grains. (Moroccans allow the couscous to dry at this point; Tunisians don't.) Pile the couscous back into the pot and continue steaming, covered if called for in the directions, until fully cooked. (The color of the couscous becomes lighter.)

5.

Dump the couscous into a wide serving dish. Fluff it up with a fork and moisten with some of the prepared broth. Cover and allow the couscous to swell for 10 minutes longer before serving. You can completely assemble couscous in advance and reheat portions in the microwave, uncovered.

One last but very important note: The stew in the bottom of the *couscousier* may be fully cooked before the couscous is ready. If so, transfer the stew to a separate saucepan, keep it warm, and continue steaming the couscous over boiling water.

Kuski Ffawwar

Couscous with greens (Tunisia)

◻

Of the numerous North African couscous recipes I've come across since writing *Couscous and Other Good Food from Morocco,* this red and green Tunisian specialty is one of my favorites. The mélange of dill and fennel tops, celery leaves, red pepper flakes, and spices makes for a light and delicious couscous.

In winter, in Tunisia, large fennel bulbs produce 18-inch stalks bearing bushy bunches of thin fernlike greens. You may have tried fennel tops and found they have little taste, but when you use 2 pounds of these greens for every pound of couscous you will discover that they have flavor and can contribute real earthiness to a dish.

There are numerous variations on this recipe. In Sfax, they make it with *malthouth,* or grilled and cracked barley grits, instead of couscous grains. I have also tasted it when made with whole wheat couscous. But the best version is this recipe given to me by Aziza ben Tanfous, curator of the Sidi Zitouni Museum on Jerba, who learned it from her grandmother.

Since this type of couscous tends to be slightly dry, you may want to serve it with glasses of buttermilk, the traditional way.

SERVES 6

- ½ pound dill and fennel (anise) leaves
- ½ pound parsley
- Handful of celery leaves
- Handful of carrot tops
- ½ pound scallions and leeks
- ½ cup olive oil
- 1 cup chopped onion
- 3 tablespoons tomato paste
- 2 tablespoons crushed garlic
- 2 teaspoons sweet paprika
- 2 teaspoons salt, or more to taste
- 2 teaspoons ground coriander or tabil (page 197)
- 1 teaspoon ground caraway
- 1½ to 2 teaspoons dried red pepper flakes, preferably Aleppo, Turkish, or Near East pepper for best flavor
- 2½ cups (about 1 pound) medium-grain couscous

1 fresh green chili, stemmed, seeded, and minced
1 red bell pepper, stemmed, seeded, and cut into 6 parts
6 garlic cloves, peeled and left whole

1. Wash the greens under running water. Drain and roughly chop. Wash and chop the scallions and leeks. Fill the bottom of a couscous cooker with water and bring to a boil. Fasten on the perforated top; add the greens, scallions, and leeks and steam, covered, for 30 minutes. Remove from the heat and allow to cool, uncovered. When cool enough to handle, squeeze out the excess moisture and set aside.

2. Heat the oil in a 10- or 12-inch skillet and add the onion. Cook 2 to 3 minutes to soften, then add the tomato paste and cook, stirring, until the paste glistens. Add the crushed garlic, paprika, salt, coriander or tabil, caraway, and red pepper flakes and cook slowly until the mixture is well blended. Add 1 cup water, cover, and cook for 15 minutes.

3. Remove the skillet from the heat. Stir the *dry* couscous into the contents of the skillet and stir until well blended. Stir in the steamed greens, leeks, and scallions and mix well. Fold in the green chili, red pepper, and garlic cloves. Fill the bottom of the couscous cooker with water and bring to a boil. Fasten on the perforated top, add the contents of the skillet, and steam, covered, for 30 minutes.

4. Turn out the couscous onto a large warm serving dish. Use a long fork to break up lumps; fish out the whole garlic cloves and red pepper slices, reserving them. Stir 1 cup water into the couscous, taste for seasoning, and cover with foil. Set it in a warm place for 10 minutes before serving.

5. Decorate the couscous with the red pepper slices in a star pattern and place the whole garlic cloves on top. Serve with glasses of buttermilk.

Mesfouf de Jerba

Savory couscous with kadid *and vegetables*

(Tunisia)

This delightful couscous, the most popular one on the Tunisian island of Jerba, is eaten "from one day to the next," according to the local cook who taught it to me.

Made with fine-grain couscous, it is flavored with red pepper, coriander, tomatoes, fresh green chili, lamb, olive oil, and two unusual ingredients—*kadid,* a lamb jerky that contributes a pungent flavor and a pastramilike texture, and *ouzef,* dried baby sardines and a distinctive fishy taste that acts as a taste stimulant and catalyst. You can, if necessary, eliminate the dried fish, but not the jerked meat, which gives the dish its unique flavor and a mildly crunchy texture.

This couscous can be made in advance, reheated in small quantities, uncovered, in the microwave.

With thanks to Mme. Najiba Chanmmakhi of Jerba and Tunis

SERVES 6

4 strips *kadid* (pages 33–34), with ¼ cup of their oil

¼ cup olive oil

½ pound onions, peeled and thinly sliced

2 shoulder lamb chops, trimmed of excess fat and cut into ½-inch pieces

2 tablespoons tomato paste

¾ cup crushed canned or fresh tomatoes

2 teaspoons dried red pepper flakes, preferably Aleppo pepper or
    Near East pepper for best flavor

1½ teaspoons tabil (page 197)

1 teaspoon ground caraway
    Fine sea salt

2½ cups fine-grain couscous

1½ cups diced carrots

1½ cups diced potatoes

15 *ouzef* (dried baby sardines) (see note), soaked in warm water
    10 minutes and drained (optional)

1 cup green peas, shelled or defrosted

3 tablespoons chopped parsley

2 to 4 tablespoons minced green chili, to taste
   Freshly ground black pepper

1. Soak the *kadid* in warm water until soft, about 15 minutes; drain and discard the bones. Cut the meat into small chunks.

2. Heat 3 tablespoons of the olive oil and the oil from the *kadid* in the bottom of a couscous cooker. Add the onions and lamb and sauté for 5 minutes. Cover and cook over low heat until the meat gives off its moisture and reabsorbs it. Add the *kadid* and the tomato paste and cook, stirring, until the meat is well coated and glossy.

3. Add the crushed tomatoes, red pepper flakes, tabil, caraway, salt and 1 cup water. Cover and cook 5 minutes; then add 1 quart water and bring to a boil.

4. Meanwhile, rinse the couscous in a sieve, spread it on a baking pan, and let it sit until grains swell, 5 to 10 minutes.

5. Break up the lumps by raking the couscous through your fingers. Lightly oil the inside of the perforated top and fasten it onto the couscous cooker; seal the two containers, if necessary, with a strip of wet cheesecloth. When steam is rising through the perforated holes, pile the couscous into the top container. Cover and steam the couscous for 20 minutes.

6. Transfer steamed couscous onto a baking pan. Gradually break up large lumps with a long spoon while sprinkling couscous with 1 teaspoon salt and 1½ cups cold water. When the couscous is cool enough to handle, break up any lumps with moistened fingertips. Allow the couscous grains to swell for 5 minutes, then sprinkle with remaining 1 tablespoon olive oil and lightly rake the couscous grains with your fingertips.

7. Add the carrots, potatoes, and drained *ouzef,* if using, to the simmering broth and check that there is enough water to cover all the solids by 1 inch. Bring the broth back to a boil; fasten on the perforated top, pile the couscous into the top container, cover, and steam for 15 minutes.

8. Lift the top container, slip the peas, parsley, and green chili into the simmering broth, return the top container, and steam another 5 minutes.

9. Tip the couscous into a wide serving dish. Taste the cooking liquid and correct the seasoning with salt and pepper. The broth should be just thick enough to lightly coat the back of a wooden spoon. Add the contents of the cooker to the

(continued)

couscous and gently toss to combine. Cover and let stand 15 minutes before serving.

Note: Ouzef, the silvery dried fish, are the size of whitebait, and can be found in oriental food stores, where they are called *niboshi* (in Japanese), *ca com* (in Vietnamese), *joetkal* (in Korean), and *chao pai* (in Chinese). Look for bright, shiny-skinned firm fish, which will keep indefinitely in a dry place. Though it is not necessary to remove the heads from the Tunisian *ouzef* (unless they are sandy), it is wise to do so with the oriental substitutes because, according to Jacki Passmore, author of *The Encyclopedia of Asian Food and Cooking,* some fish heads will turn bitter when cooked.

Mesfouf

Sweet semolina with dates, nuts, and rose water pudding (Tunisia)

The special texture and lightness of small-grain couscous make it an ideal substance for desserts. Often Tunisians will substitute coarse-grain semolina. You can find coarse semolina at Middle Eastern groceries or see Mail-Order Sources (pages 296–97).

Dessert couscous is more popular in Tunisia than Morocco. In Morocco, it is rich with butter and sugar, and eaten warm or even hot. Tunisian couscous is less sweet and is served cool or even chilled, often mixed with seasonal fresh fruits or pomegranate seeds mixed with seedless black raisins.

This sweet couscous comes from the city of Sfax on the eastern coast. What I especially like about it is that, while Tunisian sweet couscous dishes tend to be a little on the dry side, this one is moist due to a layer of creamy pudding.

SERVES 6 TO 8

PUDDING
> 2 cups low-fat milk
> 2 egg yolks
> 2 tablespoons sugar
> Salt
> 2 tablespoons cornstarch
> A few drops of pure vanilla extract
> 1 teaspoon rose water

    1 cup coarse-grain semolina
 1½ tablespoons olive oil
  ½ cup blanched almonds
  ½ cup grated walnuts
  ¼ cup seedless black raisins
  8 pitted dates, chopped
  1 tablespoon unsalted butter
  2 tablespoons granulated sugar, or more to taste
  2 tablespoons grated pistachios

1. Bring the milk to a boil in a medium saucepan. While the milk is heating, place the egg yolks, sugar, and a pinch of salt in a mixing bowl or workbowl of a food processor; beat until pale yellow and thick. Add the cornstarch; beat until smooth. Gradually pour the hot milk into the egg yolk mixture. Pour back into saucepan, set over medium heat, and cook, stirring constantly, until boiling. Continue to stir vigorously until the custard is smooth, about 45 seconds. Remove from heat and continue to beat vigorously for 30 seconds longer. Stir in the vanilla and rose water. When cool, place a sheet of plastic wrap directly on the pudding to inhibit the formation of a skin. Keep in the refrigerator until ready to use.

2. In a bowl, mix the coarse semolina and olive oil, blending well. Heat plenty of water in the bottom of a *couscousier* and bring to a rolling boil. Fasten the perforated container on top and scatter the semolina grains over the holes (they will not fall through if steam is rising), and steam, covered, for 30 minutes.

3. Toast the almonds in a low oven or in a microwave until golden brown. Grate the almonds; mix the almonds and walnuts with the raisins and chopped dates and set aside.

4. Transfer the entire steamer container with the semolina to a side bowl. Remove the cover, moisten the grains with an 8-ounce ladle of the boiling water, allowing water to drain through the holes. Return the container to the *couscousier,* cover tightly, and steam the semolina another 10 minutes.

5. Dump the semolina grains into a wide bowl, add another ladle of boiling water and the butter; stir with a fork until butter melts. Leave the grains to cool.

6. Sprinkle the grains with ½ cup cold water and a pinch of salt; fluff with a fork. Dip your fingertips into cold water and rub out the lumps. Fork in the 2

(continued)

tablespoons granulated sugar. Smooth out the grains and leave to dry in a cool place. Makes about 4 cups. Up to this point, the recipe can be prepared 3 hours in advance.

7. To assemble the dish, spread a layer of rose-scented pudding on the bottom of a 10- or 12-inch round serving dish. Spread half the steamed semolina over the pudding and scatter the nut mixture evenly on top. Top with a layer of semolina. Press the pistachios through a fine sieve and run lines of pistachio over the top. Cover with plastic wrap and set in a cool place until ready to serve.

Kuski bil Kabaar

Couscous with meatballs as prepared at the gateway to the Sahara (Tunisia)

In a private home in the dusty Tunisian town of Gabès, take-off point for trips into the Sahara, I found a lavish version of couscous that surprised me. The grain, accompanied by a hot spicy sauce, was gloriously garnished with vegetables, homemade meat sausages, and meat *boulettes,* topped off with delicious fried green peppers. I offer here an abbreviated version.

SERVES 8 TO 10

    1 cup dried chick-peas
    ½ teaspoon baking soda
    1 pound onions, sliced
    2 tablespoons olive oil
    2 tablespoons tomato paste
    4 pounds lamb neck
    1 teaspoon cayenne
    3 tablespoons *hrous* (pages 97–98)
    Coarse salt
    4 cups medium couscous (1½ pounds)
    6 whole New Mexican green chilies
    2 red ripe tomatoes, quartered and seeded
    1 pound carrots, cut into 1-inch pieces
    ½ pound turnips, peeled and cut into 1-inch pieces
    6 tablespoons yellow raisins

3/4 teaspoon ground cinnamon

3/4 teaspoon ground rosebuds

3/4 teaspoon freshly ground black pepper

2 pounds pumpkin or banana squash, peeled and cut into 2-inch chunks

2 tablespoons butter

Olive oil for frying

1 lemon

Lamb boulettes (see page 161)

1. Pick over the chick-peas and toss with the baking soda. Soak overnight in soft water. Drain, rinse well, and remove the skins by submerging the chick-peas in a bowl of cold water and gently rubbing them between the fingers. Discard the skins.

2. In a large pot, sauté the onions in olive oil until soft. Add the tomato paste, lamb, cayenne, *hrous*, 1/2 teaspoon salt, drained chick-peas, and 6 cups water. Simmer, covered, for 1 1/2 hours.

3. Place couscous in a fine strainer and rinse under cool running water. Dump into a large bowl and let stand until grains swell, 10 to 20 minutes. Break up any lumps with your fingertips.

4. Place the couscous in a perforated steamer and cook, covered, over simmering broth for 15 minutes.

5. Put couscous into a roomy pan and sprinkle with 1 1/2 cups cold water. Use a long pronged fork to break up any lumps. Sprinkle with 1 teaspoon salt, toss, and set aside until 30 minutes before serving.

6. Remove the broth from the heat and cool quickly. Skim off the fat that rises to the top. Bone the lamb and return chunks to the broth. Up to this point the couscous can be prepared early in the day.

7. About 1 hour before serving, prepare the chilies for frying. With a small knife, puncture each whole pepper near the stem end. Slip a good pinch of coarse salt into the hole and set chilies aside.

8. Forty minutes before serving, reheat the meaty broth. Add the fresh tomatoes, carrots, turnips, and raisins. Season with 1 tablespoon salt, cinnamon, rosebuds, and black pepper. Bring the broth to the boil, adding boiling water if necessary to keep all the vegetables covered. Return the perforated top, add the couscous, and steam, covered, for another 20 minutes.

(continued)

9. In a saucepan, cook the chunks of pumpkin squash in salted boiling water until just tender. Remove from the saucepan and keep warm.

10. Place the couscous on a very wide serving dish and toss with the butter, using a fork to smooth out any lumps. Readjust the seasoning of the broth, adding lemon to taste. Strain 3 cups of the broth over the couscous, cover, and let stand 10 minutes.

11. While the couscous is resting, heat 1 inch of olive oil in a heavy skillet. Add the chilies and fry until golden brown on all sides. Remove to a side dish. (You can then fry the lamb boulettes in the same oil, as directed on page 161.)

12. With a perforated spoon, lift the meat from the broth and place on top of the couscous. Scatter the vegetables on top. Surround with the pumpkin and the boulettes. Make a star pattern with the fried peppers on top of the couscous. Serve remaining sauce on the side.

KABAAR
Lamb boulettes *for couscous (Tunisia)*

These *boulettes* (meatballs) were prepared for me by Myriam Sebti, famous in Gabès for her fine cooking. During the colonial period, she had been the cook for the French governor, who, she told me, liked Gabesian food as much as he liked French cuisine.

Her *boulettes* are extremely light and aromatic due to the addition of mashed potatoes and the Tunisian spice mixture *bharat* (ground cinnamon and dried rosebuds), along with plenty of fresh coriander and parsley. They must be fried at the last minute, but the mixture can be made ahead.

        9   to 10 ounces lean lamb or veal
        1   small onion, peeled
            Salt
            Freshly ground black pepper
      1/2   teaspoon dried rosebuds
      1/2   teaspoon ground cinnamon
        3   to 4 garlic cloves, peeled
        2   small waxy potatoes, boiled, peeled, and mashed (still warm)
        2   tablespoons chopped fresh coriander
      1/4   cup chopped fresh parsley
        2   tablespoons fresh bread crumbs
        1   whole egg and 2 egg whites
            Flour for dusting
            Oil for frying

1. In a food processor, grind the meat, onion, salt, pepper, spices, and garlic until pasty. Turn into a mixing bowl; add potatoes, herbs, bread crumbs, whole egg, and egg whites, blending well. The mixture should be soft. Season with salt and pepper, cover, and refrigerate for at least 30 minutes.

2. Lightly handling the meat with moistened palms, divide the mixture into 8 or 10 patties. Dredge lightly in flour and fry in 1/2 inch of very hot but not smoking oil until crisp and well browned, about 5 minutes. Drain on paper towels. Place *boulettes* in a warm oven until all are fried.

Seksu Tanjaoui

Couscous in the style of Tangier (Morocco)

▣

This is a good all-around North African couscous, made with lamb and pumpkin, carrots, turnips, zucchini, onions, and chick-peas. It's topped by a glazed dressing of almonds, raisins, and onions. The sauce is hot, spiced with lots of pepper, ginger, and saffron. The play of this spicy sauce against the sweet glazed topping is one of the many delights of this dish.

SERVES 8 TO 10

   1 cup dried chick-peas
  ½ teaspoon baking soda
     Salt
   4 cups medium couscous (1½ pounds)
 1½ pounds lamb neck or shank
   2 rounded teaspoons freshly ground black pepper
   1 teaspoon ground ginger
  ⅛ teaspoon pulverized saffron
   3 onions, quartered
   2 sprigs each parsley and fresh coriander, tied together with thread
   8 tablespoons unsalted butter
   1 large Spanish onion, quartered and thinly sliced lengthwise
  ½ teaspoon ground cinnamon
  ½ cup black raisins
  ¼ cup sugar
   6 small carrots, scraped and quartered
   6 small turnips, scraped and quartered
 1½ pounds pumpkin, peeled, cored, and cut into 2-inch chunks
   3 to 4 small zucchini, halved
     Oil
   1 cup whole blanched almonds

1. Pick over the chick-peas and toss with baking soda. Soak the dried chick-peas overnight.

2. The next day, cover the chick-peas with fresh cold salted water and cook, covered, for 1 hour. Drain, cool, and remove the skins by submerging the chick-peas in a bowl of cold water and gently rubbing them between the fingers. The skins will rise to the top of the water. Discard the skins and set the chick-peas aside.

3. Place couscous in a fine strainer and rinse under cool running water. Dump into a large bowl and let stand until grains swell, 10 to 20 minutes. Break up any lumps with your fingertips.

4. To prepare the broth, place the lamb, 2 teaspoons salt, pepper, ginger, saffron, quartered onions, herbs, and 3 tablespoons butter in the bottom of a deep pot or *couscoussier*. Heat over a low flame, swirling the pan once or twice to let the spices and meat mix gently. When the butter is melted, cover the lamb with 3 quarts water and bring to a boil. Add the drained chick-peas, cover, and simmer 1 hour.

5. Place the couscous in a perforated steamer and cook, uncovered, over the simmering broth for 15 minutes. Place couscous in a roomy pan and sprinkle with 1½ cups cold water. Use a long pronged fork to break up any lumps. Sprinkle with 1 teaspoon salt, toss, and set aside until 30 minutes before serving.

6. Remove the broth from the heat and cool quickly. Skim off the fat that rises to the top. Bone the lamb and return chunks to the broth. Up to this point the couscous can be prepared early in the day.

7. Begin the preparation of the glazed topping. After the lamb has cooked 1 hour, transfer 2 cups of the simmering lamb broth to a saucepan. Add the Spanish onion, ground cinnamon, raisins, sugar, 3 tablespoons butter, salt, and freshly ground black pepper to taste. Cook, covered, for 1 hour, then remove the cover and continue cooking until the liquid has evaporated and the onions have a dark glazed appearance. This takes about 30 minutes. Set aside, uncovered.

8. Thirty minutes before serving, add the carrots, turnips, pumpkin, and zucchini to the lamb broth. With wet hands, break up any lumps of couscous by working the grains lightly between your fingers. Bring the broth to the boil, reseal the two containers, and steam the couscous another 20 minutes.

9. Reheat the glazed onions and raisins. Heat the oil in a skillet and fry the almonds until golden brown. Drain and set aside.

10. Dump the couscous onto a very wide serving dish and toss with 2 table-spoons butter, using a fork to smooth out any lumps. Readjust the seasoning of the broth. Strain 3 cups of the broth over the couscous, cover, and let stand 10 minutes.

11. With a perforated spoon, lift the meat from the broth and place on top of the couscous. Scatter the vegetables on top. Spread the glazed topping on top and sprinkle with almonds.

TUNISIAN BRIKS

The *brik* is the Tunisian snack *par excellence*—a delicious pastry dish that can be prepared in innumerable ways, eaten anytime of the day, and bought on the street or on the beach. It consists of a paper-thin sheet of dough filled with any one of a hundred stuffings, fast fried, served up hot, and eaten with the hands.

The delicate crisp pastry leaves are not made like *phyllo* (although phyllo can be substituted), but by kneading semolina flour and water until enormous elasticity develops and then systematically tapping pieces of this dough onto a heated pan, leaving slightly overlapping disks to cook on only one side. This pastry is called *malsouqua,* which means "to adhere."

It is exactly the same as the Moroccan *warka,* and surprisingly close to Chinese spring roll skins.

Here, first, is a master recipe for *briks* with a stuffing of onion, egg, and brains.

Briks bil Mohk
Brain and egg turnovers (Tunisia)

SERVES 4

> ¾ pound lamb, calf, or beef brains
> Salt
> Freshly ground black pepper
> Vinegar
> 2 tablespoons unsalted butter
> ¼ cup finely chopped onion
> 1 tablespoon finely chopped parsley
> 1 tablespoon grated Parmesan cheese
> 2 phyllo leaves, or 4 Chinese spring roll skins
> 4 eggs
> Oil for frying
> Lemon quarters

1. Soak the brains for 30 minutes in several changes of water. Remove the membranes, then rinse and drain. In a saucepan, bring 1½ quarts seasoned and acidulated water to the simmer. Slip in the brains, cover, and cook over low heat for 20 minutes. Drain, cool, and dice.

2. Melt the butter in a medium saucepan and cook the onion over low heat until soft but not browned. Add the brains, parsley, and salt and pepper to taste. Cook gently for 10 minutes, stirring often. Stir in the cheese. Mix and mash, then separate into four equal parts.

3. Spread out the pastry leaves and cut them in half; if using spring roll skins, leave them whole. Fold each of the pastry leaves in half and place a quarter of the filling 2 inches away from one corner. Flatten the filling slightly to make a hollow in the center. Break an egg into the hollow. Fold over the pastry to cover the egg; dab the edges in the egg white, press the edges to adhere, and fold each rim over ½ inch for a secure closing, being careful not to break the egg inside. If you are using spring roll skins, fold in the left and right sides in order to make a square, then proceed as directed above. Repeat with the 3 remaining pastry leaves.

4. Heat oil to the depth of 1 inch in a large deep skillet. When hot but not smoking, slide in one *brik*. Lightly push it down into the oil, then press one corner in order to make the *brik* swell. When golden brown on both sides, transfer to paper towels to drain. Repeat with the 3 remaining *briks*. Serve hot with lemon quarters.

Variations

SWEBA
Ground meat and egg turnovers

For each brik, mix 2 tablespoons ground beef cooked with a little onion and parsley and seasoned with salt and pepper. Mix in 1 tablespoon grated Parmesan cheese and a few drops of lemon juice. A sliced hard-boiled egg is used instead of a raw one.

BRIKS bIL STHUM
Anchovy and egg turnovers

For each brik, cook 6 fillets of anchovies and 1 tablespoon chopped onion in butter. Mix with 1 tablespoon grated Parmesan cheese and freshly ground black pepper, and top with a raw egg.

Maasems

Fatima's little fingers (Tunisia)

These crisp golden appetizers, filled with a mixture of chicken, eggs, and herbs, are all the rage in modern Tunisia. In French they are called *doigts de Fatima*.

MAKES 12, SERVING 6

2 hard-cooked eggs, shelled and chopped
3/4 cup finely chopped cooked chicken breast
1/3 cup chopped parsley
2 eggs, lightly beaten
1½ tablespoons grated Parmesan cheese
Salt
Freshly ground black pepper
3 phyllo leaves, or 9 or 18 large, very thin spring roll or egg roll skins, depending upon size
1 egg white
Olive oil
Lemon quarters

1. In a mixing bowl, combine the chopped eggs, chicken, parsley, raw eggs, and cheese. Season with salt and pepper. The mixture should be quite loose. Refrigerate, covered, for at least 30 minutes before assembling and frying the pastries.

2. Unroll one sheet of phyllo, keeping the others under a damp kitchen towel to prevent the pastry from drying out. Cut the sheet into 4 quarters, then fold each part in half. (If using spring roll skins or egg roll wrappers, cut to 5-inch squares.) Place a heaping tablespoon of the chicken mixture at the bottom of each doubled piece of phyllo dough, leaving about 1 inch at each side. Lightly froth an egg white and brush the edges. Fold the bottom over and roll over again. Do not fold in the sides. Do not brush phyllo or wrapper with oil or butter. Press on each end so that they will adhere. Using a small plastic brush, lightly dab the top with oil to keep phyllo from drying out. Repeat with the remaining phyllo or wrappers and the filling (Each stuffed pastry should measure about 1 by 5 inches.)

3. Meanwhile, heat 1 inch of oil in a deep pan. When hot but not smoking (about 350 degrees) transfer each pastry to the pan by holding the two ends and letting the center drop first into the hot oil. Fry four or five at a time (to avoid

lowering oil temperature). Turn over as soon as crisp on the first side. When golden brown on both sides, transfer to paper towels to drain. Repeat with remaining pastries and serve at once with lemon quarters.

Chorba bil Frik
Green wheat soup (Tunisia)

In Tunisia, some wheat and barley are harvested in their immature state, boiled, dried in the sun, then lightly roasted for use in soups, such as this "masterpiece of Ramadan," so nicknamed for its delicious and unique gentle smoky flavor.

This soup, from the northwestern part of Tunisia, is earthy and luscious. It is flavored with a turmeric-based spice mixture that provides a hot pungent taste and a beautiful warm color. It is thickened at the end with a creamy-textured paste of garlic, veal marrow, ground almonds, coriander, and stale bread. This method of thickening, reminiscent of Moorish cooking in Spain, probably dates back to the time of the Christian reconquest when the Moors sailed into Kalaat el Andaleus, a village near Bizerte, which was once on a headland to the sea.

SERVES 5 TO 6

  1 cup green wheat *frik* (see note)
1⅓ pounds veal shanks, cut into 1-inch slices
    Coarse sea salt
  1 teaspoon turmeric-flavored spice mixture (see following recipe)
  3 tablespoons olive oil
  2 tablespoons minced parsley stems
  1 small celery rib, minced
  1 tablespoon tomato paste

FINISHING LIAISON
10 blanched almonds
  2 garlic cloves
  1 teaspoon ground coriander
    Coarse sea salt
    Freshly ground pepper
  1 slice of stale French, Italian, or Spanish bread
⅔ cup snipped flat-leaf parsley for garnish

(continued)

1. To clean green wheat: Place the wheat in a coarse sieve or tamis and shake to remove dust, dirt, and tiny stones. Set in a deep basin filled with cool water and let stand a minute or two. Skim off the husks and debris that float to the top of the water. Vigorously rub the wheat kernels between your fingers to feel for stones or other foreign matter. Wash in several changes of water until the water runs clear. Drain, then rake the wheat through your fingers to be sure it is free of all gritty matter.

2. Season the meat with salt and spice mixture. Heat the oil in a large saucepan or pressure cooker and sauté the meat with the parsley and celery for 5 minutes, stirring often. Add the tomato paste and stir until glistening. Pour in 7 cups water and the green wheat and bring to a boil, skimming carefully. Cover the pot and cook at the simmer for about 1½ hours, or until the meat is tender. (If using a pressure cooker, cook under pressure for 20 minutes.)

3. Remove the veal shanks from the soup. Dice the meat, release the marrow, and mash it with a tablespoon of the soup to a purée; set aside. Return the meat to the pot, discarding the bone and any gristle or fat. Reheat the soup, adjust the seasoning, and keep hot until ready to finish the soup.

4. In a stone mortar with a strong pestle or in a spice mill, combine the almonds, garlic, coriander, salt, and pepper to form a smooth paste. Soften the slice of bread with water and squeeze dry. Combine 1 tablespoon squeezed bread with the marrow and the seasoned almond paste and pound until smooth. Stir the paste into the soup and cook over low heat until thick and creamy. Serve with a good sprinkling of chopped parsley.

TURMERIC-FLAVORED SPICE MIXTURE

MAKES ABOUT 5 TEASPOONS

1½ teaspoons ground turmeric
¼ teaspoon aniseed
¾ teaspoon ground coriander seeds
½ teaspoon ground caraway seeds
2 cloves
Pinch of ground cinnamon
2 teaspoons black peppercorns
½ teaspoon dried red pepper flakes

Combine the ingredients in a spice mill or mortar and grind to a powder. Place in a clean jar, cover tightly, and keep in a cool cupboard.

Notes: In southeastern Turkey, Syria, Egypt, and Jordan immature wheat kernels are set ablaze in order to endow them with an even stronger, smokier flavor. The result is *fereekah.* Though not exactly the same, *fereekah,* which you can find at Middle Eastern stores or at Dean & DeLuca, makes a good substitute for the *frik,* which can be difficult to find.

If purchasing *frik,* be sure to ask to sniff it. It should smell smoky and fresh, not stale and acrid. Store in a cool place to maintain quality (it keeps for about a year). *Frik* or *fereekah* must be cleaned, so be sure to set aside time to follow the cleaning instructions in step 1 above.

Health note on using veal marrow: I was delighted to learn that the luscious marrow of veal is not as bad for you as previously thought. Eileen Stukane, *Health News* reporter, writes: "According to Ray Field, professor of meat science at the University of Wyoming, about half of the veal marrow's fatty acids are unsaturated, and most of them are beneficial monounsaturated fatty acids, which preserve 'good' high-density lipoprotein and reduce the 'bad' low-density lipoproteins." Though veal marrow contributes niacin, it is also fattening in large quantities.

Tabbouleh

Parsley and bulgur salad (Lebanon)

In my view, a really good *tabbouleh* is made with large amounts of greens, scallions, spices, good olive oil, a small amount of fine-grain bulgur, then made tart with fresh lemon juice. This is a fortifying salad. It will, as the Arab saying goes, "put nails into your joints."

SERVES 6

- ²/₃ cup fine-grain bulgur
- 8 scallions, finely sliced
- Scant 2 cups chopped flat-leaf parsley
- ½ cup slivered fresh spearmint leaves
- ½ cup shredded sorrel leaves (optional)
- 1 medium cucumber, peeled, halved, seeded, and finely diced
- ¾ teaspoon freshly ground black pepper
- Scant ¼ teaspoon ground red pepper
- Scant ¼ teaspoon ground allspice
- Scant ¼ teaspoon ground cinnamon
- Scant ¼ teaspoon grated nutmeg
- 3 tablespoons extra-virgin olive oil
- 3 tablespoons freshly squeezed lemon juice, or more to taste
- Salt
- 2 medium tomatoes, peeled, seeded, and chopped

1. Pick over the bulgur and place in a fine sieve. Shake it to remove any dust.

2. In a mixing bowl, combine the scallions, parsley, mint, sorrel if using, cucumber, spices, olive oil, and lemon juice.

3. Rinse the bulgur under cold running water. Drain and squeeze between the palms of your hands to remove moisture. Immediately mix with the contents of the mixing bowl and cover. (This allows the grains to swell slowly in the oil dressing and keep the grains from turning mushy.) Add salt and pepper to taste and blend well. Refrigerate overnight. Just before serving, add the tomatoes and more salt, if necessary.

Kisir

Bulgur salad with tomatoes and red peppers

(Turkey)

Here is a red-hued, peppery version of the famous Middle Eastern *tabbouleh* salad, as it is prepared in Turkey. The rich red pepper paste base provides it with its magnificent color, while pomegranate molasses and lemon juice contribute a fruity tartness. This *kisir* needs less oil than most versions of bulgur salad and is thus less caloric.

MAKES ABOUT 6 CUPS, SERVING 8

1½ cups fine-grain bulgur
2 vine-ripened medium tomatoes
¾ cup red pepper paste *(biber salcasi)* (page 94)
2 scallions, trimmed and thinly sliced
½ cucumber, peeled, seeded, and chopped
¾ cup chopped parsley
6 tablespoons lemon juice
1 tablespoon pomegranate molasses (see note)
⅓ cup olive oil
1 teaspoon salt
 Hot Hungarian paprika
 Tender romaine lettuce leaves or boiled vine leaves as garnish

1. Place the bulgur in a fine sieve and shake to remove dust. Dampen with cold water and let stand 30 minutes. Squeeze out excess moisture.

2. Cut the tomatoes in half and gently squeeze to remove seeds. Grate tomato halves, cut side facing coarsest side of a four-sided grater or flat shredder. (You should be left with just the tomato skin in your hand; discard.)

3. In a mixing bowl, combine bulgur, pepper paste, tomato pulp, and all the remaining ingredients except lettuce and pita. Blend the mixture with your hands or two forks. Cover tightly with plastic wrap and chill for a few hours before serving. Correct the seasoning and serve surrounded by lettuce or vine leaves and pita bread.

Note: Pomegranate molasses is available at Middle Eastern groceries and fine food stores, or refer to "Mail-Order Sources" (pages 296–97).

Koupas

Ovals stuffed with lamb, parsley, and fennel

(Cyprus)

◫

Levantines love to stuff one thing into another. One of the most unusual dishes is the Arab *kibbeh* and its Cypriot version, *koupas*—a blend of ground lean lamb, bulgur, grated onion, and spices, molded on the index finger into little football shapes, stuffed, and fried.

In this Cypriot version, the crisp shell is made with very little meat and a high proportion of well-saturated bulgur. The method for making the shell is unconventional: Bulgur is soaked in salty hot water, making the grains swell without turning mushy. When mixed with the small amount of meat, it binds quickly and smoothly and can be molded around the finger with ease.

MAKES ABOUT 18 3-INCH ROLLS, SERVING 4 TO 6 AS PART OF A MIDDLE EASTERN BUFFET

SHELL

- 1 cup fine-grain bulgur
- 3 cups hot water
- 1 teaspoon fine salt
- 3 ounces extra-lean ground leg of lamb
- 2 level tablespoons flour
- 1/4 teaspoon freshly ground black pepper

FILLING

- 1/3 cup chopped onion
- 1 tablespoon olive oil
- 5 ounces ground lamb shoulder
- 2 tablespoons butter
- 2 tablespoons pine nuts
- 1/8 teaspoon ground cinnamon
- 1/4 teaspoon freshly ground black pepper
- Salt
- 1/4 cup cubed tomato
- 1/3 cup coarsely chopped flat-leaf parsley
- 1 1/2 tablespoons chopped fresh dill

  Oil for deep-frying
  Lemon quarters

1. Rinse the bulgur to remove any dust; drain and put in a deep bowl. Mix the 3 cups hot water with the salt, pour over the bulgur, and let stand 2 hours.

2. Meanwhile, prepare the filling: place chopped onion and oil in a medium skillet and cook until golden and soft. Add the ground lamb shoulder and brown lightly, breaking up the meat with a fork, about 5 minutes. Add 1/2 cup water and cook, uncovered, over low heat for 15 minutes, or until all the water has evaporated and the meat begins to brown in its own fat. Add the butter and pine nuts and allow meat and nuts to brown lightly. Add the spices, salt, tomato, and herbs. Cook 1 to 2 minutes longer, stirring. Remove from the heat to cool. Makes about 1 cup.

3. Drain the bulgur and squeeze to remove moisture. Mix lean lamb with bulgur, flour, and pepper in the workbowl of a food processor. Process 30 seconds, or until the mixture mounds on the metal blade. The texture should not be sticky but firm and somewhat smooth. Place in a bowl, cover, and chill thoroughly before proceeding.

4. To form the *koupas:* Dip your hands into a bowl of ice water and pinch off a walnut-size piece of the lamb-bulgur mixture. Knead gently, then use the wet palm of the other hand to mold it around your forefinger, making a thin, even cylinder about 2½ inches long. Seal any breaks by briefly dipping the shell into the ice water and smoothing the dough. Carefully slide the shell from your finger with your other hand. Quickly push about 2 teaspoons of the stuffing into the shell. Pinch the ends to seal, using a few drops of cold water to help it bind. Gently squeeze the roll with wet palms to form an elongated football shape. Place the *koupas* on a flat tray. Repeat with the remaining lamb-bulgur mixture and stuffing. Cover the stuffed *koupas* with plastic wrap and partially freeze for 10 minutes to help prevent the shells from cracking.

5. In a large skillet, heat ¼ inch of oil to 325 degrees. Add half the *koupas* to the skillet. Fry, turning, until they are copper colored and crisp all over, about 5 minutes. Remove with a slotted spoon and drain on paper towels. Serve hot or at room temperature, with lemon quarters to squeeze over the *koupas.*

Kabak u Pilau

Squash with bulgur pilaf (Turkey)

◻

There are three indigenous American ingredients that grow magnificently around the Mediterranean, where, due to differences in soil and climate, they acquire a particularly "Mediterranean" personality and taste: tomatoes, peppers, and pumpkins.

Take, for example, the Italian San Marzano tomato with its rich and aromatic flavor. Even canned, it is superior to many of our brands (though Redpack is a very good substitute).

The red peppers of Syria, southeastern Turkey, Catalonian Spain, and northern Greece are rich in flavor and yet are truly different in taste and aroma from those grown in our Southwest. Some of these peppers in their dried form are available at fine food stores and Middle Eastern groceries.

And so too with pumpkins. From North Africa to France to southeastern Turkey, the hard-skinned Mediterranean-grown squash are flavorful without being too sweet. Our own Hubbard squash and butternut squash are decent substitutes for the Turkish variety, as demonstrated in this hearty pilaf from the town of Nizip, not far from the Euphrates.

MAKES ABOUT 2 QUARTS, SERVING 12

1	large butternut squash
1½	cups chopped onions
2	tablespoons unsalted butter or olive oil
1	fresh New Mexican chili, stemmed, seeded, and finely diced (⅓ cup)
¾	pound cherry tomatoes, chopped (2 cups)
2	teaspoons dried red pepper flakes, preferably Near East or Aleppo pepper for best flavor
	Salt
	Freshly ground black pepper
2	cups chicken stock
1¾	cups large-grain bulgur
4	tablespoons olive oil
3	medium onions, thinly sliced
3	cups plain yogurt, drained to 2 cups
1½	teaspoons crushed garlic

1. Peel the squash and cut the flesh into 1-inch chunks. You should have about 2 quarts.

2. In a nonstick, covered large skillet, sweat the chopped onion in the butter or oil for 2 minutes. Add the cubed squash and cook, stirring it to lightly sear on all sides, for 2 minutes. Add the chili, tomatoes, Near East pepper, and 1 cup water. Season with 1 teaspoon salt and ½ teaspoon black pepper. Bring to a boil, partially cover, and cook over medium heat for 15 minutes.

3. Bring the stock to a boil. Stir the bulgur into the skillet. Add the stock, return to a boil, and stir once. Cover the pan, lower the heat, and cook 20 minutes, or until all the liquid has been absorbed.

4. Meanwhile, heat the olive oil in a second skillet. Add the sliced onions and sauté until golden and crisp. Drain and set aside.

5. Remove the first skillet from the heat; place a folded kitchen towel over the pilaf, cover tightly, and set in a warm place for 15 to 20 minutes, until the bulgur is completely swollen.

6. Reheat the onions for a second in a dry skillet and spread over the pilaf. Serve hot or warm with a bowl of well-chilled yogurt beaten with crushed garlic.

Crni Rizot
Black rice (Dalmatia)

This first cousin to risotto gets its color from the ink sacs of the cuttlefish and squid used in its preparation. Cuttlefish, available at fishmongers in Italian, Portuguese, and Greek neighborhoods, are preferred because of the greater amount of ink they contain, but squid makes a satisfactory substitute. The smaller the squid or cuttlefish, the more ink sacs and the blacker the rice will be. If only large squid are available, it's best to wait for another day—the taste and look of this rice is best when it is really dark in color—almost black.

To serve, dip serving spoon first into cheese, then into rice. Dip spoon into cheese before each serving.

(continued)

- 2 pounds whole small cuttlefish or squid, with ink sacs intact
- ½ cup olive oil
- 1½ cups chopped onions
- ½ cup dry white wine
- 1½ teaspoons chopped garlic
- 1½ tablespoons tomato paste
- 7 cups homemade fish stock (see following recipe)
- 2½ cups long-grain rice
- 6 ounces kefalotyri cheese, grated (about 1½ cups), or substitute grated Parmesan

1. To clean cuttlefish or squid, follow directions on page 12. Place ink sacs in a sieve set over a large bowl filled with 2 tablespoons water. Pierce ink sacs, pressing out ink; leave to drain. Cut cuttlefish or squid body and tentacles into bite-size pieces.

2. Heat oil in a heavy saucepan over medium-high heat. Add onions and sauté, stirring frequently, until soft and golden, 6 to 8 minutes. Add cuttlefish or squid; cook, stirring, for 5 minutes to boil off moisture. Add wine, garlic, and tomato paste; heat to boiling. Cook, stirring constantly, until moisture is evaporated, about 10 minutes. (Up to this point the dish can be prepared 1 to 2 days in advance.)

3. About 45 minutes before serving, preheat the oven to 300 degrees.

4. Heat fish stock in a large saucepan over low heat to simmering; keep hot.

5. If necessary, reheat the cuttlefish mixture. Stir rice into saucepan and reduce heat to medium. Cook, stirring constantly, for 2 to 3 minutes. Stir 1 cup of the hot fish stock into reserved ink; add to rice, stirring. Add another cup of stock to rice. Cook, stirring, about 5 minutes, until all liquid is absorbed. Add another 2 cups of stock and continue cooking in this manner until all the stock is used and rice is just tender and creamy, about 15 minutes. Cover the saucepan and place in the oven for 15 minutes.

6. Remove the rice from the oven and turn into a warmed serving dish. Dip spoon into cheese before each serving. Pass more cheese separately.

HOMEMADE FISH STOCK

MAKES ABOUT 7 CUPS

   2 quarts water
   1 pound nonoily fish frames and heads
   1 celery rib, halved
  ½ small onion
  ½ bay leaf
   1 fresh parsley sprig

1. Combine all ingredients in a large saucepan; heat over medium heat to boiling. Reduce heat to low; simmer, uncovered, skimming surface occasionally, until rich stock is produced, about 30 minutes.

2. Strain stock through a sieve lined with a double thickness of dampened cheese-cloth; discard solids. Cool to room temperature. Store in a closed container. Refrigerate up to 2 days, or freeze up to 2 months; reheat to boiling before using.

POTATOES

Patatas al Caldero
Andalusian potatoes in tomato and pepper sauce (Spain)

This is a simple potato dish traditionally served to field-workers during the olive harvest. *Caldero* refers to a big wide pan used to cook the potatoes. You can present it in soup plates as a first course much as pasta or risotto is served in Italy.

In the original recipe, the potatoes are sliced thin, quickly deep fried in olive oil, and then simmered in a savory and aromatic tomato and pepper sauce. The

(continued)

potatoes soften and the flavors meld, resulting in one of those simple, miraculous, melt-in-the-mouth dishes one finds occasionally around the Mediterranean.

In my version I use a lot less oil, but the flavor is still delicious. The tomato-pepper sauce can be made a day or two in advance.

SERVES 6

Extra-virgin olive oil
6 yellow potatoes, such as Yukon Gold (about 2 pounds)
1 large, crusty, stale dinner roll
2 garlic cloves, peeled and cut in half lengthwise
⅓ cup diced red bell pepper
⅓ cup diced green bell pepper
3 tablespoons chopped onion
1 large vine-ripened tomato, cored, seeded, and diced (about 1 cup)
½ bay leaf
Scant ¼ teaspoon ground cloves
¼ teaspoon ground cumin
¼ teaspoon freshly ground white pepper
¼ teaspoon Spanish paprika (*pimentón*) or Hungarian paprika
Pinch of cayenne
Salt
Pinch of sugar (optional)
2 to 3 flat-leaf parsley sprigs

1. Brush a baking sheet with olive oil. Preheat the oven to 425 degrees.

2. Peel the potatoes and slice them by hand to make ⅛-inch-thick rounds. Cover the prepared baking sheet with a layer of overlapping potatoes and set on the top shelf of the oven to bake for 20 minutes. Turn the potatoes over and bake for 20 to 25 minutes, or until the potato slices are lightly browned and tender. Remove from the oven.

3. While the potatoes are baking, prepare the tomato sauce. Slice the dinner roll into three or four pieces. Lightly brush 1 of the garlic cloves and the pieces of bread with olive oil and set them on a baking sheet. Bake for about 15 minutes, or until brown on all sides. Set aside.

4. Heat 2 teaspoons olive oil in a deep wide pan or wok over medium heat. Add red and green peppers and 1 tablespoon water, cover, and cook for 2 minutes, or until softened. Add onion and 2 more tablespoons water and continue cooking, uncovered, for 4 to 5 minutes, stirring, or until all moisture evaporates and the onions are lightly browned. add the tomato, bay leaf, cloves, cumin, white pep-

per, paprika, and cayenne and cook, stirring, for 5 to 7 minutes, or until tomatoes are softened and pasty. Remove from the heat and discard the bay leaf.

5. Soak the browned bread in 2¾ cups water for 5 minutes to soften. In the food processor, purée the bread, along with 1 cup of the soaking water, the baked and unbaked garlic cloves, and the tomato-pepper mix. Push the purée through a strainer back into the large pan or wok. Add the remaining soaking water and correct the seasoning with salt and sugar. Bring to a boil, then lower heat to medium. Slip the browned potatoes into the sauce, stirring gently to separate them. Cook for 5 minutes. Serve hot in wide soup bowls with a sprinkling of parsley.

"Tiella" di Patate e Cozze
Apulian casserole of potatoes, rice, and mussels
(Italy)

"**T**his is one of the hardest dishes to get right," says Camillo Guerra, the sophisticated and caring proprietor of the magnificent spa and hotel Il Melograno, situated in Monopoli in the southern part of Italy. "It depends on the glazed deep earthenware casserole that allows the proper evaporation of moisture during cooking, the quality of the rice, the quality of the potatoes, and the cooking time that must be perfectly calculated so that everything becomes meltingly tender and yet the mussels in their half-shells are not overcooked."

I use an earthenware paella dish, called a *cazuela,* as a substitute for the deeper wider pan that Camillo used, and I have reduced his recipe accordingly. Camillo used very small mussels that had been pried open without any cooking. I have opted for a quick steaming until the mussels open just a crack, then I slide a thin-bladed knife into the mussel to remove the top shell. The mussels are then nestled between the layers of potatoes, which act as insulation. Because the mussels I use are larger than his, the dish remains in balance.

Here is a trick for this *tiella* (and for all *tiellas,* too): Sprinkle olive oil over the assembled dish after the liquid in the pan comes to a boil; the top will be beautifully glazed.

Tiella is a great dish for parties, because you can make it ahead and serve it warm, at room temperature, or even cool. Serve this captivating dish as a first

(continued)

course in place of pasta, or as a main dish along with sautéed vegetables, such as broccoli rabe.

SERVES 8 TO 10 AS A FIRST COURSE, 4 TO 6 AS A MAIN DISH

- 3 dozen medium-size mussels, washed and scrubbed
- 3 to 3½ pounds boiling potatoes, such as white rose or red bliss
- 5 tablespoons olive oil, plus more for brushing the pan
- ¾ pound onions, peeled and thinly sliced (1¼ cups)
  Salt
  Freshly ground black pepper
- 2 tablespoons chopped flat-leaf parsley
- ½ cup grated pecorino cheese
- 1 ripe tomato, peeled, seeded, and crushed (½ cup)
- ¾ cup medium-grain rice, washed, drained, and soaked in cold water until ready to use

1. Put the mussels in a large skillet, cover, and shake over high heat. When they just begin to open, remove from the heat, discard the upper shells, and set the mussels on a large flat plate. Strain and reserve the liquor.

2. Peel the potatoes and cut crosswise into ⅛-inch slices. Lightly brush a 12-by-2-inch earthenware pan with olive oil. Scatter a small amount of the onion slices in the paella pan. Layer one third of the potatoes on top of the onions and sprinkle with salt, pepper, and 1 tablespoon of the parsley. Scatter half the mussels in their shells in one layer; sprinkle with 1 tablespoon olive oil, ¼ cup pecorino cheese, half the onions, and half the crushed tomato. Drain the rice, reserving the soaking liquid, and scatter half the rice on top.

3. Layer another third of the potatoes and repeat with the salt and pepper, the remaining parsley, mussels, rice, cheese, onion, and crushed tomato. Sprinkle 1 tablespoon of the olive oil over all and cover with the remaining potatoes. Season well with salt and pepper. Pour over the reserved mussel broth. Measure the soaking liquid for the rice and add enough water to make 6 cups; pour down along the insides of the pan. Press down on the potatoes so there will be some room for expansion. (The liquid should just barely cover the potatoes.)

4. Preheat the oven to 400 degrees.

5. Place the pan over low heat and slowly bring to a boil, about 15 minutes. Spoon the remaining 3 tablespoons olive oil on the bubbling liquid and set the pan on the top rack of the oven to bake for about 20 minutes. Lower the oven

heat to 350 degrees and continue baking for 35 minutes. Turn off the oven and let the *tiella* rest another 30 minutes before removing from the oven. Serve warm, at room temperature, or cool.

Note: *Cazuelas* can be purchased by mail order from Dean & DeLuca and Williams-Sonoma. It is essential that you season and "cure" a new *cazuela* before using. *Cazuelas* are fragile—sooner or later they break—but proper curing will harden them enough so that they can be used (with caution) directly over a gas flame. Here are the rules: never put a hot *cazuela* on a cold surface; never pour hot liquid into a cold *cazuela;* when you use your *cazuela* over an open flame, start the flame very low, then very gradually increase the heat. If you follow these rules you will enjoy your *cazuela* for a long time.

To cure: Soak the entire earthenware dish in water to cover for 12 hours. Drain and wipe dry. Rub the unglazed bottom with a cut clove of garlic. Fill the dish with water to ½ inch below the rim, then add ½ cup vinegar. Place the dish on a Flame Tamer over low heat and slowly bring the water to a boil. Let the liquid boil down until only about ½ cup remains. Cool slowly and wash. Your *cazuela* is now ready for use—the garlic has created a seal.

To clean, soak in sudsy water and scrub with a soft brush to remove any hardened food.

Pescado al Horno
Fish, potatoes, tomato, and peppers
roasted in the oven (Spain)

In the Andalusian town of Jerez de la Frontera, a type of sea bream called *pargo* is a much-favored fish. I've substituted a thick fillet of tilefish, which, being quite dense, takes longer to cook than the recommended 10 minutes to the inch. Monkfish also works well in this recipe.

Around Jerez, the food often includes sherry. Here the fish baked with potatoes, onions, peppers, and tomatoes is finished with a splash of sherry, which provides a wonderful aroma.

(continued)

    3 yellow potatoes, such as Yukon gold (about 1 pound), peeled and cut
          into $1/8$-inch slices

    3 garlic cloves, thinly sliced

   $1/4$ cup chopped fresh parsley

    1 small onion, sliced

    1 large vine-ripened tomato, chopped (about 1 cup)

    1 Italian (sweet frying) pepper, cored, seeded, and cut into rings
       Salt
       Freshly ground black pepper

 $1 1/2$ pounds 1-inch-thick tilefish fillets with skin on

    4 thin lemon slices

    1 tablespoon olive oil

    1 bay leaf, broken in half

    4 to 5 fresh thyme sprigs, or $1/2$ teaspoon dried

   $1/4$ cup fino (dry) sherry

1. Preheat the oven to 375 degrees. Lightly oil a 3-quart shallow baking dish.

2. Rinse and drain potatoes. Spread half of the sliced potatoes on the bottom of the prepared baking dish. Scatter garlic, parsley, onion, tomatoes, and peppers on top and season with salt and pepper. Finish with the remaining potatoes. Pour 1 cup of water over the mixture and cover with foil. Bake for 1 hour.

3. Meanwhile, season fish with salt and pepper and make four to five slashes on each side of the fillet. Let stand 10 minutes.

4. After the potatoes have baked for 1 hour, raise the oven temperature to 425 degrees. Nestle the fish, skin side down, in the bed of potatoes and vegetables. Lay the lemon slices on top and drizzle with oil. Tuck the bay leaf and sprigs of thyme under the fish and return the dish, uncovered, to the oven's uppermost rack. Bake for about 15 minutes, until the fish flesh is opaque. It is not necessary to turn the fish in the pan. The surrounding potatoes should be crusty and browned.

5. Spoon sherry over the fish and return to the oven for 2 minutes. Remove the bay leaf. Serve directly from the dish.

HERBS, SPICES, AND AROMATICS

Look around an American kitchen. Rosemary, basil, thyme—all the herbs are there in a dried state, usually in a rack of neatly labeled uniform little jars.

But go around behind a house in Provence, Italy, or Greece. Somewhere near the kitchen door you'll find the herbs growing in little pots. You're in the Mediterranean world, where herbs and spices are important, not afterthoughts to pep up food.

Before getting into specific flavorings and some recipes that show what they can do, I think it is a good idea to take a little Mediterranean tour, and see the picture as a whole.

In Andalusia, the spicing is simple: cinnamon, paprika, saffron. Olive oil and garlic are vitally important. Next door in Catalonia, the spicing becomes more intricate, with sharper contrasts and stronger flavors. Bitter orange peel, chocolate, and almonds are used to balance the spices.

In Languedoc, goose fat and garlic are used to hold flavor in the main dishes and aniseed in the desserts. Provence, on the other hand, is a land of herbs, and perfumed waters are used.

In Italy, herbs are king. Liguria is full of basil and marjoram, which are used in numerous imaginative ways. Farther south we find red pepper and the stronger flavored oregano. And in Sardinia, there are traces of Spain—saffron in the rice, the pasta, and the soups.

The Slavs use lots of caraway and paprika, an influence from Austro-Hungarian ties. All over the Levant we find cinnamon, allspice, and mint in rice, meats, and desserts, a heritage of the distinguished and wonderful cuisine of the Turks.

Egypt, Lebanon, Syria, and Palestine are strong on cinnamon, showing a preference for sweet spices and perfumed waters, too. But as we move toward Tunisia things begin to heat up: tabil and red hot harissa sauce. The Algerians use black pepper and cinnamon, the old formula of the Turks, then combine it with the red hot paprika of the Tunisians to create a synthesis between Maghreb and Levant.

Finally Morocco, truly a land of spices, with its *ras el hanout*—a mixture of more than twenty different exotic flavorings. The Moroccans go further with spices than any country except India. For their snail dish *boubouche* ("little slippers"), they combine crushed gum mastic, whole hot peppers, crinkled peels of sweet and bitter orange, crumbled mint leaves, verbena, thyme, anise, licorice, and caraway.

ANISEED

The best aniseed is the fragrant green variety from Spain with its strong warm flavor and licorice taste. It's used in cakes, breads, cookies, and spice drinks.

In Languedoc, in southwestern France, aniseed is used in rustic cakes like *le soleil d'anis,* often served on hot summer afternoons along with a glass of cold sparkling wine from Limoux.

The Syrians use aniseed to flavor their sugary spice drink, *miglee,* and include it in the making of fig jam, not only because of the refreshing association, but because they believe that aniseed wards off the hatching of worm larvae in figs.

The Corsicans like cookies sweetened with aniseed-flavored sugar, and in Calabria, *mostaccioli* cookies, made with flour and honey, are flavored with an anise liqueur called Sambuca. Sambuca is a popular after-dinner drink that Italians serve *con la mosca.* Literally this means "with flies," an image for the coffee beans they float on top.

The Mediterranean is famous for its anise-flavored apéritifs. The Catalonians make one of the best anisettes in the world, *anís del mono.* The French produce *pastis,* a close relative of the forbidden absinthe. Greek *ouzo,* Turkish *raki,* and French *pastis* all turn milky when diluted with water. They are all quite powerful, should be drunk in small quantities, and are best when served with something to eat.

Melon con Anís del Mono
Melon with anisette (Spain)

Anís del mono, literally "the monkey's anise," is the name of a famous Catalan anisette.

SERVES 4

- 2 ripe cantaloupes
- ½ tablespoon anisette
- 1½ tablespoon confectioners' sugar
- 3 tablespoons water

(continued)

Halve the melons and remove the seeds. Scoop out the melon flesh in balls and place in a glass serving dish. Combine the anisette, sugar, and water and pour over the melon balls. Allow to stand in a cool place about 1 hour before serving.

BASIL

In ancient Greece, basil was called "the royal herb," since no one but a king could cut it, and then only with a golden sickle. Pliny regarded it as an aphrodisiac and suggested feeding it to horses during their mating season. Around most of the Mediterranean, the royal herb was used chiefly as a perfume and insect repellent. When I lived in Morocco, basil was plentiful, but not in the kitchen. Part of the Moroccan reluctance to eat basil may be based on superstition: until recently people believed that if you ate basil in the morning and were bitten by a scorpion in the afternoon, you would not survive the night.

The great aficionados of basil are the Italians and the French. The herb goes beautifully with fresh cheese, oil, garlic, and tomatoes, and can be used to flavor vinegar, bean soups, meat and fish dishes, and as a component in numerous salads. A special use is to substitute basil butter for the traditional parsley butter on mussels: mash sweet basil leaves in a mortar with garlic, nuts, and butter, spread on steamed mussels set on half shells, then set under a broiler until bubbly hot.

The larger so-called lettuce-leaf basil has the most delicate flavor; smaller varieties are spicier but less versatile. In some eastern Mediterranean homes a dark variety is presented on a platter without dressing for nibbling.

Pesto

Ligurian basil sauce from Nervi (Italy)

This recipe for pesto comes from Nervi, a small town a little south of Genoa. In Nervi they make pesto with a touch of cream, creating a light, smooth, avocado-green sauce that makes a good change from the usual recipe. For the best flavor, it is preferable to make pesto in a large mortar, but it can be made in the food processor, too. Try it over *fettuccine, trenette,* semolina gnocchi, and broad lasagne noodles.

Tender lettuce-leaf basil is recommended for this dish; it is finer in flavor. If the leaves are tough, drop them into simmering water; leave them 10 seconds, then drain. This tenderizes the leaves. Squeeze gently to remove the moisture.

SERVES 4

- 2 packed cups (3 ounces) stemmed basil leaves
- ½ packed cup stemmed Italian parsley
- ½ cup pine nuts
- 2 tablespoons shelled and chopped walnuts
- 2 garlic cloves, peeled, halved, and green shoots removed
- ½ cup extra-virgin olive oil
- ½ cup grated cheese (⅓ cup grated Parmesan and 2½ tablespoons grated pecorino)
- Fine sea salt
- 4 tablespoons light cream
- 1 pound pasta

1. If using a mortar: Pound the basil and parsley to release their tasty juices, until they turn pasty. Add the nuts and garlic and pound until smooth. Blend in the oil, cheese, salt, and cream.

2. If using a food processor: Purée the basil, parsley, nuts, garlic, and oil to a smooth paste. Add the cheese, salt, and cream and pulse to blend completely.

3. Cook the pasta in boiling salted water until al dente. Meanwhile gently warm the pesto sauce in a wide skillet. Loosen the pesto by stirring in ½ cup boiling pasta water and remove from the heat. Drain the pasta and immediately add the pasta to the pesto sauce. Turn the pasta in the sauce and serve at once.

(continued)

Follow the directions in step 1 or 2, omitting the cheese, garlic, and salt. Pack into plastic cartons. Close tightly and freeze. Thaw completely before using; add the garlic, cheese, and salt, and dilute as directed.

Pistou Marseillaise

Vegetable soup with basil (France)

In Provence, the specialty is *pistou,* a thick vegetable soup embellished with a spoonful of crushed basil and garlic mixed with oil, called a *pommade.* I always thought *pistou* an overrated soup until I tasted this version from Marseilles. Claude Thomas, a good friend from Provence, who gave me the recipe, told me the trick is to use a ratatouille as the base. The eggplant, tomatoes, and green pepper should cook down until they're in a juicy liquid state. Then, and only then, should you begin to make the soup.

SERVES 8 TO 10

½ pound dried white beans
   Salt
½ pound eggplant, peeled and cut into small chunks
¼ cup olive oil
3 cups chopped onions
1 tablespoon chopped garlic
¾ pound small, firm zucchini (about 4 or 5), peeled and cut into small pieces
1 medium sweet green pepper (or 2 small elongated light-green Italian peppers), seeded, deribbed, and cut into small chunks
2½ cups peeled, seeded, and chopped tomatoes
3 quarts boiling water
1 cup diced carrots
⅔ cup diced celery ribs
1 cup string beans, cut small
1 cup wax beans, cut small
   Bouquet garni: 3 basil leaves, 5 parsley sprigs, 1 bay leaf, and 2 thyme sprigs, tied together

Freshly ground black pepper
¼ teaspoon grated nutmeg
1 pound potatoes, peeled and diced
¾ cup elbow macaroni

POMMADE
1 cup fresh large basil leaves, torn into small pieces
1 to 2 teaspoons finely chopped garlic
About 1 cup olive oil
⅓ cup grated Parmesan or Gruyère cheese
Salt and freshly ground black pepper
Bowl of freshly grated Parmesan cheese

1. Cover the beans by 1 inch with water. Allow to soak overnight.

2. Salt the eggplant pieces and let drain for 15 minutes in a colander. Rinse and squeeze gently to remove the bitter juices.

3. Heat the oil in a large soup pot. Add the onions and cook them gently until soft. Add the garlic and cook, stirring, for 2 minutes longer. Add the eggplant and cook, stirring, for 3 to 4 minutes. Add half the zucchini and cook 3 minutes longer. Add the green pepper and cook 3 minutes longer, stirring often. Stir in the tomatoes and allow the mixture to simmer 5 minutes, stirring often. Cover the pot and cook at the simmer for about 30 minutes.

4. Pour the boiling water into the simmering mixture, stirring briskly. Drain the beans and add to the pot. Cook, covered, over gentle heat for 1½ hours.

5. Add the carrots, celery, string and wax beans, bouquet garni, pepper, and nutmeg and continue to cook at the simmer for 20 minutes. Salt to taste.

6. Add the remaining zucchini and the potatoes and continue to cook 10 minutes longer. Stir in the macaroni and continue to cook at the simmer until tender.

7. Meanwhile make the *pommade:* Pound the basil leaves and garlic to a paste in a large mortar or bowl. Slowly add half the oil, alternating with the cheese. Add the remaining olive oil, stirring, until the mixture is well blended and thickened. Season with salt and pepper. Scrape into a small serving bowl or serve directly from the mortar.

8. Correct the seasoning of the soup. Serve hot and pass a bowl of grated Parmesan cheese and the *pommade.*

BAY LEAVES

Imported bay leaves from Turkey are milder than our California ones. In all the recipes in this book I used Mediterranean bay leaves. If you buy imported ones, the proportions will always be right; if you use California bay leaves, halve the amounts.

The French *bouquet garni* is the standard herb bouquet comprising a bay leaf, thyme, a few parsley sprigs, and sometimes a few celery leaves tied together and added to stocks, stews, soups, and pot-au-feu. In Provence, a dried orange peel is added to daubes and bouillabaisse.

The Turks alternate bay leaves with skewered fish, then broil the fish kebabs over hot coals.

Fegato di Vitello con Foglie di Lauro
Calf's liver with laurel leaves (Italy)

In this recipe for calf's liver you can enjoy bay leaves in a prominent role. Lamb, pork, or beef liver may be substituted and will be just as good.

SERVES 3 TO 4

  10 imported bay leaves
    1 pound calf's liver, cut into 1-inch cubes
       Salt
       Freshly ground black pepper
       Pinch of grated nutmeg
       Vegetable oil
    1 lemon, quartered

1. In a mortar, pound 3 of the bay leaves until almost a powder.

2. In a mixing bowl, toss the liver cubes with the ground bay leaves, salt, pepper, grated nutmeg, and 3 tablespoons oil. Allow to stand 1 hour.

3. Cut the remaining 7 bay leaves into 1-inch pieces. Thread seasoned liver cubes alternately with bay leaves. Brush with oil. Broil quickly on all sides, 3 inches from a broiler flame, until the first drops of light pink liquid ooze up, about 6 to 8 minutes. Serve at once with lemon quarters.

CAPERS

Capers are the small closed green flower buds of small wild shrubs that grow all around Mediterranean shores. The biggest and fleshiest grow in Sicily, and as a result the Sicilians use them the most. They salt or pickle them and use them in salads, as a base for sauces for chicken and game, as additions to fish tarts, in tomato sauces, and on their famous pizzas.

Capers are much appreciated in Apulia, in southeastern Italy, where they're used inside meatballs. They're delicious on boiled green vegetables, especially string beans. Gently sauté a little chopped parsley and a spoonful of rinsed capers in a few tablespoons of butter for a minute or two. Then sprinkle them with lemon juice, season with salt and pepper, and pour the bubbling mixture over freshly boiled green beans.

Capers are popular in the Spanish Mediterranean island of Ibiza, too. A smooth sauce of sieved crushed capers, ground almonds, crushed garlic, and chopped parsley is poured over freshly fried pollock *(mero)*.

Tapenade
Provençal olive paste (France)

This is a typical Provençal method of treating capers (in Provence the word *tapéno* means "capers") with olives, resulting in a somewhat salty, sharp spread, delicious with toast.

Small, oval, unctuous, Nyons olives, with their distinctive winy flavor, make a wonderful *tapenade,* fully warranting the title "Provençal caviar." You can also substitute wrinkled Moroccan or Greek olives with excellent results. The smooth round Greek black olives can also be used.

In parts of Provence, *tapenade* is used in a fresh curd cheese tart, brushed onto the pastry with olive oil, spread with cheese, sprinkled with herbs, then baked in the oven. It also is served with boiled new potatoes, cold fish, or simply spread on grilled bread.

MAKES 1 CUP

- 1 cup wrinkled black olives, pitted
- 1 2-ounce can anchovy fillets
- 4 tablespoons capers
- 2 tablespoons lemon juice
- ½ teaspoon Dijon mustard
  Freshly ground black pepper
- 1½ tablespoons Cognac or dark rum
- ¼ cup fruity olive oil

1. Soak the olives, anchovies, and capers to remove excess salt. Rinse, drain, and pat dry.

2. In a food processor or blender, combine olives, anchovies, capers, lemon juice, mustard, pepper, and Cognac and blend until pasty. With the machine on, pour in just enough olive oil in a steady stream to obtain a smooth thick sauce. Scoop into a pretty pottery bowl and allow flavors to mingle at least 1 hour before serving.

Variation

TAPENADE WITH SMOKY EGGPLANT

Some Provençal cooks, finding the flavor too bold and assertive as a topping for bread, add a small amount of homemade tomato paste and a pinch of sugar, or a small amount of crumbled canned tunafish. Others add the mashed pulp of a well-baked medium-size eggplant.

MAKES ABOUT 2 CUPS

   1 large eggplant
   1 cup *tapenade*

Grill or bake the whole eggplant until it is black, blistery, and collapsing. Peel under running water and squeeze out any bitter juices. Place in a bowl, preferably wooden, and pound until well mashed. Gradually whisk in the *tapenade*.

CARAWAY SEEDS

═══

Houriya
Spiced carrot salad with feta cheese and black olives
(Tunisia)

In this unusual and delicious salad, garden fresh carrots are cooked in very little water (in a pressure cooker, a microwave, or a small, heavy pot), highly seasoned, crushed to almost a purée, and served cold with small black olives and feta cheese. The dish is extremely healthy; I recently learned that the best way to prepare carrots, in terms of full beta-carotene benefits, is to both cook and crush them (see note) before eating.

    If carefully stored, this salad will keep up to a week in the refrigerator.

(continued)

> 2 pounds fresh garden carrots, trimmed and pared (see note)
> 3 large unpeeled garlic cloves
> Fine salt
> 1 teaspoon homemade or top quality commercial harissa (pages 200–201), or more to taste
> 2 teaspoons ground caraway seed
> 7 teaspoons mild vinegar, such as malt or cider vinegar
> 2 to 3 tablespoons fruity olive oil
> 2 dozen small black olives, preferably the French niçoise or the Greek elitses
> 4 ounces imported feta cheese, cubed

1. Cut the carrots into thin rounds. Arrange in layers in a pressure cooker, steamer, pot, or covered glass dish. Add 3 tablespoons water, the garlic, and a pinch of salt. Cover and cook until carrots are tender (3 minutes in a pressure cooker; 10 minutes on High in a microwave, or in a steamer with an extra ½ cup water). If using the microwave, remove and stir the carrots for even cooking. Remove the garlic, peel, and set aside.

2. Drain the carrots, reserving 1 tablespoon of the cooking liquid. Allow the carrots to cool, then crush with a fork or pulse in a food processor.

3. Blend the harissa with the reserved cooking liquid. Add the carrots, caraway, cooked and peeled garlic, and the vinegar, blending well. Gradually beat in the oil. Correct the seasoning with salt. Keep covered in the refrigerator. Return to room temperature before serving.

4. To serve, mound the carrots in a round shallow serving dish. Surround with drained olives and cubes of feta cheese.

Notes: According to James Olson, professor at Iowa State University, "Cooking carrots makes 25 percent of the beta-carotene available to the body, and puréeing cooked carrots allows your body to absorb about 50 percent."

The dish is especially delicious when made with home-grown carrots. You can also purchase carrots marked "organically grown." If you don't plan to cook them right away, bury them up to their green shoots in your garden until ready to use. Once picked, remove the feathery tops as soon as possible to prevent loss of moisture.

Variation

Purée the carrots to a creamy consistency for a different texture.

Gambri Sghir

Shrimp with sauce kerkennaise (Tunisia)

On the Kerkenna Islands off the coast of Tunisia, this very spicy sauce accompanies grilled shrimp.

MAKES 2 CUPS, SERVING 4

2 large ripe tomatoes (1 pound)
½ cup chopped scallions (1 bunch)
2 teaspoons minced banana pepper, or other mildly hot fresh chili
¾ teaspoon ground coriander seed
¼ teaspoon ground caraway
1 small garlic clove, peeled and crushed with ¼ teaspoon salt
¼ cup chopped flat-leaf parsley
Pinch of sugar
1 tablespoon mild vinegar, or more to taste
1 teaspoon sea salt
3 tablespoons olive oil, plus oil for brushing shrimp and grill
1½ pounds jumbo shrimp, shelled if desired
1 teaspoon capers, drained

1. Halve tomatoes crosswise, squeeze gently to seed, and grate on a large-holed grater. Mix with remaining ingredients except the shrimp and capers and let stand for at least 1 hour.

2. Prepare an outdoor grill or preheat the broiler. Brush grill and shrimp with olive oil and grill or broil the shrimp until evenly cooked through, 2 to 3 minutes. Serve shrimp with sauce and garnish with capers.

CORIANDER

Please remember that coriander is both an herb and a spice, that the taste of each is different, and that the one cannot be substituted for the other.

Fresh coriander is widely available, sometimes under the names "cilantro" or "Chinese parsley," and you can easily grow it fresh by simply planting the seeds.

There is no substitute for the special flavor of the coriander herb. It's one of the most important ingredients in Moroccan food and, to a lesser degree, the food of Algeria, Tunisia, and the Middle East. The Palestinians serve fresh fava beans with a dusting of chopped fresh coriander and garlic.

Ground coriander seeds (the spice) form the base for a delicious paste for Moroccan roasted lamb. For a 10-pound forequarter, blend 1½ tablespoons ground coriander seeds with 1 tablespoon chopped garlic, 2 teaspoons ground cumin, 1 teaspoon paprika, and 5½ tablespoons softened butter. Rub the forequarter with salt and pepper, then spread with this paste before roasting.

H'mam M'Douzane

Squab with coriander and spices (Algeria)

This recipe is adapted from the *Grandes Recettes de la Cuisine Algérienne,* by Youcef Fehri.

SERVES 4

4	ready-to-cook squabs
	Salt
	Freshly ground black pepper
⅛	teaspoon ground saffron
1	teaspoon ground aniseed
⅓	cup olive oil
1	tablespoon chopped fresh coriander
2	tablespoons finely chopped scallions
	Juice of 1 lemon

1. Quarter the squabs. Rub all over with a mixture of salt, pepper, saffron, aniseed, and some of the oil.

2. Heat the remaining oil in a shallow earthenware dish or heatproof serving skillet with a tight-fitting cover. Slowly brown the squab pieces on both sides, which takes 10 to 15 minutes. Add 1½ cups water, ½ tablespoon coriander, and 1 tablespoon scallions. Cook, covered, at the simmer for 30 minutes, turning the pieces often to cook evenly.

3. Uncover the dish and allow the cooking juices to reduce to a thick gravy, about ¾ cup. Sprinkle with the remaining coriander, scallions, and lemon juice. Serve at once.

Tabil (Twabil)

Spice mixture (Tunisia)

In 1492, when the last Moorish kingdom fell in Spain, not all the Andalusian Moors fled to Morocco. Some sailed into the bay of Tunis to settle south of the city in a town called Testour. These Moors introduced numerous spices to the Tunisian culinary spectrum. The most important is this spice mixture called *twabil,* used in recipes for salads, stews, and couscous.

Here is a confusing note: In the Tunisian dialect, the *tabil* or *twabil*—which means "spices" in Arabic—is often applied to green coriander alone, but it's also the name of this spice mixture:

MAKES ABOUT 3½ TABLESPOONS

  2 tablespoons ground coriander seeds
  2 teaspoons ground caraway seeds
¼ teaspoon garlic powder (optional)
½ teaspoon ground red pepper
¼ teaspoon crushed fennel seeds
¼ teaspoon crushed aniseed
¼ teaspoon ground cumin
¼ teaspoon ground turmeric
½ teaspoon freshly ground black pepper

Mix and store in a tightly covered jar.

CUMIN

Cumin seeds smell like old hay, but when they're ground in a mortar a marvelous aroma is released. The mixture of cumin, coriander, and garlic is very popular in Morocco, Cyprus, and Greece. The Cypriot ham, *loutsa,* is a boned pork loin rubbed with salt, pepper, garlic, lemon, coriander, and cumin, baked in the oven, and served cold in thin slices. Cumin, along with coriander and garlic, is the essential flavoring in the spicy Greek sausage, *soutzoukakia.*

In Morocco, when you order *mechoui* you will be served a crusty roasted lamb, a small bowl of ground cumin, and a bowl of salt. The lamb, still very hot, should be eaten with the fingers—you dip the morsels of meat into the cumin and salt. And all across North Africa from Cairo to Tangier, shelled hard-boiled eggs sprinkled with cumin and salt are a popular street snack.

Autumn is the time to eat freshly killed quail and the Egyptians have a special way of flavoring them. They blend cumin, ground coriander, grated onions, and chopped parsley, then rub the mixture into the quail flesh before grilling over hot coals.

In her excellent *A Book of Middle Eastern Food,* Claudia Roden describes her mother's recipe for *dukkah,* an Egyptian spice mixture served with bread and olive oil as a breakfast treat. The *dukkah* contains sesame seeds, hazelnuts, coriander seeds, and cumin seeds, all roasted and pounded together well.

Algerians use cumin in many of their stews. A particularly interesting one is made of thin slices of leg of lamb rubbed with ground cumin, dusted with bread crumbs and grated cheese, then rolled in beaten eggs and fried in oil. Afterward the meat is simmered in a cumin, cinnamon, and pepper-flavored onion sauce.

FENNEL

Fennel appears in various forms: dried or fresh stalks; seeds or bulbs; wild or cultivated. You can discover the way its mild licorice flavor can excite the palate by slicing a bulb into thin strips, soaking the strips in ice water until crisp, then serving them with lemon juice and salt.

The seeds, stalks, or leaves are particularly delicious in Provençal fish soups. Long, dry, straw-colored fennel stalks are set alight under a grilled bass, imbuing it with a lovely aroma and a delicate taste. You can always tuck a few fennel seeds into the cavity of an oily fish to eliminate its "fishy" taste.

Fennel greens grow wild in California and are available in Italian markets around March 19, the day of the Sicilian feast of St. Joseph. A popular St. Joseph's Day dish is *pasta con le sarde,* which should be made with highly aromatic wild fennel, although a combination of farmers' fennel, fennel seed, and dill will get you by. One of my favorite quick lunches is a Tunisian salad of fresh fennel, olives, and sardines, which is either the inspiration or a playback of the great Sicilian pasta specialty.

Slatit Bisbas

*Fresh fennel salad with green olives
and sardines (Tunisia)*

SERVES 2 TO 3

  1 fresh fennel bulb, about 7 ounces
18 Sicilian-style green olives, drained
  1 tablespoon mild vinegar
  2 to 3 tablespoons extra-virgin olive oil
 ¼ teaspoon crushed garlic
     Pinches of dried red pepper flakes or ground red pepper
     Salt
     Freshly ground black pepper
  2 tablespoons minced tender celery
  1 tablespoon chopped parsley, plus additional for garnish
  1 can sardines packed in olive oil, drained
     Lemon wedges

1. Cut the fennel lengthwise in half; remove the stalks and leaves and trim the base. Use a sharp knife to cut each half bulb crosswise into thin slices. Discard the tough center core. You should have about 2 cups. Soak in cold water for about 5 minutes.

2. Meanwhile, wash the olives and drain. Loosely wrap the olives in a kitchen towel, gently crush with a mallet, and press out the pits. Soak the olives for 10 minutes in water, or until the excessive briny flavor is muted; drain and chop roughly.

(continued)

3. Drain the fennel and place in a bowl. Add the vinegar, oil, olives, garlic, and red pepper flakes. Toss and chill for a few hours. (This can be refrigerated for up to 3 days.)

4. Just before serving, correct the seasoning with salt and pepper. Add the celery and 1 tablespoon parsley and toss once. Mound loosely in the middle of a flat serving plate. Carefully place sardines around the mounded salad. Garnish with lemon wedges and sprinkle with parsley.

HARISSA

Harissa
Hot chili paste (Tunisia)

In Tunisia, fiery hot red peppers play a role in almost every dish, usually in the form of the famous harissa paste, a mixture of sun-dried peppers pounded with spices and garlic and packed into jars under a coating of oil.

The Tunisian/French harissa sauce sold in cubes and tubes bears little resemblance to a true homemade harissa paste. In fact, I find commercial harissa pretty dreadful.

I used to use Indonesian *sambal oelek* as a sort of workhorse for most of my Tunisian cooking, adding ground coriander, caraway, and garlic to give it the proper pungent, full-rounded taste. Now that dried New Mexican peppers are available, I make my own. I soak the peppers, then grind them with a little garlic, salt, tabil, oil, and roasted red bell pepper for an even richer texture. This sauce is better than one you will find in the Central Market of Tunis. It is almost as good as the homemade versions in Nabeul, a town famous throughout Tunisia for its delicious peppers and the best harissa.

Incidentally, in Tunisian home cooking, many soups, stews, and sauces begin the same way: The cook stirs some tomato paste into a spoonful of hot oil; when the paste turns glossy and gives off a good aroma, some harissa, diluted with water and stirred until smooth, is added to the pot, along with the vegetables, liquid, herbs, and spices. This method not only tames the harissa, but creates a creamier sauce.

MAKES ABOUT 1 CUP

> 3 ounces dried mild and hot chilies, preferably a mixture of anchos, New Mexican, and guajillos or all anchos
> 1 small garlic clove, peeled and crushed with ¼ teaspoon salt
> 1 teaspoon ground coriander seed
> 1 teaspoon ground caraway seed
> 1 roasted red bell pepper, stemmed, seeded, chopped, wrapped in cheesecloth, and pressed until dry
> 1 teaspoon fine sea salt
> Olive oil

1. Stem, seed, and break up the chilies. Place in a bowl and pour over boiling water. Cover and let stand 30 minutes. Drain; wrap in cheesecloth and press out excess moisture.

2. Grind chilies in a food processor with the garlic, spices, red bell pepper, and salt. Add enough oil to make a thick paste. Pack the mixture into a small dry jar; cover the harissa with a thin layer of oil, close with a lid, and keep refrigerated. Will keep 2 to 3 weeks in the refrigerator under a thin layer of oil.

Table Harissa Sauce:

To serve harissa sauce at the table as an accompaniment to meat or fish, to heighten the flavors of salads, or as an accompaniment to Tunisian couscous: Combine 4 teaspoons harissa paste, 4 teaspoons water, 2 teaspoons olive oil, and 1 or 2 teaspoons fresh lemon juice in a small bowl and blend well. Makes ¼ cup.

Hout Moquli Bil Zeitoun
Fish fillets with harissa and black olives
(Tunisia)

◻

Harissa—thick, red, pasty, and fiery—is a pillar of the Tunisian kitchen. In this delicious and quickly made dish, the heat is softened by the addition of imported juicy black olives packed in salt brine.

Any boneless fish fillet can be used, but I particularly like this sauce on farmed catfish.

SERVES 4 TO 6

> 1½ pounds thick fish fillets
> Salt
> Freshly ground black pepper
> Flour
> Olive oil for frying
> ½ cup chopped onion
> 2 garlic cloves, minced
> 1 cup tomato sauce
> ½ teaspoon harissa (pages 200–201)
> 1 bay leaf
> 1 cup juicy black Tunisian or Greek olives, washed, drained, and pitted
> Juice of ½ lemon, or more to taste
> Chopped parsley

1. Season fish with salt and pepper. Dust with flour and fry in hot olive oil until golden brown on both sides. Transfer fish to a side dish. Pour off all but 2 tablespoons oil.

2. Add onion and garlic to the skillet and cook, covered, for 2 to 3 minutes. Add the tomato sauce, harissa, bay leaf, and ½ cup water. Cook for 10 minutes. Add the olives and fish fillets and continue cooking, uncovered, until the fish is tender and the sauce thick. Add lemon juice to taste. Discard the bay leaf. Serve with a sprinkling of chopped parsley.

MILOUKIA

—

Miloukia, a green leafy vegetable similar to spinach, has been eaten almost daily in Egypt since the time of the Pharaohs. Like okra it gives a viscous texture to soups. Frozen miloukia leaves are available in Middle Eastern food stores.

A soup broth made from rabbit, goose, chicken, meat, or duck and chopped miloukia is popular in Egypt, Syria, Lebanon, and Palestine. A Lebanese friend told me that it's best to add miloukia slowly and then shake rather than stir the pot. In Lebanese homes this soup is served like an Indian curry dinner, with bowls of boiled rice, pieces of the meat or chicken or rabbit that made the broth, and chopped vegetables on the side. Often a *taklia,* a mixture of green coriander or mint and garlic, is sautéed in butter and added to the soup just before it's served. Sometimes hot chilies and chopped onions are added, too.

In Palestinian homes, finely chopped cooked miloukia leaves are surrounded with bowls of chopped onions in vinegar, toasted bread cubes, rice, and chicken or meat.

MINT

—

Mint is so easy to grow you often see pots of it outside the kitchens of American homes. If you buy a fresh bunch of mint, leave a few leaves on the stalks, then push them about one inch into fresh soil and keep them moist. Soon your "cuttings" will root and from then on you'll have fresh mint whenever you need it. Mint is essential to Moroccan tea, which will help with "tourist tummy" if you get it.

The Romans have enjoyed mint-flavored zucchini since ancient times and the Greeks make a beef broth memorable because of the addition of mint. Yogurt and fresh mint make a refreshing combination and are eaten a great deal in the Levant.

Dried pulverized mint is much used in Tunisia and gives surprisingly good flavor to salads and *tagines*.

Tagine Nana

Lamb and mint tagine in the style of Kairouan
(Tunisia)

Many readers are familiar with Moroccan *tagines*—stews of meat, poultry, or fish smothered with one or two vegetables or fruits, cooked in an earthenware dish with a conical cover.

Tunisian *tagines* are different. Tunisian cooks, when speaking of *tagines,* will refer to their having a "beginning," a "middle," and an "end."

The "beginning" is usually a mini-stew of veal or lamb cut into very small pieces and cooked with onions and spices such as sweet-smelling dried rosebuds and cinnamon or a robust combination of ground coriander and caraway. Then something starchy is added to thicken the juices—white beans, chick-peas, bread-crumbs or cubed potatoes. When the meat is tender, it is combined with whatever ingredient has been chosen to be the dominant flavoring—in this case, dried mint.

The "middle" part is the enrichment of the stew with cheese and eggs.

The "end" is the final baking in a deep pie dish, either on the stove or in the oven until both top and bottom are crisply cooked and the eggs are just set, somewhat like an Italian *frittata.*

When the *tagine* is ready, it is turned out onto a plate and sliced into squares, accompanied by wedges of lemon.

In rural parts of Tunisia, home cooks place their shallow earthenware *tagine* dishes over glowing olive wood, covered with flat earthen pans, and then piled high with hot coals. The resulting *tagine* is crusty on top and bottom, moist within, and is infused with a subtle smoky fragrance.

SERVES 4

  1 pound boneless lean lamb, cut into 1-inch cubes
    Salt
    Freshly ground black pepper
  2 tablespoons vegetable oil
  1 cup chopped onion
  4 ripe medium tomatoes, peeled, seeded, and chopped
  1½ teaspoons sweet paprika
  1½ teaspoons tabil (page 197)
  6 eggs

½ cup bread crumbs

¼ cup grated Parmesan or Gruyère cheese

1½ tablespoons pulverized dried mint leaves

    Clarified butter

1. Trim the lamb of excess fat. Season the chunks with salt and pepper. Heat the oil in a small casserole and brown the lamb with the chopped onion. Stir in the tomatoes, paprika, tabil, and 1 teaspoon ground black pepper. Cover tightly and set over low heat to simmer for 1 hour, adding a little water if needed.

2. Transfer the lamb to a 1-quart ovenproof serving dish, cover, and keep moist. Reduce the cooking juices to ½ cup and let cool.

3. Preheat the oven to 350 degrees.

4. Beat the eggs to a froth, add the cooled cooking juices, the bread crumbs, grated cheese, and mint. Season with very little salt and pepper. Pour the egg mixture over the lamb. Set on the middle shelf of the oven and bake for 15 minutes.

5. Raise the oven heat to the highest setting, remove the dish, dribble over the clarified butter, and return the dish to the highest shelf in the oven. Bake 10 minutes. Serve hot cut into wedges.

Slatit Tounsiya
Mixed salad (Tunisia)

◻

This is the Tunisian version of a mixed tomato, cucumber, onion, and pepper salad. It is a personal favorite because I like the addition of a tart green apple and the taste of powdered dried mint.

Here is a delightful recipe I learned from a Tunisian cook on the island of Jerba.

MAKES 2 CUPS

1 or 2 ripe tomatoes, peeled, seeded, and cut into small dice
  (about ¾ cup)
1 small cucumber, peeled, seeded, and cut into ⅛-inch dice (1 cup)
4 whole scallions, thinly sliced
1 small apple, peeled, cored, and cut into ⅛-inch dice (1 cup)
2 tablespoons minced fresh green chili
  Fine sea salt
  Freshly ground black pepper
  Juice of ½ lemon
2 tablespoons extra-virgin olive oil
1 tablespoon dried mint leaves, pressed through a fine sieve to make 1
  teaspoon powder

Toss the ingredients in a salad bowl, cover with plastic wrap, and refrigerate up to 2 hours.

PAPRIKA

===

Red pepper *capsicums* grow so well on Mediterranean shores that there are regions that have become famous on account of their peppers, such as Tarragona in southern Spain, Nabeul in Tunisia, Maras and Urfa in Turkey, Aleppo in Syria, and Florina in Macedonia.

Hungarian paprika is unique for its intense flavor. There are two varieties—the sweet and the hot.

South Slavs use lots of paprika because of the Austro-Hungarian influence on their cuisine. It's also used a lot in Morocco, where it is blended with ground cumin and used to season soups, tagines, and salads.

Arnavut Ciğeri
Albanian-style liver (Turkey)

This *mezze,* popular in Istanbul, is reminiscent of Venetian-style liver. According to food historian Arto der Haroutunian, it is "one of the best hors d'oeuvres from the time of the Ottomans and was introduced by the mountain people of Albania."

SERVES 8 AS PART OF A MIDDLE EASTERN *MEZZE*

- 1 pound calf's or lamb's liver
  Coarse salt
- 1/4 cup olive oil
- 1/2 cup minced scallions or red onions
- 1/4 cup flour
- 3 to 4 teaspoons sweet Hungarian paprika
- 1/4 teaspoon hot Hungarian paprika
  Freshly ground black pepper
- 2 tablespoons finely chopped parsley

1. Soak the liver in salted water for 10 minutes. (This helps to express some of the blood and tightens the flesh of the liver.) Peel off any of the thin transparent skin and cut away any tubes and hard pieces. Pat dry and cut into 3/4-inch cubes.

(continued)

2. Heat the oil in a wide skillet over high heat. Rub the scallions or red onions with a pinch of salt and set aside to soften.

3. Meanwhile, put the flour, sweet and hot paprika, and ½ teaspoon black pepper into a plastic bag and shake to blend. Add the liver and toss so that each cube is well coated. Dump the contents of the bag into a sieve over a bowl and shake to remove excess flour. Immediately fry the liver cubes until well browned on the outside and juicy and pink inside, about 2 minutes.

4. Tamp the sieve to remove any flour and set sieve over a bowl. When the livers are brown on the outside but still very juicy within, dump the entire contents of the skillet into the sieve to drain. Transfer the liver to a serving dish, toss with the scallions or onions and another pinch of coarse sea salt, and mix lightly. Sprinkle with parsley and serve.

Cordornices Guisados
Double marinated quail (Portugal)

In this delicious specialty of the Azores, the quail is marinated in sweet- and hot-paprika-scented beer for an intense flavor, then cooked in the marinade and left to marinate again up to two days. When ready to serve, the quail may be broiled or grilled quickly until the skin crisps.

SERVES 4

- 4 quail (4 ounces each), fresh or defrosted
  White vinegar
- 3 garlic cloves, peeled and crushed with 1 teaspoon salt
- 2 teaspoons sweet paprika
- ½ teaspoon hot Hungarian paprika, or more to taste
- 6 fluid ounces (½ can) domestic beer
- 1 tablespoon vinegar with 7 percent acetic acid
- ¼ cup olive oil
  Coarse salt
  Sprigs of parsley or watercress as garnish
- 8 lemon wedges

1. Cut the quail in half, wash them in vinegared water, drain, and pat dry with kitchen towels.

2. Combine the garlic and sweet and hot paprika and rub over the quail thoroughly. Combine the beer and vinegar in a bowl, add the quail, and marinate for at least 8 hours, turning occasionally.

3. Put the quail, marinade, and the ¼ cup olive oil in a large skillet and bring to a boil. Reduce the heat and cook, covered, for 10 to 15 minutes. Transfer the quail to a deep bowl. Boil the cooking liquid until it coats a spoon. Add more hot paprika to taste. Pour over the quail; cool, cover, and refrigerate up to 2 days.

4. Remove the quail from the soaking marinade and, without drying, broil them close to the heat, turning once and basting with the marinade until crisp and well browned. Serve at once, sprinkled with coarse salt and surrounded by parsley and lemon wedges.

PARSLEY

Flat-leaf parsley is widely used around the Mediterranean and is often the basis of such salad as *fattouch* and *tabooli*.

In Provence, ragouts, sautés, and roasts as well as a wild mushroom sauté, a few slices of calf's liver, or some string beans are all at their best when served with a *persillade*—a mixture of parsley and garlic.

In Greek Macedonia, chunks of lamb or veal are prepared with a sauce that contains more than two pounds parsley bound with lemon and eggs, and the Spanish make a simple sauce of crushing parsley with garlic and lemon for fried fish.

Tagine Maadnous

Lamb and parsley tagine in the style of Sfax
(Tunisia)

Traditionally this *tagine* is served with a *mechouia* salad of grilled peppers and tomatoes (pages 88–89).

SERVES 8 AS PART OF A TUNISIAN BUFFET

¼ cup dried white beans, soaked overnight
8 ounces lean boneless lamb shoulder, coarsely ground
½ teaspoon salt
½ teaspoon freshly ground black pepper
2½ tablespoons olive oil
½ cup minced onion
2 teaspoons tomato paste
¼ teaspoon cayenne
3 packed cups chopped flat-leaf parsley
½ cup soft bread crumbs
1 ounce Parmesan cheese, grated (about ⅓ cup)
3 ounces Gruyère cheese, cubed (about 1 cup)
½ teaspoon Tunisian *bharat* (see note)
6 large eggs
6 lemon wedges

1. Drain the beans, cover with fresh water, and cook until they are half tender, about 30 minutes. Meanwhile, cut the lamb into ½-inch cubes and toss with salt and pepper.

2. Heat 1¼ tablespoons oil in a 10-inch skillet. Cook the onion until translucent, add the meat, and sauté for 5 minutes. Cover the skillet and cook over low heat until the meat gives off its moisture and reabsorbs it. Add the tomato paste and cook, stirring, until lamb cubes are well coated. Add cayenne, the beans, and about 1 cup of the bean cooking liquid. Cover the skillet and cook over medium heat for 20 minutes longer, or until the meat and beans are fully cooked and the juices are thick. Remove from the heat and allow to cool. (Up to this point the dish can be made 1 day in advance. Return to room temperature before proceeding.)

3. Place the oven rack in the second highest position and preheat the oven to 350 degrees.

4. In a mixing bowl, combine the contents of the skillet, the parsley, ⅓ cup of the bread crumbs, grated Parmesan, and cubed Gruyère, mixing well. Season highly with salt, pepper, and sieved *bharat*. Beat the eggs to a froth and add to the mixture.

5. Use the remaining oil to coat the bottom and sides of a 5- or 6-cup baking dish, or an attractive 9-inch well-seasoned ovenproof skillet. Place the prepared mixture in the dish, sprinkle with reserved bread crumbs, and set in the oven to bake for 12 minutes. Raise the oven heat to the highest setting, remove the *tagine* from the oven, tilt the dish so that the oil collects in one place, then brush this oil over the surface of the *tagine*. Return the dish to the oven and bake for 8 minutes. Serve hot directly from the dish.

Note: Bharat is dried rosebuds rubbed through a sieve and mixed with ground cinnamon. Rosebuds that have not been sprayed are available by mail order from Aphrodisia (see "Mail-Order Sources," pages 296–97).

MYRTLE

Myrtle, with an aroma close to rosemary and juniper, is used a lot on the Mediterranean islands of Sardinia, Corsica, and Crete. It's good as a flavoring for lamb, and the Sardinians are fond of it with small birds. But the flavor of myrtle is quite strong, so rather than adding it directly the Sardinians wait until the birds are roasted, then, still hot, place them under a bed of myrtle leaves to absorb the aroma. They do the same with small roasted pig, but feel free to stuff the leaves directly into a wild boar, since that creature has a strong flavor of its own.

Corsican *pâté de merles* is flavored with a liqueur made from myrtle called myrthe.

ORANGE FLOWER WATER

In North Africa, orange flower water is often made in the home. Arabs invented the distilling process, and their alembic stills are pretty much the same as the sort of distilling apparatus you might find in a modern chemistry laboratory.

Orange flower water is used to flavor cakes and cookies in Provence and in Lebanon. It is used to flavor almond pastries in the Maghreb—even the pastry dough wrapped around the almond paste. The Algerians perfume meatballs with it, and in Morocco it's used to perfume the water with which you rinse your hands after a grand *diffa*.

Roummaniya bil Zhar
Pomegranates with orange flower water (Tunisia)

André Gide, who spent much time in North Africa, wrote of pomegranates in his *Les Nourritures terrestres:* "Sections of beehives, guarded treasure, richness of savor, pentagonal architecture. The shell splits, the seeds fall. Seeds of blood in azure bowls. And some like drops of gold on plates of enameled bronze."

To make this popular Tunisian dessert, buy the largest, flame-red pomegranates you can find. Lacking azure bowls and bronze plates, you can serve the pomegranate seeds in small crystal cups, in which they will resemble glistening rubies.

SERVES 4

- 2 pomegranates
- 1 tablespoon orange flower water
- 2 tablespoons granulated sugar

1. To remove seeds from a pomegranate without coloring everything in sight, cut each pomegranate into 3 or 4 pieces and place in a deep pan of water. One piece at a time, give a gentle whack on the skin side, which will loosen the seeds. Remove all the peels and "flake" the seeds apart with your fingers.

2. Drain seeds in a colander and divide among four serving dishes. Sprinkle evenly with orange flower water and sugar. Let stand 1 hour before serving.

PIMENTÓN

This is the Spanish paprika so beloved by the Andalusians—a paprika that is extremely flavorful and can be either sweet or hot. The peasants of Almería are famous for their light *pimentón*-flavored dark red fish soup made with fresh anchovies, firm, white-fleshed fish, sardines, fried onions, tomatoes, garlic, and cumin.

The Spanish call second-quality *pimentón* "*arena*," or "sand." *Pimentón* is a little stronger then Hungarian paprika and is essential in the justly famous Andalusian boiled bean soup, *berza*.

Berza

Mixed vegetable, chick-pea, bean, and sausage soup (Spain)

There is a remarkable variety of pork products in Andalusia, including an extraordinary cured ham produced in the town of Jabugo, made from the Iberian black pig fattened on acorns. Jabugo ham has a nutty, earthy, sweet flavor that, to my mind, rivals that of the very best hams of Parma or Bayonne.

I learned a good use for Andalusian pork products on a visit to Castellar de la Frontera, a beautiful mountainous area known for producing bulls for the bullfight as well as for the cultivation of cork. I was told of the delicious home cooking available in the hotel La Amoraima, a magnificent place recently converted from a privately owned hunting lodge, which in turn had been converted from an old convent.

When I arrived, I was told that the regular cook had taken ill. A local woman had been brought in. She was solemn, not at all shy, a little intimidating. When I asked her what she was preparing, she answered, "My best dish."

It turned out to be a *berza*, a thick bean and vegetable soup enriched with chunks of *chorizo* and black sausage. With slow cooking, the pork fat mingled with, but did not bind with, the cooking juices, and was easily removed by degreasing. The dish was not heavy at all, but the spicing was strong—lots of cumin, nutmeg, cloves, and *pimentón*.

(continued)

The ham hocks and blood sausage are more like condiments than main ingredients in this nourishing soup, but they are necessary for the deep flavor. The soup is best made a day ahead and allowed to mellow overnight. This will also help you to remove much of the fat.

SERVES 12

3/4 cup dried chick-peas, soaked overnight in water to cover
1½ pounds meaty ham hocks
1½ pounds meaty pork neck bones
½ cup dried white kidney beans or Great Northern beans, soaked overnight
    in water to cover
1 pound Swiss chard, with thick stalks, washed
2 large celery ribs, strings removed
4 garlic cloves, minced
1 bay leaf
1 tablespoon Spanish paprika *(pimentón)* or Hungarian paprika
¼ teaspoon ground cumin
¼ teaspoon ground cloves
¼ teaspoon grated nutmeg
¼ teaspoon freshly ground black pepper, or more to taste
¼ teaspoon dried red pepper flakes, or more to taste
2 teaspoons coarse sea salt
3 ounces *morcilla* or other blood sausage
5 carrots, peeled and cut into bite-size chunks
½ pound pumpkin, Hubbard, or butternut squash, peeled and cut into
    bite-size chunks
3 waxy potatoes, peeled and cut into bite-size chunks
6 ounces fully cooked *chorizo* sausage
2 tablespoons chopped fresh parsley

1. Drain the chick-peas, rinse well, and place in a soup pot. Add the ham hocks, neck bones, and 3 quarts cold water; bring to a boil. Simmer for 30 minutes, skimming the surface often to remove scum. Drain the kidney beans and add to the pot; cook for 30 minutes longer.

2. Cut off the leaves from the chard stalks. Slice the leaves into long ½-inch-wide strips. Set aside.

3. Add chard stalks to the soup pot, along with celery, garlic, bay leaf, paprika, cumin, cloves, nutmeg, black pepper, red pepper flakes, sea salt, and whole piece

of *morcilla*. Bring to a boil. Reduce heat, cover, and cook gently about 1 hour, or until ham hocks and pork meat are tender.

4. Carefully transfer the ham hocks and pork meat to a work surface and cool slightly. Add carrots, pumpkin or squash, potatoes, and the reserved Swiss chard leaves to the pot and slowly boil, covered, for 30 minutes, or until the vegetables are tender.

5. Meanwhile, pierce the *chorizo* and cook it in boiling water for 7 minutes, or until it has cooked through. Drain, thinly slice, and set aside.

6. Trim the ham hocks of all fat, bones, and gristle and cut the meat into bite-size chunks. Return meat to the soup along with the sliced *chorizo*. Let the soup cool, cover, and refrigerate overnight.

7. Remove hardened fat from the surface of the soup. Reheat, remove the bay leaf, and adjust the seasonings. Ladle into soup bowls and sprinkle with parsley.

ROSEMARY

In Tunisia there's an interesting rosemary variant called *kilil,* which is extremely aromatic. It's used in a regional dish of lamb cubes rubbed with paprika, then steamed over a bunch of *kilil* in the top of a *couscousier.* The broth below is full of onions and seasoned with cinnamon, pepper, and salt. Later couscous is added to the top and steamed through the *kilil,* too.

Rosemary has such a powerful aroma you needn't eat it to get the point. It penetrates everything that is cooked with it. The Italians use it a great deal, tucking great bouquets of it under roasts of lamb, veal, or pork.

In Abruzzi, in central Italy, there's a famous lamb dish made with rosemary and chili peppers. The people there also like to rub lamb with a rosemary and honey paste before putting it in to roast. In Tuscany there's a popular chestnut flour cake flavored with rosemary, pine nuts, and sultanas and served with a generous helping of ricotta cheese, and in Rome there's a superb way of serving rosemary-flavored rib steaks.

Costata di Manzo alla Romana
Rib steaks in the style of Rome (Italy)

An Italian approaches his food with "winged nostrils." He can tell by the aroma when his dinner is seasoned and cooked to perfection. He will nonchalantly stop the *girarrosto,* the roasting spit, or remove a casserole from the stove, and announce to nobody in particular: "This is now ready for me."

SERVES 4 TO 5

> 2 1-pound rib steaks, 1 inch thick
> 1 tablespoon finely chopped fresh rosemary
> 2 garlic cloves, peeled and chopped
> ½ cup olive oil
> ¼ teaspoon freshly ground black pepper
>   Salt
>   Juice of 1 lemon

1. The day before serving, pound the slices of meat between sheets of wax paper until somewhat thinner. In a mortar, pound the rosemary and the garlic to a paste. Stir in the olive oil and season with the pepper and a little salt. Marinate the meat at least 12 hours in the oil mixture, turning the meat once or twice.

2. Remove the meat and pat dry with paper towels. Broil 4 minutes on each side, or until done to taste. Place on a warmed serving dish, sprinkle with lemon juice, and serve at once.

SAFFRON

Saffron, the dried stigmas of *Crocus sativus,* should be set on a flat dish over a pan of boiling water. When the stigmas become brittle, pound them to a fine powder. This is the best way to get the full use of every thread of saffron—the world's most expensive spice.

In Tunisia there's a *tagine* with "bananas": Mashed potatoes are mixed with ground meat and grated cheese, then combined with chopped hard-boiled eggs and seasoned with salt and pepper. Saffron is used to make the mixture yellow, then it's formed into a banana shape and cooked in boiling oil.

In Languedoc and Périgord, *le mourtairol* is a beef, chicken, ham, and vegetable casserole simmered for many hours. Some of the cooking juices are removed, cooked until creamy with saffron and a loaf of toasted French bread, then dolloped by the spoonful back into bowls of the soup.

Paella is the most famous saffron dish, and rightly so. There are as many ways to make it as there are Spanish cooks, but the common ingredient is always the saffron that permeates paella and gives it its distinctive taste.

The history of paella is long and complicated. It was invented in southern Spain, and in its early form was not made with chicken, pork, sausage, or seafood, but with rabbit, snails, and freshwater eels. It was traditionally made outdoors over an open fire, and rather than being accompanied by salad, it was eaten while chewing on a raw wild scallion.

Paella
(Spain)

When I lived in Tangier, I learned this recipe, a rendition from Murcia, from an old cook and refugee from Franco's Spain.

SERVES 8

- 3/4 cup olive oil
- 1 cup grated onion
- 1/2 pound boneless pork shoulder, cut into 1-inch cubes
- 1 3-pound chicken, cut into 8 pieces
- 1 teaspoon finely chopped garlic
- 2 cups peeled, seeded, and chopped tomatoes
- 2 bay leaves
- 4 fresh parsley sprigs
  Salt
  Freshly ground black pepper
- 1/2 teaspoon pulverized saffron
- 12 mussels, well scrubbed
- 1/2 pound small clams, scrubbed and soaked in cold water for 30 minutes to eliminate sand
- 1/4 pound sweet green peppers, seeded, deribbed, and cut lengthwise into thin strips
- 1/4 pound green beans, trimmed and cut into 1-inch lengths
- 3 cups raw medium- or short-grain rice
- 1 7-ounce jar roasted red peppers, drained and cut into thin strips
- 1/2 pound shelled and deveined shrimp
- 1/4 pound fully cooked *chorizo* sausage, skinned and thinly sliced
- 2 lemons, quartered

1. In a large casserole, heat 1/3 cup of the olive oil and cook 1/2 cup of the grated onion for 2 minutes, stirring. Add the pork and chicken and sauté for 5 minutes, stirring. Then add the garlic, tomatoes, herbs, salt, pepper, and saffron. Cover and cook over medium heat for about 25 minutes, stirring from time to time.

2. Meanwhile, steam the mussels and clams in 1 cup water until they open, about 5 minutes. Discard any that do not open. Reserve the mussels, clams, and cooking liquid and discard the shells. Strain the liquid.

3. Add the green peppers and green beans to the casserole. Cook, covered, for 5 to 10 minutes longer.

4. Meanwhile, heat the remaining olive oil in a 15- to 16-inch paella pan and cook the remaining ½ cup grated onion for 1 minute. Add the rice and cook, stirring until all the grains are coated, 8 to 10 minutes.

5. Add the mussel and clam liquid plus 7 cups water to the casserole. Bring to the boil. Slowly pour the bubbling sauce over the rice. Then slide the remaining contents of the casserole evenly over the sizzling rice. Add the red peppers, shrimp, *chorizo* slices, mussels, and clams. Stir once. Cook, uncovered, over brisk heat until the liquid is absorbed and the rice is tender, about 20 minutes. Rotate and shake the pan from time to time to cook the rice evenly. Allow the contents to rest 5 minutes before serving. Serve directly from the pan with the lemon wedges.

SAGE

Sage, like myrtle and rosemary, is a strong herb and needs careful handling. The Tuscans say that their famous *fagioli all'uccelletto,* with a seasoning of sage, garlic, and tomato, makes white beans taste like small game.

Acqua Cotta di Maremma
Tuscan vegetable soup with olive oil and sage (Italy)

◻

This dish, favored by workmen in the countryside around Maremma in Tuscany, is for lovers of olive oil. It's from the *Petit Breviaire de la cuisine,* by my good friend Mario Ruspoli, who counsels that the bread chunks must fill half the soup tureen.

SERVES 4 TO 6

2	bunches of fresh sage leaves
½	cup virgin olive oil
3	garlic cloves, unpeeled
1	cup shelled green peas
1	cup shelled fava or lima beans
1	cup diced carrots
½	cup diced celery
4	raw artichoke hearts, cleaned and halved
2½	quarts water
	Salt
	Freshly ground black pepper
1	dried red pepper, crumbled
8	large chunks of coarse country-style bread, toasted in the oven then rubbed with garlic
4	to 6 fresh eggs
	Grated Parmesan or pecorino cheese

1. Scatter the sage leaves on the bottom of a 5½-quart casserole or deep wide earthenware dish set over a Flame Tamer. Pour over the olive oil. Add the garlic. Cook over very low heat for 5 minutes. Add all the vegetables and cook, stirring, over brisk heat for 2 to 3 minutes. Add the water, salt, pepper, and red pepper. Slowly bring to the boil and cook at the simmer until the vegetables are tender.

2. Fill a soup tureen halfway with the prepared country-style bread. Poach the eggs in the simmering soup for 5 minutes. Carefully transfer the soup and the eggs to the tureen. Sprinkle with grated cheese. Serve lukewarm or, better still, cold the next day.

Sesame Seeds

═══

Tahini, or sesame paste, an emulsion of sesame seeds and oil, is much used in the Middle East. Before you use it be sure to stir the mixture in the can until it's well blended and smooth.

The simple tahini cream sauce, the base of such dishes as *hummus, baba ghanoush,* and a sauce for cold poached fish, makes a delightful dip when mixed with lots of chopped parsley.

Combine 1 cup of well-mixed tahini with 1 teaspoon finely chopped garlic and ½ teaspoon salt. Beat well, then stir in enough cold water (about ⅔ cup) to make a thick sauce. Thin it with lemon juice, still stirring, and you'll have a flavorful sauce for grilled foods, cooked cold vegetables, and fish.

Sesame seeds are used in halvah, the famous Turkish sweet. The Moroccans toast them and sprinkle them over sweet *tagines,* and the Israelis use them to coat chicken.

Oaf Sum Sum
Fried chicken with sesame seeds (Israel)

SERVES 4

> 4 leg and thigh pieces of chicken, separated
> Salt
> Freshly ground black pepper
> 1 egg, lightly beaten
> ⅔ cup all-purpose flour
> 1 cup sesame seeds
> 2 teaspoons paprika
> Oil for frying

1. Preheat the oven to 350 degrees.

2. Rub the chicken pieces with salt and pepper. Beat the egg with ½ cup water in a shallow bowl. Combine flour, sesame seeds, paprika, and salt to taste in a plastic bag, mixing well. Place the chicken pieces, two or three at a time, in the

(continued)

egg mixture and then in the plastic bag. Close and shake until the chicken is nicely coated with the sesame seed mixture. Remove to a dish. Repeat with the remaining pieces of chicken.

3. In hot but not smoking oil, brown the chicken pieces on both sides. Transfer to a baking sheet, set on the middle shelf of the preheated oven, and bake for about 20 minutes. Serve hot.

Samak bi Taheeni

Fish fillets baked in sesame seed sauce
(Lebanon)

SERVES 2

> ½ pound lean, white-fleshed fish, preferably thick fillets
>   Sea salt
> 1 large onion, halved lengthwise and sliced thin
> 2½ tablespoons olive oil
> 1 garlic clove, sliced
> 3 tablespoons sesame seed paste (tahini)
> 2 tablespoons lemon juice
> 1 tablespoon chopped parsley

1. Sprinkle the fish fillets with sea salt and refrigerate for at least 1 hour.

2. Preheat the oven to 375 degrees.

3. In a nonstick skillet, cook the onions with olive oil, ¼ teaspoon salt, and ½ cup water for 10 minutes, or until onions are soft and water has evaporated. Allow the onions to slowly turn a deep, golden brown, stirring occasionally. Add the garlic and cook, stirring, for another minute.

4. Meanwhile, steam the fish over boiling water until the flesh is barely flaky. Cool and break into small pieces. Mix fish with the onions and spread in a 9-inch oiled baking dish.

5. In a mixing bowl, combine sesame seed paste and ¼ cup water, beating well. Gradually stir in the lemon juice until smooth and creamy. Pour over the fish mixture and set in the oven to bake for 15 minutes. Allow to cool to room temperature. Serve cool or chilled with a garnish of chopped fresh parsley.

SUMAC

Sumac is a nonpoisonous red berry that gives a distinctive, delicious, sour-lemony flavor to shish kebab and yogurt sauces. Middle Easterners add it to fried onions to turn them a lovely yellow mustard shade. It is sometimes used along with lemon juice to reinforce an astringent tart flavor without liquid.

The quality of sumac can vary enormously. It should smell somewhat like lemon. Mixed with pungent herbs such as thyme, savory, oregano, or marjoram, it's called *za'atar* (not to be confused with the oregano hybrid of the same name). Buy it from a reputable grocer or mail-order source (see pages 296–97). Store sumac in your freezer.

If you obtain sumac in grain form, soak it in water, strain it, then press the mixture. Use it like lemon juice over tomato and cucumber salads and as part of the cooking liquid for stuffed tomatoes and green peppers.

Fatayer bi Sabanekh
Spinach and sumac triangles (Syria)

◻

The unique flavor of this popular snack or luncheon dish is the result of, first, the wilting of the spinach by salting, and second, the combination of sumac and lemon juice.

With thanks to Imam Najjar of Amman, Jordan, for sharing this recipe

MAKES 9 TRIANGULAR PIES

DOUGH

- 1 teaspoon active dry yeast
- 1/2 teaspoon sugar
- 2 tablespoons water
- 2 1/2 cups all-purpose flour
- 1/2 teaspoon salt
- 1 teaspoon baking soda
- 1/4 cup olive oil
- 3/4 cup low-fat plain yogurt, beaten until slightly liquid

SPINACH AND SUMAC FILLING

- 1 pound bunch of fresh spinach
  Coarse salt
- 1/4 cup chopped parsley
- 1 cup finely chopped onion
- 1/2 teaspoon ground allspice
- 1 1/2 teaspoons sumac
  Juice of 1 lemon (about 3 tablespoons)
- 3 tablespoons olive oil, plus more for brushing the pastry
- 1/2 cup finely chopped walnuts
  Freshly ground pepper

1. In the workbowl of a food processor, combine the yeast, sugar, and water, pulsing once. Spread 2 cups of the flour mixed with the salt and baking soda over the yeast and place the bowl cover on top. Let stand 15 minutes. With the machine running slowly add the oil and then the yogurt. Process until smooth, about 20 seconds. Turn the dough out onto a lightly floured surface and knead

until smooth and springy in texture, about 5 minutes. Cover with a heavy kitchen towel and put in a warm place until dough rises, about 1 hour.

2. Wash and stem the spinach. In a large colander, rub the spinach with 1½ tablespoons salt; let stand for at least 30 minutes.

3. Squeeze the spinach to remove excess moisture; rinse to remove excess salt and finely chop. Squeeze the spinach until dry. Add the parsley, onion, allspice, sumac, lemon juice, olive oil, nuts, and pepper to taste. Correct the seasoning.

4. Preheat the oven to 350 degrees.

5. Divide the prepared dough into nine equal parts. On a lightly floured work surface, roll each into a smooth round and allow to rest for 10 minutes.

6. Roll each to a 5-inch round. Place an equal amount of filling in the shape of a long triangle in the center of each round. Fold two sides in toward the center, and the remaining short side down to form a triangle. Crimp the seams with fingertips. Brush with olive oil. Bake on a nonstick pan until golden brown, about 30 minutes.

7. Remove from the oven, set the pan on a rack, cover with a damp towel, and let stand 10 minutes. Serve hot or cold.

Pirpirim Salatasi

Purslane, tomato, and sumac salad (Turkey)

Purslane is a leafy succulent, exceptionally rich in nutrients and deliciously tart. In early summer you can eat the leaves and tender stems and unopened buds. In August, only the leaves are tender enough to eat raw. This tangy salad is a perfect accompaniment to grilled fish, lamb kebabs, or just good bread.

MAKES 4 CUPS

- 1 medium summer green onion
  Salt
- ½ pound purslane
- 1 cup peeled, seeded, and cubed ripe tomatoes
- 1 small green bell pepper, stemmed, seeded, and finely chopped
    (about ½ cup)
- 3 teaspoons sumac
- ½ teaspoon mildly hot dried red pepper flakes or Aleppo pepper
- 4 to 6 tablespoons fresh lemon juice
- 2 tablespoons olive oil

1. Peel and chop the onion; sprinkle with salt and leave for 10 minutes.

2. Meanwhile, wash, stem, and chop the purslane. Rinse the onion; drain well. Combine the onion with the purslane, tomatoes, peppers, sumac, red pepper flakes, lemon juice, and olive oil, mixing well. Add salt to taste. Serve cold.

ZA'ATAR AND OTHER MEDITERRANEAN DRIED HERBS

Za'atar, along with marjoram, savory, oregano, thyme, and hyssop, grows wild on the mountain slopes of Mediterranean lands; these herbs are used a great deal in Mediterranean cooking. They are so close in spirit that they can be spoken of together; they are sometimes interchangeable when marinating meats or fish before grilling and for sprinkling over olives, cheese, and salads.

In Morocco, *za'atar*, which is a sort of hybrid of oregano and marjoram, is used with zucchini and as an herbal drink after a heavy meal. In the Middle East, pungent *za'atar* is a popular seasoning on breads and salad. It is also one of the essential ingredients in the Turkish spice blend, *baharat*, and the Lebanese version of the bread salad, *fattoush*. Though often confused with other herbs in the thyme-oregano-marjoram-savory family, it should not be confused with the spice blend called *za'atar*, a mixture of sumac and *za'atar*. (The blends may also include toasted sesame seeds, pistachios, and other spices. In the Syrian city of Aleppo, there are shops that sell nothing but *za'atar* blends to be mixed with olive oil and used as a dip for pita.)

Middle Eastern grocers sell plain *za'atar* and *za'atar* blended with sumac. See "Mail-Order Sources" (pages 296–97).

Fattoush

Bread and parsley salad (Lebanon)

I learned this tart, pungent salad from Mrs. Wadad Fakhreddine, who comes from the Chouf Mountains above Beirut.

The special tangy edge of this salad comes from the combination of lots of lemon juice and pungent herbs, including *za'atar* and sumac. When purchasing *za'atar* blends at Middle Eastern grocers, check for tartness. (Some blends contain a lot of sumac, while others contain hardly any.) If necessary, buy some sumac as well and adjust the recipe accordingly.

SERVES 6

> 2 cups parsley
> 1 garlic clove, peeled and crushed with ½ teaspoon salt
> ⅓ cup fresh lemon juice, or more to taste
> 1 tablespoon *za'atar* blend or 1 teaspoon plain *za'atar* and 2 teaspoons
>   sumac
> ⅓ to ½ cup olive oil
>   Freshly ground black pepper
> 1 packed cup fresh mint leaves
> 1 cucumber, peeled and finely diced
> 1 cup chopped scallions
> ⅔ cup roughly chopped purslane leaves (optional)
> 2 ripe tomatoes, cored, seeded, and diced
> 1 cup chopped tender celery or bell pepper
> 1 large pita, separated, toasted, and crumbled

1. Wash and spin-dry the parsley. Remove all stems. Finely chop the parsley by hand. In a mixing bowl, dissolve the garlic in the lemon juice. Beat in the *za'atar* seasoning and the oil. Season with pepper.

2. Toss in the parsley, mint, cucumber, scallions, purslane, if using, tomatoes, and celery or bell pepper; mix well. Scatter the crumbled pita on top. Fold the bread into the salad about 5 minutes before serving.

YOGURT

Yogurt is a Turkish word, and though it's eaten now all over the world, it probably comes from the Middle East. The Indians use it in great quantity, of course, and over the last several decades it has become hugely popular in Western Europe and the United States. I still think the Bulgarians make the best tasting yogurt in the world—I'd go a long way to find some Bulgarian yogurt culture to start a batch for myself at home.

In the Middle East, yogurt is made with cow's milk, goat's milk, sheep's milk, or even the milk of a camel. Cow's milk seems best, though a Greek might argue on behalf of the quality of his sheep's-milk yogurt, called *proveio.*

The Turks have infinite uses for it, and most of the great Mediterranean yogurt dishes have origins in Turkish cuisine. Besides serving it plain or mixed with fruit preserves, yogurt is marvelous as a cooking medium, a sauce thickener, a cooling agent, and a drink.

The Turks serve it often with their pilaf, made of cooked lamb, fried onions, raisins or currants, pine nuts, tomatoes, and garlic. They use it as a sauce on eggplant slices fried in batter or in a hot soup made with mint, garlic, onions, lamb, and rice. They mix it with sugar and then pour it on fresh fruits and berries, or concoct it in a dessert, *yogurt tatlisi,* an orange-flavored cake in which the yogurt substitutes for milk.

There are all sorts of stories about the origins of yogurt, most of them having to do with astonished Middle Eastern nomads who find the milk in their goat-skins curdled to a delicious substance when they return to their tents at the end of a hot summer day. *Voilà!* Yogurt, the great health food, is born, and thus begins the tradition of preserving fresh milk in a curdled state—a tradition that has brought us the glories of cheese.

Today most people buy their yogurt in the supermarket, or else make it themselves in a yogurt-making machine. The supermarket varieties cost too much, especially if you're a big yogurt eater like me. And as for the machines, they're quite all right, but the truth is that you can make yogurt yourself without any special equipment and for a fraction of the supermarket cost. The only thing you have to remember is to keep the yogurt culture alive. I've told my children many times: "Eat as much yogurt as you want, but *never* eat the last one in the fridge."

Here's how to make your own yogurt, the simplest, least expensive way. And on the following pages I've put together a group of recipes in which yogurt is the prime ingredient and the key. Some are very simple, like *labni,* the fresh Lebanese cheese, or *tarator,* a delicious Slavic yogurt and cucumber soup. Others are more complicated like *shish barak bi laban,* a fine Lebanese dish of lamb dumplings and *kibbeh* in a tasty yogurt sauce. And another, *laban oummo,* a modern-day version of the classic "baby lamb cooked in its mother's milk."

Yogurt
Homemade yogurt

MAKES 1 QUART

    1 quart milk, whole or skimmed
    ¼ cup commercial yogurt

1. Simmer the milk for 5 minutes, stirring often. Cool to about 110 degrees, or until a few drops of milk on the inside of the wrist feel warm. Stir the yogurt into the milk, then pour into a large bowl. Cover and wrap in towels. This helps the culture to ferment the milk. Place in the warmest part of the kitchen. Do not disturb for 6 hours.

2. Uncover the bowl. Cover the bowl with plastic wrap and set in the refrigerator to chill completely. The yogurt will keep fresh for a few days.

3. To make more yogurt, use some of your homemade yogurt as a starter.

Labni
Fresh cheese made from yogurt (Lebanon)

MAKES ½ CUP

    2 cups yogurt
    ½ teaspoon salt

1. Combine the yogurt and salt. Pour into a cheesecloth sack, tie up, and suspend over a large bowl. Let drain overnight. The bowl will catch the dripping liquid.

2. In the morning, discard the water. Unwrap the cheese and use as a spread on *pita* or form into small balls and serve with olive oil and chopped fresh mint or with black olives.

Yogurt Çorbasi

Hot yogurt soup (Turkey)

I am fond of the yogurt soups of Gaziantep, a town in southeastern Turkey where the yogurt is particularly sweet. The soups here are silky and creamy because the local cooks use only drained yogurt, and they often add a little milk to make the soup even sweeter. All sorts of vegetables can be cooked in these soups—leeks, peas, green garlic, and fava beans.

In this recipe, only rice is added so as not to detract from what I call the "flourish"—the final swirling in of sizzling mint and black pepper, which heightens the aroma of the herbs and spice and gives the soup a delicious flavor and an elegant appearance.

MAKES 6 CUPS

    4   cups whole or low-fat plain yogurt
        Salt
    ¼   cup raw medium or small-grain rice
    1   quart rich chicken or lamb stock, degreased
    1   tablespoon cornstarch
    1   whole egg
    ½   cup milk
    2   tablespoons unsalted butter or olive oil
    1½ tablespoons crumbled dried mint, pressed through a sieve to make
            1¼ teaspoons powdered mint
    1   teaspoon freshly ground black pepper, pressed through a sieve to make
            about ¾ teaspoon powdered black pepper

1. One day before serving, drain the yogurt. In a cheesecloth-lined sieve set over a medium bowl, combine the yogurt with ½ teaspoon salt. Let drain at room temperature to 2 cups. (Discard the whey or save for cooking vegetables or bread baking.)

2. Cook the rice in the stock for 20 minutes.

3. In a second saucepan, make a smooth paste with the cornstarch and ½ cup cold water. Beat in the yogurt, whole egg, and milk until smooth. Set the yogurt over low heat and turn off the heat under the stock. Gradually stir 2 cups of the hot stock into the yogurt in order to raise its temperature. When the temperature

of the yogurt is hotter than the temperature of the stock, pour the yogurt into the remaining stock and set it on medium heat. Stir until it just comes to a boil, about 15 minutes. Remove from the heat. Correct the seasoning with salt. Transfer to a soup tureen.

4. Heat the butter or oil in a small skillet, bring to a sizzle, and add the mint and pepper. Remove from the heat, stirring, and pour over the soup, stirring gently to create swirls. Cover the soup and wait 5 minutes before serving.

Tarator

Yogurt and cucumber soup (Macedonia)

The combination of yogurt and cucumbers is popular through all the Middle East. In Turkey they make *cacik,* without the walnuts but with a good sprinkling of chopped fresh dill. In Greek *tavernas* you will be served *tzatziki,* a thick cucumber and yogurt dip.

In the former Yugoslavia I've eaten an excellent variation on *tarator*—the soup was spiked with raw chopped hot green pepper instead of chopped mint.

SERVES 4

   ½ cup walnut halves
   3 large garlic cloves, peeled
   2 tablespoons olive oil
   4 cups plain yogurt
   2 firm cucumbers, peeled and seeded
     Salt
     Freshly ground black pepper
     Chopped mint

1. In a mortar, pound the walnuts with the garlic until pasty, then start adding the oil, drop by drop, stirring constantly.

2. Dump the yogurt into a large mixing bowl and beat until liquid. Beat in the walnut-garlic paste.

3. Dice or grate the cucumbers; drain, then fold into the yogurt soup. Season with salt and pepper. Chill well. Garnish with chopped mint before serving.

Çilber

Poached eggs with yogurt (Turkey)

I think this is an enchanting way to serve poached eggs, unusual and delicious, particularly good as a light supper late at night.

SERVES 2 TO 4

>   1 cup whole milk plain yogurt
>   1 small garlic clove, crushed
>   Salt
>   4 large eggs
>   1 tablespoon vinegar
>   Freshly ground black pepper
>   2 tablespoons unsalted butter
>   1 teaspoon hot paprika

1. Heat the oven to 300 degrees.

2. Combine the yogurt, garlic, and salt. Put equal amounts in 4 ovenproof ramekins and set them in the oven to heat gently.

3. Meanwhile, poach the eggs in acidulated water. Drain and set 1 egg in each ramekin. Sprinkle with salt and pepper to taste. Keep hot in the oven.

4. Quickly melt the butter in a small pan. Stir in the paprika to make the butter a bright red color. Dribble the butter over each egg, leaving the paprika powder behind in the saucepan. Serve at once.

Variation:

Substitute fried chopped onions for the garlic.

Shish Barak bi Laban

Lamb dumplings and kibbeh in yogurt sauce (Lebanon)

SERVES 6

DUMPLINGS

- 2 cups all-purpose flour, sifted
- 1 teaspoon salt
- 1 tablespoon clarified butter or oil
- ⅔ cup warm water (approximately)
- 10 ounces ground lamb or beef
- ½ cup finely chopped onion
- ½ teaspoon Lebanese spice mixture: 2 good pinches of cayenne, 2 good pinches of ground cinnamon, and 1 good pinch of grated nutmeg
- 2 tablespoons butter
- ¼ cup pine nuts

KIBBEH

- 1 pound boned lamb cut from the leg, ground twice
- 1 medium onion, finely chopped
- Salt
- Freshly ground black pepper
- 1 cup fine-grain bulgur
- 2 ice cubes

YOGURT SAUCE

- 2 quarts homemade yogurt
- 1 tablespoon cornstarch
- 1 egg

TAKLIA

- 2 teaspoons finely chopped garlic
- 3 tablespoons finely chopped fresh coriander or mint
- 2 tablespoons butter, melted

1. To make dumplings, mix the flour with the salt on a flat workspace and make a well in the center. Slowly work in the melted clarified butter or oil and enough warm water to make a soft ball of dough. Add more water, if necessary. Knead

(continued)

the dough until it forms a smooth ball. Allow to rest 30 minutes under an inverted bowl.

2. Meanwhile prepare the stuffing: Brown the meat with the onion and spices in butter. Season with salt. Use a fork to break up the lumps of meat. Stir in the pine nuts and toss with the meat over high heat until lightly toasted. Allow to cool.

3. Knead the dough again until very elastic. Separate into four parts and roll each into ⅛-inch-thick sheets. Cut into 2-inch squares. You should have 36. Place 1 teaspoon stuffing in the center of each square, fold to form a triangle, and press the edges to adhere firmly. Set aside to dry for 1 hour.

4. To make the kibbeh, grind the ground lamb with the onion and season with salt and pepper. Wet the bulgur with water, drain, and squeeze out all the moisture. Mix into the meat and knead well. Traditionally the kibbeh is pounded in a mortar until smooth. I use an electric beater with a dough hook attachment. Knead the kibbeh 10 minutes at medium speed. During the final part of the kneading, add 1 or 2 ice cubes. After the kibbeh has been thoroughly kneaded, form into 18 walnut-size balls. Set aside in a cool place.

5. To make the sauce, beat the 8 cups yogurt in a large casserole using a wooden spoon until thin and smooth. Dilute the cornstarch in a little cold water. Whisk the cornstarch and the egg into the yogurt. Slowly bring to the boil, stirring constantly.

6. Drop the dumplings and the kibbeh into the yogurt (there is enough room!) and allow to cook at the simmer for 20 to 25 minutes. Season with salt and pepper.

7. Meanwhile, for the *taklia,* sauté the garlic and the coriander or mint in melted butter for 1 minute. Stir into the yogurt mixture just before serving. Serve in a large deep serving dish with rice pilaf as an accompaniment. This dish can be served hot, tepid, or cold.

Notes: You may substitute 1½ 12-ounce packages of frozen ravioli for the home-made dumplings.

Raw kibbeh is delicious mixed with chopped fresh mint and oil as a sandwich filling.

You can prepare the kibbeh mixture in a food processor. Process until the mixture is completely smooth.

Ispanak Kavurmasi

Sautéed spinach with yogurt-garlic sauce (Turkey)

Simple, nutritious, and extremely tasty, this Turkish dip can be part of a large buffet or an accompanying dish to grilled fish or poultry.

Be sure to chop the onions until very fine; after they're sautéed and added to the spinach, they should be invisible.

SERVES 4 TO 6

- 1½ pounds fresh spinach with stems attached
  - Coarse salt
- 4 teaspoons olive oil, plus more for drizzling
- 2 large onions, peeled and finely chopped
- ½ cup water
- ½ teaspoon freshly ground black pepper
- ½ cup plain yogurt
- 1 garlic clove, peeled and crushed with salt to a purée
  - Hot Hungarian paprika

1. Wash the spinach and stems until water runs clear; drain. Cook the spinach and the stems for 10 minutes in boiling salted water; drain, refresh, drain, squeeze, and chop fine.

2. Meanwhile, heat 4 tablespoons olive oil in a 10-inch skillet and cook the onions, a pinch of salt, and ¼ cup water, covered, for 10 minutes. When the water evaporates, slowly let the onions turn golden, stirring occasionally. Add the spinach, and cook, stirring, for 2 to 3 minutes. Blend in the remaining ¼ cup water and adjust the seasoning with salt and pepper. Remove from the heat and allow to cool to room temperature.

3. In a small bowl, beat together the yogurt and the garlic. Spread the spinach on a small serving plate, smooth it, and top with the yogurt. Decorate with hot paprika and a drizzle of olive oil.

Moussaka

*Baked meat and eggplant casserole with
yogurt sauce (Greece)*

It's impossible to write a Mediterranean cookbook without including a recipe
for Greek moussaka. The yogurt sauce, from Sarah Scoville, is in my opinion the
best way to make the dish.

Be sure not to confuse Greek moussaka with the Arab dish called *musakká*.
The latter is simply a stew of squash, tomatoes, and chick-peas.

SERVES 8

    1½ pounds eggplant
        Salt
     5 tablespoons olive oil, plus more for cooking eggplant
    1½ cups minced onions
     1 teaspoon chopped garlic
     1 pound ground lean beef or lamb
    ¾   teaspoon ground cinnamon
    ¼   teaspoon ground allspice
    ½   teaspoon freshly ground black pepper, or more to taste
    ½   cup tomato purée
    ¼   cup chopped parsley
     4 medium red-skinned potatoes (about 1½ pounds)
     2 tablespoons butter
    ¾   cup grated cheese, such as kefalotyri or Parmesan
     3 eggs
     2 cups whole or low-fat plain yogurt, beaten until smooth
     1 cup milk
        Pinch of hot Hungarian paprika

1. Peel the eggplants and cut into ½-inch rounds. Soak them in salted water for
at least 30 minutes.

2. In a heavy large skillet, heat 3 tablespoons olive oil with the onions and garlic
and cook, covered, until the onions are soft, about 10 minutes. Add the meat and
cook, stirring, until nicely browned. Stir in the spices, tomato purée, ½ cup

water, parsley, and salt to taste. Cook, stirring, until you get a thick sauce, about 30 minutes.

3. Heat the broiler. Drain the eggplant slices, squeeze gently, and pat dry with paper towels. Lightly oil a baking sheet; arrange the eggplant slices on the sheet in a single layer and brush with olive oil. Broil until golden brown on both sides. Transfer to a side dish.

4. Peel the potatoes and cut into ⅛-inch rounds. Rinse and pat dry. Put the remaining 2 tablespoons oil in a large nonstick skillet, set over moderate heat, add the potatoes, and cook, tossing and turning the slices often so each becomes pliable and golden brown, about 5 minutes. Transfer to a side dish. Sprinkle with salt and pepper.

5. Use half the butter to grease a 10 by 14 by 2-inch baking dish. Cover the bottom completely with an even layer of potatoes. Spread the meat on top and arrange the eggplant over the meat. Top with an even layer of cheese.

6. Preheat oven to 375 degrees. Thoroughly beat the eggs. Slowly stir in the yogurt, milk, and season with salt, pepper, and hot paprika. Pour the sauce over the top and dot with remaining butter. Let settle about 10 minutes. Bake, uncovered, until the top is golden brown, about 45 minutes. Remove from the heat, let settle, then cut in large squares and serve.

Laban Oummo

Lamb cooked in its mother's milk (Lebanon)

This is one of those legendary Middle Eastern dishes, comparable in a way to the famous delicacy "squid cooked in its own ink." T. E. Lawrence mentions eating it in Arabia, and there are variations in other countries, too. Among the most interesting, a dish called *caldariello,* which Waverley Root found in the Apulia region of Italy. There, cut-up lamb is cooked in a fat-bellied cauldron (hence the name *caldariello*) along with olive oil, onion, parsley, wild fennel, and sheep's milk.

(continued)

Among the dishes I read about and tasted in the Mediterranean was this easy, delicious family-style recipe for lamb smothered in yogurt and flavored with garlic and fresh mint. It is a wonderful dish to serve with rice pilaf.

SERVES 4 TO 6

2 pounds boned leg of lamb, cut into 1-inch pieces
1 cup chopped onion
  Salt
  Freshly ground white pepper
1 tablespoon cornstarch
1 egg
1½ cups plain yogurt
1 tablespoon butter
2 garlic cloves, crushed to a paste with a little salt
1 tablespoon chopped fresh mint, or 1½ teaspoons crumbled dried mint
  leaves

1. Place the lamb and the onion in a heavy 4-quart casserole. Add ½ cup water, 1 teaspoon salt, and ¼ teaspoon pepper. Cook, covered, for about 1 hour, or until the meat is very tender.

2. In a saucepan, whisk the cornstarch and the egg into a little yogurt, beating until smooth. Stir in the remaining yogurt. Bring to the boil over medium heat, stirring constantly. Lower the heat and continue to cook, stirring, until the yogurt is thick and creamy. Fold in the meat, onion, and cooking juices. Continue to cook for a few minutes to blend flavors.

3. Heat the butter in a skillet and sauté the garlic and the mint for 1 minute. Stir into the yogurt mixture. Readjust the seasoning and serve very hot with rice pilaf.

CHEESE

The proverbial Mediterranean picnic (for which all of us urban Americans forever long) takes place beneath an olive tree overlooking some wondrous unspoiled lagoon, and consists of a full-bodied "honest peasant" wine, a crusty "honest peasant" loaf of bread, and, of course, a tangy hard or pungent creamy "honest peasant" cheese. It's a beautiful image that evokes our nostalgia for the sensuous life most of us crave. And sometimes, if we're lucky, we actually bring it to life.

The Mediterranean countries produce a wide range of soft fresh cheese. In North Africa, you'll often see a country-made goat's cheese, moist and formed into a cake resting on palm leaves in a basket. When you buy it, you must specify whether you want it strong or mild. It's very good with olives, or stuffed into pastry leaves and fried, and in Tunisia, where they call it *gouta,* it's actually cooked in meat stews or tagines.

The Italians make ricotta, similar to our own fresh white cheeses in texture, but with a taste all its own. They eat it fresh on bread for breakfast, and use it to stuff ravioli or in dishes like *gnocchi di spinaci.* Mascarpone is like our cream cheese mixed with sour cream and is sold in Italy in little muslin bags. It's delicious mixed with strawberries and raspberries or scooped on top of other fruits.

The Corsican broccio is much like ricotta except a bit more salty. Elizabeth David suggests it be beaten up with eggs and a little chopped wild mint and made into a flat, round, oil-fried omelet. The Corsicans mix it with raisins and use as a stuffing for guinea hen, or mix it with herbs as a stuffing for floured fried artichoke bottoms.

Looking around the Mediterranean at other soft fresh cheeses, we mustn't forget the Greek mezithra, or the yogurt-based cheeses of the Middle East (see *labni,* page 231). In Serbia and Turkey, the soft fresh cheese is kajmak. When it's young and white, its flavor is mild, but as it ages it turns pungent and becomes the color of straw.

In both Malta and Sardinia, the country people make a similar tasting soft fresh goat cheese, for which they each have their respective uses. In Sardinia they make an Easter peasant dish called *pardulas,* in which the cheese is stuffed into pastry along with sugar, lemon, eggs, and saffron, then baked and served hot covered with country heather honey. The Maltese, on the other hand, use their fresh goat's cheese in their so-called Widow's Soup, with eggs, herbs, vegetables, and broth.

Of the firmer fresh Mediterranean cheese the buffalo-milk mozzarella is probably the most famous. Excellent domestic varieties are now available, sold by Italian grocers directly from the keg. Mozzarella, when very fresh, is delicious uncooked. Try a salad of fresh mozzarella, sliced tomatoes, and fresh basil.

Greek feta runs a close second to mozzarella in terms of fame. This white, semisoft, crumbly, salty goat's milk cheese is much used in cooking and is excellent in salads or with olives. It's imported from Greece in tubs and kept moist in milk whey.

The Egyptian cow's milk cheese, domiati, is preserved in salt milk whey brine, as is the Turkish tulim, made from the milk of sheep. Tulim, though, is not sold from the tub, but from small sheepskin bags. The Spanish manchego (which I heartily recommend when well aged) is firmer than these others and splinters when cut. Another great Spanish cheese is the Asturian gamonedo, made of a mixture of cow's, sheep's and goat's milks. Smoked and blue-veined, its flavor is sharp and rich.

All the cheeses we've looked at so far fall into the fresh or perishable category. The Mediterranean has its share of fine ripened cheeses, too. The soft French banon is justifiably well-known. It's made from goat's milk, cured in brandy, and ripened in grape or chestnut leaves.

In Italy, the semisoft ripened Bel Paese is smooth and mild, delightful to eat with fruit. The Cypriot haloumi gets better and better as it ages, and can be put to good use with mint as a stuffing for ravioli.

Of the firm ripe Italian cheeses, the sausage-shaped provolone is the best known, and can be purchased either mild or sharp. But don't forget about the round caciocavallo. Both are soft and smooth when they're young and both can be steamed and eaten hot. Greek kasseri is similar in flavor and grain, and can be fried because of its high melting point.

This brings us finally to one of my favorite Mediterranean cheeses, the unsurpassable Parmesan. There are lots of imitations, and though some of them are passable, it's best to shop for the real thing. Look for the words *parmigiano reggiano* on the rind and check for the traditional straw color and moist feeling of the grain. Don't grate Parmesan until you're ready to use it.

Young Parmesan is soft and has a wonderful nutty flavor. As it ages it becomes very hard, and then it's ready for grating. True Parmesan never becomes stringy when it's cooked, which is one reason it turns up in so many recipes.

Pecorino romano and pecorino sardo are two other Italian hard-ripened cheeses. Romano is sharper than Parmesan, and more aggressive, while sardo is even more pungent. In Nuoro, the capital of Sardinia, there's a special sort of dry crumbly bread as thin as a communion wafer, called *o pan carasau*. It's dipped into warm water, then served with a sauce of eggs and grated sardo cheese. An extraordinary dish, I think, which is called *pillonca*.

In this brief summary I've not been able to mention all the Mediterranean cheeses, but I hope I've given some notion of their great variety and usefulness.

Mozzarella in Carrozza

Cheese sandwiches (Italy)

◘

This is a delicious Italian snack, the Roman version of a grilled cheese sandwich.

Another Roman specialty, popular in the old section of the city, is *crostini di mozzarella alla romana*. Slices of mozzarella cheese are placed over sliced Italian bread, then heated in the oven. A spoonful of anchovy paste is spread on top and the *crostini* are returned to the oven to bake for a couple of minutes.

SERVES 4

8 thin slices of crustless stale white bread, each 3 inches square
²⁄₃ cup milk
4 ounces mozzarella cheese (4 slices 2½ by 2½ by ¼ inch)
1 large egg, beaten
  Salt
  Freshly ground black pepper
  Bread crumbs
  Oil
  Lemon wedges

1. Dip the bread slices in milk and let drain on a wide plate.

2. Sandwich each slice of cheese between 2 bread slices, pressing down firmly around the edges so that they adhere.

3. Season the egg with salt and pepper. Dip the sandwiches in egg and coat them with bread crumbs.

4. Heat oil to the depth of ½ inch in the skillet and fry the sandwiches until golden on both sides, about 4 minutes. Drain on paper towels and serve hot with lemon wedges.

Note: Slices of prosciutto can be added to the sandwiches.

Salatit Michoteta
Cheese salad (Middle East)

Claudia Rodin describes a similar recipe in her fine book on Middle Eastern food. She recommends that it be served with *ful medames,* an Egyptian brown bean dish, available in cans from Middle Eastern shops.

MAKES 1½ CUPS, SERVING 4

  1 small cucumber
     Salt
  ½ cup (4 ounces) small-curd cottage cheese or ricotta
  ½ cup (4 ounces) crumbled feta cheese
  ¼ cup grated and drained onion
  1 tablespoon minced green pepper
  ¼ cup lemon juice
  ¼ cup olive oil
     Freshly ground black pepper
     Sprigs of fresh mint
     Sprigs of fresh dill

1. Peel the cucumber, halve lengthwise, score with the tines of a fork, sprinkle with salt, and let stand ½ hour.

2. Combine the cheeses with the grated onion, green pepper, lemon juice, and oil; mix thoroughly. Season with pepper and a little salt.

3. Drain, rinse, and cut the cucumber into small cubes. Mix into the cheese mixture. Place in a shallow serving dish and decorate with a ring of mint and dill sprigs. Let stand in a cool place 30 minutes before serving.

Spinaci con Parmigiana

Spinach with Parmesan cheese (Italy)

Here is the Florentine method for adding lightness and wonderful flavor to spinach. I learned this lovely dish from Pablo Zappi-Manzoni.

SERVES 4

1½ pounds fresh spinach
¾ cup light cream
¾ cup grated Parmesan cheese
Salt
Pinch of grated nutmeg
Freshly ground black pepper
2 egg whites

1. Trim off any spinach stems. Wash spinach thoroughly and gently squeeze to remove most of the water. Place in a saucepan and cook until tender. Drain spinach well.

2. Place spinach in a food processor. Add the cream and process for 20 seconds. Return to the saucepan and mix in the cheese. Season with salt, nutmeg, and black pepper.

3. Stiffly beat the egg whites and fold into the spinach. Cook over low heat 2 to 3 minutes. Place in a warmed serving dish and serve at once.

Sfirya
Chicken tagine with potato-cheese croquettes (Algeria)

This is an Algerian family dish, an unusual approach to a typical North African *tagine*. In Morocco, *tagines* or stews are often decorated with hard-boiled eggs, while in Tunisia they are spread with a blanket of cheese and beaten eggs. In a *sfirya*, the cheese and eggs are bound together with potatoes to make embellishing croquettes.

SERVES 6

- 1 3½-pound chicken, cut up
- 2 tablespoons clarified butter
- 2 onions, grated and drained
- ½ teaspoon ground cinnamon
- ¼ teaspoon cayenne
- 1 garlic clove, peeled and chopped
- 1 15-ounce can cooked chick-peas, drained and rinsed
  Salt
  Freshly ground black pepper

CROQUETTES

- 2 pounds potatoes, peeled and quartered
  Salt
- 2 eggs
- ⅔ cup grated Gruyère cheese
- ¼ cup grated onion
- 2 tablespoons chopped parsley
  Pinch of grated nutmeg
  Freshly ground black pepper
  Flour for dredging
  Oil for frying

1. In a casserole or heavy pan, sauté the chicken pieces in hot butter until golden brown on all sides. Add the onions, spices, and garlic. Cook, covered, 5 minutes. Add the chick-peas and 1 cup water. Season with salt and a little black pepper. Bring to the boil and cook at the simmer, covered, for 1 hour.

(continued)

2. Meanwhile, cook the potatoes in boiling salted water until tender. Drain, push through a ricer, and allow to cool. Combine with eggs, cheese, onion, parsley, nutmeg, salt, and black pepper. Form into 2-inch rounds, dust with flour, and fry in 4 to 5 tablespoons hot oil until golden brown.

3. Arrange the chicken in a deep bowl. Readjust the seasoning of the sauce and pour over the chicken. Surround with the hot cheese croquettes and serve at once.

Garides à la Turkolimano

Shrimp in tomato sauce with feta cheese (Greece)

◻

Turkolimano is an area about twenty minutes out of Athens where one is inevitably taken to eat fresh fish. There's a street along the harbor filled with seafood restaurants, some of them rather touristy, others extremely chic. (Of course they all look the same—fashionability depends on where the countesses and film stars choose to dine.) They make a big production at these places of letting you choose your own fish, but no matter what you order you receive *garides,* too.

SERVES 4

- ½ cup chopped onion
- 1½ tablespoons olive oil
- 1 garlic clove, chopped
- 2 cups fresh or canned tomato sauce, or a mixture of fresh tomato sauce, tomato paste, and water
- ¼ cup dry white wine
- ¼ cup chopped parsley
  - Salt
  - Freshly ground black pepper
  - Pinch of cayenne
- 1½ to 2 pounds raw shrimp (about 50)
- 1 cup crumbled feta cheese

1. Preheat the oven to 450 degrees.

2. In a skillet, cook the onion in olive oil until soft and golden. Add the garlic, tomato sauce, wine, half the parsley, salt, pepper, and cayenne. Cook at the simmer, uncovered, for 15 minutes, stirring often. The tomato sauce should be rather thick.

3. Meanwhile, peel and devein the shrimp. Put the shrimp, tomato sauce, and the cheese in a shallow baking dish, cover, and set in the oven to bake for 8 to 10 minutes. Sprinkle with remaining parsley and serve very hot.

Frittura di Ricotta Ruspoli
Easter ricotta cheese fritters (Italy)

These Tuscan cheese fritters are usually served along with broccoli fritters and spinach fritters.

To make a dessert variation, simply add a few ground *amaretti* (Italian macaroons).

MAKES 25

  1 cup ricotta cheese
  ½ cup all-purpose flour
2½ teaspoons double-acting baking powder
  1 egg
    Pinch of grated lemon rind
  ¼ teaspoon salt
    Pinch of freshly ground black pepper
  2 to 3 tablespoons grappa, marc de Provence, or Cognac
    Oil for frying

1. In a bowl, combine ricotta, flour, baking powder, egg, lemon rind, salt, pepper, and grappa, mixing well. Cover with a towel and let stand for 1 hour.

2. Fill the skillet to a depth of 1½ inches with oil and heat to about 375 degrees on a fat thermometer. Fry the cheese balls, one at a time, for about 30 seconds, until golden brown, being very careful to keep the temperature constant. Drain on paper towels. Serve hot or warm.

Peynirli Kabak

Zucchini stuffed with cheese (Turkey)

You can prepare parts of this refined first course the day before, but don't fill the shells until ready to set under the broiler to brown.

SERVES 8 AS A FIRST COURSE

> 4 zucchini, each about 4½ inches long
> Salt
> 1 cup feta cheese, rinsed, drained, and crumbled
> ⅓ cup grated Gruyère cheese
> 2 tablespoons flour
> 1 tablespoon chopped fresh dill
> 1 teaspoon crushed garlic
> Freshly ground black pepper
> Bread crumbs
> Butter
> 1 tablespoon paprika butter (see note)

1. Wash the zucchini. Drop into boiling salted water and cook at the simmer for 15 minutes, or until just tender. Drain and allow to cool.

2. Mix the cheeses with the flour, dill, garlic, pepper, and very little salt. Slice the zucchini in half lengthwise and scoop out the seeds. Arrange cut side up in a buttered, 9 by 12-inch ovenproof serving dish. Sprinkle the shells with pepper and very little salt. Fill with the cheese mixture. Dust lightly with bread crumbs and dot with butter. Glaze under a hot broiler until the cheese is sizzling. Dribble a tablespoon of paprika butter on top. Serve hot.

Note: To make paprika butter, melt 1½ to 2 tablespoons butter in a small saucepan. Stir in ¼ teaspoon sharp paprika. Spoon off the clear red-hued butter and discard the butter sediment and the paprika.

Figues Fraîches au Fromage

Figs and creamed cheese (France)

"The only figs worth eating in France are figs eaten while in the Midi," wrote Alexandre Dumas. Some lucky Californians have their own fig trees; the rest of us must find figs in the open market—unbruised, neither too soft nor too hard—and carry them home like the treasures they are.

SERVES 4

- 12 freshly picked black figs
- 3 tablespoons light honey
  Juice of 1 lemon
- 1 cup whipped or creamed cottage cheese
- 3 tablespoons heavy cream

1. Peel and slice the figs; put them in a shallow serving dish. Dilute the honey with lemon juice. Spoon over the figs. Let stand for 1 hour.

2. Meanwhile, sieve the cheese and beat in the cream. Serve chilled with the honeyed figs.

Note: To peel figs is not an affectation; it's preferred when they're served at the end of a meal because the skin is hard to digest.

NUTS

Imagine a Mediterranean dinner in which each course is flavored with a different kind of nut. We could begin with a thick creamy Andalusian almond soup. The main course would be *kafta snobar,* a Lebanese dish of lamb patties sprinkled with toasted pine nuts. Afterward, a walnut and fennel salad from France. And the dessert would be *bruciate briachi*—an Italian dessert of "burnt" (baked and shelled) chestnuts strewn with sugar and hot rum and flamed.

Personally I wouldn't serve such a dinner except to make the point that the people around the Mediterranean have been highly imaginative with nuts. In Corsica, they make a polenta with chestnut flour, and in Tuscany chestnut flour is combined with rosemary and pine nuts to make an interesting cake called *castagnaccio.* Israel, France, and Italy all claim the nut and raisin sauce served over boiled tongue, and the Milanaise have concocted their own version with pine nuts, cream, cinnamon, and sugar, which they pour over boiled beef.

In Turkey, cooks take sheets of strudel dough, sprinkle them with sugar and pistachios, roll them up like rugs, twist them into coils, and fry them in butter.

Almond paste, or marzipan, is used in all sorts of Mediterranean desserts and over baked fish in Morocco. And in Tunisia, there's a pine nut cream called *balweza,* which is made with toasted ground pine nuts, almonds, sugar, and milk, and perfumed with geranium-scented water.

The Spanish, in the great tradition of the Moorish empire, use almonds with fish, chicken, meats, and eggs. In *huevos a la gitanella,* the eggs are baked with a fried paste of garlic, almonds, and bread and seasoned with cumin, saffron, and nutmeg.

And while we're looking at various dishes, here's one called *le saussoun* from Escudier and Fuller's *The Wonderful Food of Provence,* acquired, they write, from the collection of the Abbé Deschamps of Roquebrune-sur-Argens. It's a spread for bread made from pounded almonds, anchovies, fennel, mint leaves, water, and oil.

The possibilities, you see, are endless, and the point, I think, is well made. Around the Mediterranean, they don't just eat nuts, serve them up as snacks, nibble them with drinks. They *cook* with them, integrate them into their cuisines, and the results can be extremely good.

I hope the recipes that follow demonstrate in highly edible terms some of the possibilities of nuts and demolish the widely held notion that nuts are for desserts.

Ajo Blanco

Chilled almond soup with green grapes (Spain)

This famous white gazpacho of Malaga is soothing and delicious. If you want to be absolutely authentic, pound the almonds in a mortar until absolutely smooth. Nowadays, the food processor and a fine sieve may be considered "gastronomically correct."

  2   garlic cloves, peeled, green shoot removed
      Coarse salt
  ½   cup shelled blanched almonds, preferably soaked in water overnight to promote creaminess
3 to 4   pieces of crustless stale Spanish or Italian-style bread, soaked in water and squeezed to extract moisture, to make ½ cup
  3   tablespoons extra-virgin olive oil
  2½   teaspoons sherry wine vinegar, or more to taste
  ½   cup green grapes, seeded, peeled, and halved

1. In a mortar, crush the garlic and ¾ teaspoon salt to a purée.

2. Place the almonds, puréed garlic, ⅓ cup water, and the squeezed bread in a blender or food processor. Purée until smooth, adding a little extra water, if necessary. With the machine running, slowly add the oil in a steady stream. Pour into a bowl; whisk in the wine vinegar, gradually adding 2 to 2½ cups cold water. Readjust the seasoning. Pour into soup bowls, garnish with green grapes, and serve chilled.

Djej bil Looz (Tarfaya)

Chicken with almonds (Morocco)

◻

In Morocco, there are two ways to combine chicken with almonds. In one, called *kdra touimyia,* the almonds are boiled in stock for a long time until they're buttery soft. In this version, they're fried in oil until crunchy and golden brown, then sprinkled on top of the prepared chicken just before the dish is served.

SERVES 4

- 1 3½-pound chicken, quartered
- 4 garlic cloves, peeled
- 2 tablespoons chopped parsley
- Salt
- Olive oil
- ⅛ teaspoon pulverized saffron
- ½ teaspoon freshly ground black pepper
- 1 cup chopped onion
- ¾ cup whole blanched almonds
- 4 hard-boiled eggs

1. Rinse the chicken well, then pat dry with paper towels. In a mortar, combine the garlic, parsley, and salt, pounding to a paste. Moisten with 2 tablespoons olive oil and add saffron and pepper. Rub this mixture into the flesh of the chicken. Cover and refrigerate overnight.

2. Heat ¼ cup oil in a 3½-quart casserole and cook the onion until soft and golden. Add the chicken. Sauté slowly until golden brown on both sides. Add 1 cup water and bring to a boil. Cover and simmer gently for 45 minutes. Turn and baste the chicken quarters often. (You may need to add water during the cooking.)

3. In a skillet, fry the almonds in 1 tablespoon oil until golden brown. Drain on paper towels.

4. To serve, cover the chicken with almonds, decorate with halved hard-boiled eggs, and serve hot.

Gambas à la Menorquina

Shrimp in tomato sauce with almonds and pine nuts (Spain)

SERVES 3 TO 4

- 1/3 cup olive oil
- 1 cup chopped onion
- 3 cups fresh or canned tomatoes, peeled, seeded, and chopped
- 1/2 cup ground blanched almonds
- 1/3 cup pine nuts
- 4 garlic cloves, peeled and chopped
- 2 tablespoons chopped parsley
- 1/4 teaspoon cayenne, or more to taste
  Salt
- 2 cups shelled cooked small shrimp
- 2 cups boiled rice

1. Heat the oil in a skillet and cook the onion until soft and golden. Add the tomatoes. Cook, uncovered, for 15 to 20 minutes, stirring often.

2. In a blender, grind the almonds, pine nuts, garlic, parsley, and 3 tablespoons water to a paste. Stir into the tomato sauce. Cook, stirring, 5 minutes. If the sauce is very thick, thin with 3/4 to 1 cup water. Season with cayenne and salt.

3. Fold in the shrimp. Allow to heat through. Serve on a bed of boiled rice.

Note: Small fresh fish such as whitings of fresh fillets of fish can be covered with the above sauce and baked in a 325-degree oven for 20 to 30 minutes.

Salsa Romesco

Almond and hot pepper sauce from Tarragona (Spain)

◻

This strong, rich, spicy sauce uses the romesco pepper, a burnished, fleshy, aromatic dried pepper rarely available—even in Catalonia, where it is grown. Most Catalan cooks settle for the less expensive and milder *nyora*, which is similar to the Mexican *cascabel*, with the same wonderful nutty, woody flavor. See "Mail-Order Sources" (pages 296–97) on where to find *cascabel* chili peppers.

This sauce is delicious on broiled and poached fish, hot or cold shellfish, and broiled meat. It's also very good spread on grilled bread.

With thanks to Rosa Grace of the Florio Restaurant in Barcelona.

MAKES ABOUT 1³⁄₄ CUPS

   2 medium onions
     Olive oil
   3 medium red-ripe tomatoes
   1 whole head garlic, unpeeled but broken into cloves
   2 dried *cascabel* peppers
   1 dried hot red chili pepper
   1 cup red wine vinegar
   3 dozen shelled whole almonds
     Sea salt

1. Preheat the oven to 450 degrees.

2. Make six lengthwise cuts through each onion from the top downward toward the root. (The onion will open like a chrysanthemum.) Arrange on a lightly oiled baking pan. Add the tomatoes and garlic cloves and sprinkle with olive oil. Roast until tomatoes and garlic are well browned but not burned, about 1 hour.

3. Meanwhile, place the *cascabel* peppers, the dried pepper, and the vinegar in a noncorrosive pan. Slowly boil down to 1½ tablespoons.

4. Remove the tomatoes and garlic from the baking pan; peel and seed the tomato and peel the garlic. Add the chili peppers and vinegar to the onions; stir once and continue roasting until onions are soft and browned, about 30 minutes.

5. Blanch the almonds and slip off their skins. Toast on a small baking sheet in the oven until golden brown. Crush to a smooth paste in a mortar. Place the

almonds in the workbowl of a food processor, add the seeded tomato and peeled garlic, and process until smooth. Add the peppers, onions, baking pan juices, and a little salt and process to blend, about 30 seconds. Press through the fine blade of a food mill. Let the sauce stand at room temperature for a few hours before serving to allow the flavors to ripen.

Pita Sa Orasima
Walnut and raisin pie (Serbia)

This dessert is made two to three days in advance of serving because it improves with age. Covered, it will keep up to a week at room temperature; do not refrigerate.

SERVES 10

- ½ cup yellow raisins
- ¼ cup *slivovitz* (plum brandy)
- 9 ounces walnuts (about 2¼ cups)
- ¼ cup plus 2 tablespoons sugar
- 1 teaspoon ground cinnamon
- 1 teaspoon grated lemon rind
- ½ pound phyllo pastry leaves
- 3 tablespoons vegetable oil, mixed with 3 tablespoons clarified butter

SUGAR SYRUP
- ¾ cup sugar
- ½ cup water
- 1 teaspoon lemon juice

1. Preheat the oven to 350 degrees.

2. Soak raisins in slivovitz until plump. In the workbowl of a food processor, grind the walnuts with raisins and ¼ cup sugar. Add remaining sugar, cinnamon, and lemon rind and process until well blended and almost smooth.

3. Oil a 9 by 13-inch baking pan. Line with half the phyllo, trimming edges to fit. Brush or sprinkle each leaf as you stack them with oil mixture.

(continued)

4. Spread the prepared nuts evenly over the pastry leaves. Cover with the remaining leaves, drizzling each with oil mixture, brushing the top leaf lavishly. With a very sharp knife, score the pie with crisscrossing lines to form the traditional diamond pattern, or cut into squares. Dip the fingers of one hand in water and shake the water over one half the surface. Repeat once more over the other half. Bake on middle oven shelf until golden brown, about 45 minutes.

5. While the pita is baking, make the sugar syrup. Combine sugar, water, and lemon juice in a saucepan; heat over medium-high heat to boiling. Boil 5 minutes, then remove from heat.

6. Remove the pita from the oven. Repeat cutting through all layers into squares, pour the warm syrup all over the pie, and return to the oven to bake 5 minutes. Allow pie to cool to room temperature.

7. Remove pieces from the baking pan. Allow the pieces to dry out on a parchment-lined baking sheet for one to two days before serving, protected by a cheesecloth tent folded around and over the pieces.

Acelgas con Piñones

Swiss chard with pine nuts (Spain)

SERVES 4

    2 pounds fresh Swiss chard, tender young beet tops, or spinach
    4 thick slices of bacon, diced
    2 tablespoons olive oil
    1 garlic clove, peeled and crushed
    ½ cup pine nuts
    2 tablespoons yellow raisins, plumped in hot water
      Freshly ground black pepper
      Salt

1. Remove the chard leaves from the stalks. Wash the leaves in two or three changes of cold water. Discard the stalks and any wilted or tough leaves. Place in an enameled or stainless steel saucepan; cover and cook, stirring once or twice, over medium heat until tender. Drain and chop roughly.

2. Sauté the bacon until crisp in a skillet. Pour off almost all the fat. Add the olive oil and garlic clove and cook 1 minute. Discard the garlic clove. Add the pine nuts and sauté briefly. Add the Swiss chard and the raisins and toss well. Season with pepper and a little salt. Serve hot.

Pouding au Nougat
Nougat pudding with chocolate sauce (France)

The best nougat is made with honey, sweet almonds, and egg whites.

SERVES 6

  ½ pound nougat
  2 cups milk
  ½ vanilla bean, or 1 teaspoon vanilla extract
  6 eggs
     Pinch of salt
  ½ cup sugar

CHOCOLATE SAUCE

  4 squares sweet cooking chocolate
  ½ cup water
  2 tablespoons unsalted butter
  1 teaspoon vanilla extract
  2 to 3 tablespoons heavy cream

1. To be prepared one day in advance of serving: Finely grind the nougat in the blender. Pour into a mixing bowl. Heat the milk in the saucepan with the vanilla bean; allow to steep for 10 minutes. Remove the vanilla bean and pour the milk over the nougat.

2. Preheat the oven to 350 degrees.

3. In another mixing bowl, beat the eggs with the salt. Gradually add the sugar, beating well. Beat until pale yellow and thick. Stir in the nougat. Pour into a buttered 1½-quart mold. Place in a pan of hot water and set in the oven to bake for 1 hour, or until a knife inserted comes out clean. Allow to cool completely, then refrigerate overnight.

(continued)

4. To make the chocolate sauce, melt the chocolate with the water in a small saucepan. Add the butter and the vanilla. Stir over gentle heat until the butter is melted. Stir in the cream. Keep warm until ready to serve. Makes about 1 cup sauce.

5. Just before serving, unmold onto a shallow serving dish. Pass the sauce separately.

Croquets de Languedoc

Hazelnut crisps from Languedoc (France)

The secret to the crispness of these lovely light cookies is not to overwork the batter after the flour is in.

MAKES 45 CRISPS

    5 tablespoons unsalted butter, softened
    1 cup sugar
    ½ cup egg whites (about 4 egg whites)
    ¾ cup ground hazelnuts
    2 teaspoons grated orange rind
    ⅔ cup cake flour

1. Preheat the oven to 425 degrees. Butter 3 baking sheets.

2. Place the butter and the sugar in a mixing bowl; beat until creamy. Beat in the egg whites. Fold in the ground nuts and the grated orange rind. Using a rubber spatula, gently stir in the flour 2 tablespoons at a time. Drop small rounds of batter onto the greased baking sheets, leaving 3 inches between each round. Using a knife dipped in cold water, flatten each into a thin oval shape. Bake until the edges are golden brown—about 10 minutes.

3. Use a spatula to detach the crisps and allow to cool on wire racks. Store in an airtight tin.

Soufflé Dolce di Amaretti

Almond macaroon soufflé (Italy)

Here's a good soufflé using the famous Italian *amaretti di Saronno,* vanilla-flavored almond macaroons. It's flavored, too, with Amaretto, liqueur distilled from bitter almonds.

This soufflé is delicious with hot chocolate sauce.

SERVES 4

    3   tablespoons all-purpose flour
    ¾   cup milk
    ½   cup sugar
    4   egg yolks
    ⅓   cup crumbled Italian almond macaroons
    ½   teaspoon vanilla extract
    2   tablespoons Amaretto or Noyau de Poissy
    6   egg whites
        Pinch of salt
        Confectioners' sugar

1. In a heavy saucepan, beat the flour with 3 tablespoons milk until smooth. Beat in remaining milk and sugar. Cook, stirring, until the mixture boils. Beat vigorously over medium heat until thick and smooth. Allow to cool.

2. Beat in the egg yolks, one by one. Then add the macaroons, the vanilla extract, and the liqueur.

3. Preheat the oven to 400 degrees. Butter and sugar a 6-cup soufflé dish.

4. Stiffly beat the egg whites with a pinch of salt. Stir a quarter of the beaten whites into the base to lighten it, then fold in the remaining whites. Transfer to the prepared dish and bake 30 to 35 minutes. After 10 minutes, lower the oven heat to 350 degrees. Remove when puffy and golden brown, about 20 minutes longer. Dust with confectioners' sugar and serve at once.

Karidopitta

Honey walnut cake (Greece)

The Greeks make all sorts of wonderful cakes with nuts—*kadaif, baklava,* and this *karidopitta,* which is very easy and *very* sweet.

SERVES 8

- 1¼ cups sugar
- ¾ cup honey
- 1¼ teaspoons ground cinnamon
- Juice of ½ lemon
- 1¾ cups chopped walnuts
- 1½ cups all-purpose flour, sifted
- 1 teaspoon double-acting baking powder
- 4 tablespoons unsalted butter, softened to room temperature
- 4 eggs, separated

1. To make the syrup, cook ¾ cup sugar and ¾ cup water in a small saucepan, stirring. Bring to the boil. Simmer 5 minutes. Stir in the honey, ¼ teaspoon ground cinnamon, and the juice of ½ lemon. Cook at the simmer 5 minutes longer. Allow to cool completely.

2. Preheat the oven to 350 degrees. Butter an 8- or 9-inch square baking pan.

3. Combine ¼ cups walnuts, remaining cinnamon, the flour, and the baking powder. Set aside.

4. Cream remaining ½ cup sugar with butter until light and fluffy. Add egg yolks, one at a time, beating well after each addition. Beat in the walnut mixture. Separately beat the egg whites until stiff. Gently fold the egg whites into the walnut mixture. Put the mixture into the prepared pan. Sprinkle the top with the remaining ½ cup chopped walnuts. Set in the oven to bake until the cake tests done.

5. Remove the cake from the oven. Cut into diamond shapes in the cake pan. Pour cool syrup over the hot cake. Cover and allow to stand overnight before serving.

Lemons, Oranges, Figs, Dates, and Other Mediterranean Fruits

There was a mini-orchard in my garden in Tangier, which I thought of as a microcosm of the Mediterranean cornucopia of fruits. There were five old grape vines growing along a stone wall, and then in clearings down a dozen grassy walks, quince trees, pears, apricots, sweet and bitter oranges, lemons, pomegranates, and figs. There were a pair of old granddaddy palms bearing dates, but because of the climate the dates didn't ripen. The same with the banana trees, though my mulberry tree exploded, and each fall I ruthlessly cut it back. I planted strawberries beside a field of daylilies, and I had an old tree that produced loquats. And the cactus along the bottom of the garden rendered prickly pears, or "barbary figs" as we called them in Morocco.

There were many gardens in Tangier like mine—there was nothing exceptional about an orchard. We didn't have tangerines, which amused us, because that's what we called ourselves, and of course we didn't have the fruit trees that need chill: apples, cherries, peaches, and plums. We didn't have grapefruit, either, though they grow well farther south.

Fresh fruits, I think, make the best dessert to follow a Mediterranean meal. Like vegetables they appeared in the markets only in their seasons—just as we tired of clementines the first strawberries came in. Wagonloads of oranges flooded the streets; great pyramids of lemons were erected beside market stalls. Mediterranean life is a festival of fresh fruit, and in the regions of the orchards it's impossible to starve.

We made sherbets of fruits and wonderful preserves, and we also cooked with them. Not only desserts, but soups, fish, poultry, and stews. Moroccan shad stuffed with dates, Middle Eastern lamb and raisin pies, Greek *avgolemono* soup, French *épaule d'agneau à l'orange,* and sangría, the Spanish national drink—they are all based on fruit, as are hundreds of other dishes.

LEMONS

==

Lemons are a big crop in North Africa, Italy, and Spain. I'll never forget walking through the lemon groves that cover the slopes of Mt. Etna and breathing in the tart fragrance of huge ripe lemons weighing down the boughs.

Lemons are used so widely that they are inevitably associated with Mediterranean cuisine. I've even seen their leaves put to use in Positano, where they're used to pack raisins in crates. Lemon juice is used in place of vinegar in dressings and sauces, and with oil as a Levantine sauce for fish. If your lemons don't seem particularly juicy, let them sit in warm water for a while before squeezing them. You may get more out of them that way, but some lemons give very little no matter what you do. I had that problem just before Ramadan in Tangier—lemons are an indispensable ingredient in *harira* soup, which North Africans use to break the fast, and someone always cornered the market on the juicy ones just before the start of holy month.

The Greeks use lemon slices as a bed for fish before putting them in the oven to bake. In Israel, there's a liver ragout flavored with garlic and lemon, and in Italy, lemon makes a famous veal scaloppine sauce. In Campania, a little lemon peel is used in the meatball mixture called *polpette,* and candied lemon peel is added to sweets and to sauces for game. In Tunisia, bits of peel are often sprinkled over freshly grilled meat, and throughout North Africa preserved or pickled lemons are an important ingredient in *tagines*.

There are numerous lemon ices, lemon-flavored rice puddings, and lemon ice cream desserts, not to mention lemon-flavored preserves, *confits,* and candies. In the Balearic Islands they serve a lovely lemony dessert called *pastel de grachonera de Ibiza,* made of egg yolks, lemon, and milk, and thickened with *ensaimades*—a lard-flavored spiral-shaped roll.

Limoun Marakad

Preserved lemons (Morocco)

Preserved lemons are a necessity if you want to make North African food. They're used in salads, chicken, and olive dishes, and many other things, including the recipe for the artichoke salad that follows. The green olives of Tunisia are often packed in jars with wedges of preserved lemons, and in my opinion this makes them among the most delicious green olives in the world.

It's possible that a white lacy growth will appear in your pickling jar as the lemons mature on your shelf. Don't worry about it—simply discard it when you open the jar and rinse the lemons before use.

> 2 ripe lemons
> 1/3 cup coarse sea salt
> 1/2 cup fresh lemon juice

Scrub the lemons and dry well. Cut each into 8 wedges. Toss them with the salt and place in a 1/2-pint glass jar with a glass or plastic-coated lid. Pour in the lemon juice. Close the jar tightly and let the lemons ripen at room temperature for 7 days, shaking the jar each day to distribute the salt and juice. To store, add olive oil to cover and refrigerate for up to 6 months. Rinse lemons before using.

Slatit Gannariya

Artichoke and preserved lemon salad (Tunisia)

The contrast of thinly sliced, slightly bitter raw artichoke bottoms and tangy preserved lemons is refreshing.

You need to make the preserved lemons about a week ahead, but they keep well in the refrigerator and are delicious in all sorts of salads, baked along with small fish, or slipped into a simple chicken stew.

SERVES 4

2 large artichokes
¼ teaspoon harissa (pages 200–201), diluted in 1 teaspoon water
3 tablespoons extra-virgin olive oil
2 tablespoons fresh lemon juice
¼ preserved lemon (page 268)
4 teaspoons capers, rinsed and drained
¼ teaspoon freshly ground black pepper
   Sea salt
   Chopped fresh coriander

1. Break off artichoke stems and thick leaves. With a thin-bladed very sharp knife, shave the bottom of the artichoke in order to trim off all the thick green exterior. The knife should cut off just the leaf, leaving the fleshy part attached to the artichoke bottom. Scrape all around the artichoke until the bottom is smooth and only the pale green cone remains on top. Cut the artichoke in half and remove choke and tender leaves. Drop prepared artichokes into a bowl of acidulated water to prevent discoloration. They can be stored in the refrigerator up to 2 hours, covered.

2. In a small bowl, combine the diluted harissa, olive oil, and lemon juice, mixing until well combined. Rinse the preserved lemon quarter under running water, removing and discarding the pulp. Mince the peel and reserve 1½ teaspoons.

3. About 20 minutes before serving, slice the artichoke bottoms as thin as for potato chips. Mix into the prepared harissa dressing. Spread out on a flat serving dish, sprinkle with preserved lemon, capers, and black pepper and let stand 10 to 15 minutes. Taste for salt. Sprinkle with chopped coriander and serve.

Koustilyat Michwi
Grilled lamb chops (Tunisia)

SERVES 4

8 rib lamb chops, each about 1½ inches thick
Salt
Freshly ground black pepper
3 to 4 tablespoons olive oil
2 teaspoons finely chopped lemon peel
½ cup finely chopped onion
2 tablespoons chopped parsley
2 to 3 tablespoons freshly squeezed lemon juice

1. Heat charcoal in an outdoor grill or heat the broiler.

2. Trim the lamb chops to remove excess fat. Sprinkle with salt and pepper and brush with oil. Arrange chops over the coals on an oiled rack. After 4 minutes, turn. Avoid overcooking the meat. Arrange the chops on a large serving dish. Scatter chopped lemon peel, onion, and parsley over them and sprinkle with lemon juice. Serve at once.

Dolmadakia me Avgolemono

Stuffed grape leaves with lemon and egg sauce (Greece)

SERVES 6 AS A MAIN DISH

1 cup finely chopped onion
3/4 pound ground lamb
1 1/2 tablespoons olive oil
1/2 teaspoon salt
2 pinches of freshly ground black pepper
1/2 cup raw rice
1/2 teaspoon dried mint leaves, crumbled to a powder between fingertips
1/2 tablespoon finely chopped parsley
1 8-ounce jar grape vine leaves in brine
1 cup rich beef stock, or more
2 egg yolks
2 tablespoons lemon juice

1. Cook the onion and the lamb in oil in a large skillet for 5 minutes, stirring. Sprinkle with salt and pepper, then stir in the rice. Cook, stirring, for 5 minutes over gentle heat. Add 1/2 cup water and continue cooking until the water is completely absorbed by the rice. Add the herbs and toss gently to mix well. Set aside to cool.

2. Rinse the grape leaves under cold running water, carefully separating each leaf. Place the leaves shiny side down, a few at a time, on a flat work surface. Fill each in the following manner: Put 1 heaping tablespoon filling on each grape leaf near the base. Starting at the base, fold bottom of leaf over filling. Fold sides over filling to center. Roll tightly toward the tip of the leaf.

3. In a heavy 3-quart saucepan, arrange rolls in layers, scattering a few torn grape leaves between each layer. When all the rolls are in the saucepan, add enough beef stock to cover them. Weight them down using a heavy plate, just large enough to fit inside, on top of the rolls. Bring to the boil, cover saucepan, and cook over very low heat for 1 hour. Add additional stock if needed. Remove from heat and let rest, uncovered, for 10 minutes.

4. In a small saucepan, whisk the egg yolks until thickened. Gradually beat in the lemon juice, then one cup of the hot cooking juices. Heat gently until mixture coats a spoon and thickens slightly, about 2 minutes. Do not allow the mixture to boil. Transfer the stuffed grape leaves to a warm serving dish and spoon over the sauce. Serve at once.

Perdices Escabechadas
Marinated partridges in piquant jelly (Spain)

SERVES 4

2 1-pound partridges, ready to cook
Salt
Freshly ground black pepper
¼ cup olive oil
3 whole garlic cloves, peeled
⅓ cup wine vinegar
2 cups dry white wine
10 whole black peppercorns
2 to 3 parsley sprigs
2 bay leaves
1 thyme sprig
Pinch of sharp paprika
6 thin slices of lemon
4 thin slices of orange
8 very thin slices of orange

1. The day before you plan to serve, split the partridges in half, rinse, and wipe dry with a cloth. Rub all over with salt and black pepper. In a 5-quart casserole, lightly brown the partridges in heated oil on both sides. Add the garlic cloves and gently fry for 1 minute, without browning. Combine vinegar, wine, spices, herbs, lemon slices, and 4 orange slices and pour over the birds. Bring to a boil, reduce the heat to the simmer, closely cover the casserole, and cook for 45 minutes, or until the partridges are tender.

2. Let the partridges cool in the liquid, then refrigerate until ready to serve. Remove cooked orange and lemon slices and replace with fresh thin slices of orange.

Barbounia Ladolemono
Red mullets with lemon oil dressing (Greece)

This is a superb way to serve broiled small fish. It's popular in Greece, Turkey, and throughout the Middle East.

SERVES 4

 2 1½-pound fish suitable for charcoal broiling, such as red mullets, small
bass, mackerel, porgies, or bluefish, split and cleaned, boned or left
whole
Salt
Freshly ground black pepper
 ⅓ cup olive oil
 3 tablespoons freshly squeezed lemon juice
 2 good pinches of dried oregano, finely crumbled between fingertips just
before using

1. Heat charcoal in an outdoor barbecue or heat the broiler.

2. Sprinkle the fish inside and out with salt and black pepper, then rub all over with a little olive oil.

3. Combine remaining oil, lemon juice, and oregano in a small bowl. Place the fish on an oiled grid over hot coals. Brush with the prepared oil dressing and let cook, without turning, about 5 minutes. Turn and baste the fish.

4. Turn the fish onto a serving dish, pour over the remaining oil dressing, and serve at once.

ORANGES

There were always bitter orange trees in Morocco, and the Moors brought them to Europe, but it took the Portuguese to import the sweet oranges they found in India and China.

Bitter oranges, or *bigarades,* or Seville oranges as we call them, are the basis for the best orange marmalade. You can find them in the middle of winter in Latino markets. The original duck *à l'orange* was first made with them in southern Spain, where chocolate was also an ingredient. The dish spread to Languedoc, where it was refined and the chocolate omitted, but bitter oranges remained the foundation of the sauce. Finally when the *bigarade* was not available, the good cooks of Paris changed the recipe and used vinegar to make sweet oranges tart.

Elizabeth David counsels that one of the best ways to use bitter oranges is in a tomato sauce as they do in southwestern France. A thick garlic-flavored tomato sauce is made, and then a handful of peeled *bigarade* pulp is added and cooked down. The sauce is used with broiled chicken or eggs.

Peel of *bigarade* is absolutely *de rigueur* in Provençal daubes, and in Perpignan they make *perdreaux à la Catalane*—partridge in orange and wine sauce.

In Spain, pollock is served with an orange sauce, and in Murcia they bake hake with slices of orange and cinnamon.

In Turkey, there is a salad of orange slices, black olives, and tiny sweet onions served in a dressing of lemon juice and olive oil. The Turks call it "the Emir's pearls" because of the colors of the dish.

Orange juice is used to flavor cookies, cakes, glazed fruits, berries, and soufflés. In Provence, Lebanon, and North Africa, orange petals are distilled to make orange flower water used to flavor all sorts of sweets, as well as Moroccan salads and *tagines*.

In Tunisia, cooks have a unique way of making *sole meunière*. Because wine can't be used in cooking on account of Koranic law, they use the juice of Seville oranges to glaze the pan drippings for the sauce.

Remojón

*Salad of oranges, salt cod, and a splash
of spring water (Spain)*

"The secret ingredient in this cooking," confided Pablo Amate, a well-known Spanish food writer, "is simply . . . the water."

We were sitting on the top floor of a restaurant in old Granada. Amate, a dark, handsome, passionate man in his forties, passed me a bottle of water from a spring high in the Sierra Nevada.

"All the food you're eating and admiring here was cooked in this water. You won't find the same dishes prepared as well in Seville or Cordoba, where they cook with water that tastes flat, that has no soul."

Well, I count myself second to none in my eagerness to make food with soul, but with all due respect to Pablo, I've decided not to worry too much about obtaining Granada spring water for this salad—I use bottled water instead.

Although the salad was originally made with either salt cod or bread flavored with the bitter orange from Seville, onion, olive oil, and garlic, I offer a somewhat more elaborate modern version using navel oranges, with the addition of sherry wine vinegar, cubed tomatoes, juicy black olives, and a pinch of hot paprika.

This dish is often touted as "Mozarab" (the cooking of the Spanish Christians who lived under Arab rule), but salt cod did not come into use in southern Spain until after the withdrawal of the Moors. A true "mozarab" version would probably be the one using bread. The word *remojón* means a sudden splash of water—in this case after the salad has been well tossed. The dish turns into a soupy dip.

The salt cod is placed under a broiler for a few minutes before soaking to make it easier to shred into plump little strips. Please note that salt cod is not cooked, but is cured and ready to eat. (This is similar to the South American dish *seviche,* where fish "cooks" in the marinade.)

(continued)

    2/3 pound salt cod
    4 small navel oranges or tangelos
    3 tablespoons chopped white scallion
    2 tablespoons extra-virgin olive oil
    2 tablespoons peeled, seeded, and cubed tomato
    1 tablespoon sherry wine vinegar
    1 garlic clove, minced
       Pinch of crushed black pepper
       Pinch of dried red pepper flakes
    1/4 cup bottled spring water
    6 juicy black olives, pitted

1. Set the dry salt cod, skin side down, under a heated broiler and allow the flesh to soften and lightly brown, about 3 minutes. Cool and soak in several changes of cold water for a few hours or overnight.

2. Drain well and remove the skin and bones. Tear the cod with your fingers into small pieces, shredding one piece at a time, pulling and tearing the cod into small plump strips. Do *not* use a knife. (Makes about 1 1/3 cups.) Place the strips in a colander under running water, and when they no longer taste salty, press out all moisture. Set aside.

3. Using a sharp knife, remove the skin and white pith from the oranges and discard. Cut the segments away from their surrounding membranes and reserve slices. Toss the cod strips with oranges, scallions, olive oil, tomatoes, vinegar, garlic, and both peppers. Refrigerate, covered, for at least 1 hour.

4. Just before serving, adjust the seasonings; add more vinegar if the oranges are too sweet and season with pepper and salt. Sprinkle with spring water and stir well. Decorate with olives and pass slices of crusty bread.

Vin d'Orange de Colette
Orange-flavored wine (France)

This recipe, adapted from Bifrous' *200 Recettes secretes de la cuisine française,* was devised by the French writer Colette, who was a very good cook.

    2 pounds oranges, quartered
    1 bottle dry white wine, preferably from Burgundy
    1 cup sugar
    2 to 3 tablespoons good Cognac or *eau de vie*

1. Pack orange quarters into a jug or pitcher. Pour in the wine, cover, and set in a shady cool place for 1 week.

2. Strain into a saucepan, add the sugar, and stir over low heat until the sugar is completely dissolved. Cool. Stir in the Cognac. Pour into a clean wine bottle, recork, and let stand 1 week in a cool dark place. Chill well before serving.

Oaf Tapuzim
Chicken with oranges (Israel)

SERVES 4

    1 3-pound chicken, quartered
    4 teaspoons sharp mustard
       Salt
       Freshly ground black pepper
    2 tablespoons olive oil
    ½ onion, finely chopped
    1 cup orange juice
    ¼ cup brown sugar

1. Preheat the oven to 375 degrees.

2. Smear the chicken quarters with mustard and sprinkle with salt and pepper. Place the quarters skin side down in one layer in a baking pan. Add olive oil,

(continued)

onion, and orange juice. Set in the oven to roast, basting often with the pan juices, for 20 minutes.

3. Turn the chicken quarters over, skin side up, add the sugar, and continue roasting and basting until the chicken is tender and golden brown.

4. Pour the pan juices into a saucepan. By way of boiling, reduce to a thick sauce, stirring. Spoon part of the sauce over the chicken. Serve hot and pass the remaining sauce in a sauceboat.

Épaule d'Agneau à l'Orange
Lamb stew with oranges (France)

This dish is from the southeast of France. The bouquet garni includes a dried orange peel, which is typical of the region. To properly dry orange peel, peel off the zest of the orange and let dry for three days in an airy place.

SERVES 4

4   ounces lean salt pork, blanched, refreshed, drained, and cut into large
        dice (½ cup)
2   tablespoons olive oil
2   small onions, quartered
2   carrots, cut into 1-inch pieces
2   pounds lean shoulder of lamb, cut into 1½-inch chunks
        Flour
1   cup dry white wine
1   cup beef stock or water
        Bouquet garni: 1 bay leaf, a few parsley sprigs, thyme leaves, a few celery
            leaves, and a 2 by 1-inch piece of dried orange peel, tied together
            with thread
1   tablespoon finely chopped garlic
        Salt
        Freshly ground black pepper
2   teaspoons sugar
2   to 3 tablespoons freshly squeezed juice of a bitter orange, or substitute
        orange juice mixed with 1 tablespoon lemon juice (see note)

Cayenne (optional)
8 peeled orange sections, preferably from bitter oranges
Chopped parsley

1. In a deep heavy skillet or casserole, lightly brown the salt pork in the olive oil. Add the onions and carrots and cook, stirring, until golden brown and soft, about 15 minutes. Set aside the salt pork and vegetables.

2. Brown the meat in the same skillet on all sides. Sprinkle with flour and allow to brown nicely, turning the pieces of meat often. Add the wine and bring to the boil, stirring. Reduce the heat, add the beef stock, bouquet garni, and garlic. Return the vegetables and the salt pork to the skillet. Season the cooking liquid with salt and pepper. Cover tightly and simmer over low heat for 1 hour.

3. After the first hour's cooking, lightly caramelize the sugar in a small saucepan. Stir in the orange juice and one quarter of the cooking liquid, mixing well. Add to the skillet and continue cooking, covered, an additional 45 minutes, or until the lamb is tender.

4. Transfer the lamb to a side dish, cover, and keep warm. Strain the cooking liquid into a saucepan, pressing down with a pestle on the vegetables to extract all their juices. Bring to the boil, reduce the heat, and simmer 15 minutes. Skim off all the fat that rises to the surface of the sauce. Correct the seasoning. Add the meat to the sauce. Add cayenne, if desired. Simmer a few minutes to blend flavors. Add the peeled orange sections and allow to heat through. Serve hot, dusted with freshly chopped parsley. Serve with rice pilaf.

Note: Bitter oranges are available in early February.

Lomo de Cerdo al Estilo de Ibiza

Roast pork with oranges (Spain)

SERVES 8

- 4 pounds pork loin
- 1 cup freshly squeezed orange juice
  Salt
- 3 tablespoons sugar
- 1 onion, quartered
- 1 bay leaf, crumbled
- 1 teaspoon chopped garlic
- ¼ teaspoon dried thyme
- 2 oranges, thinly sliced
- 2 apples, cored and thinly sliced
- 2 tablespoons butter
  Freshly ground black pepper

1. The day before you plan to serve, place the pork loin in a bowl. Combine the orange juice, ½ teaspoon salt, 2 tablespoons sugar, onion, and bay leaf. Pour over the meat, cover, and refrigerate for at least 12 hours, turning the meat once or twice.

2. Preheat the oven to 450 degrees.

3. Lift, drain, and wipe dry the meat, reserving the marinade. Rub the meat with a mixture of salt, garlic, and thyme. Place the roast fat side up in a roasting pan and set in oven. After 20 minutes, turn the oven heat down to 350. Baste often with the fat in the pan. After the first hour, drain the fat from the pan. Add the marinade, strained, and continue basting the meat every 10 minutes. The total roasting time is about 2½ hours.

4. Just before the end of the roasting time, sauté the orange and apple slices in butter in a small skillet. Sprinkle with the remaining tablespoon sugar and cook until nicely glazed.

5. When the meat is cooked, remove and keep warm. Carefully skim off any fat from the pan. Boil down the remaining pan juices. Correct the seasoning with salt and pepper.

6. Place the meat, sliced, on a heated serving dish with alternating slices of orange and apple down each side. Pour the pan juices over the meat and serve at once.

Torchi

Turnip wafers with citrus marinade (Tunisia)

Most pickled vegetables take time to make and are put up for the season. This quick pickle, called a *torchi*, is made weekly and is a staple in most Tunisian homes. Raw thin-sliced turnips tossed with tangy citrus juices go well with all the spicy and robust dishes typical of Tunisian cuisine. Quality is important here, since the taste relies almost totally on the freshness and tenderness of the purple-topped turnip.

SERVES 4 TO 6

> 4 tender small turnips, about ¾ pound, peeled
> 8 small fresh red radishes, stemmed and well washed
> 1 teaspoon fine salt
> Juice of ½ lemon
> ½ grapefruit, peeled and cubed
> 1 teaspoon extra-virgin olive oil
> ½ teaspoon dried red pepper flakes

1. Cut the turnips in half. Slice them wafer-thin, preferably with a food processor fitted with a 1-mm slicing disk or with a mandoline. Slice the radishes as thin as possible, by hand or in the food processor with the slicing disk. In a shallow bowl, combine the turnips, radishes, salt, lemon juice, and grapefruit cubes. Cover and chill.

2. Just before serving, drain off all liquid. Spread out on a flat serving dish and sprinkle with olive oil and red pepper flakes.

FIGS

In the Casbah of Tangier, there's an old fig tree in the courtyard of a house that was once the home of Samuel Pepys. It's now owned by an elderly British gentleman who is accosted every summer by the women of his neighborhood just as the figs on his tree become ripe. They want the fruit because they think it will increase their fertility. The Englishman graciously complies.

Whether or not figs of old fig trees can perform miracles in marital beds, they are unquestionably a wondrous fruit. They're grown all over the Mediterranean region and used in a great variety of ways.

Italian kadota figs are pale green, the calmyrna of Smyrna are yellow and large, French bellons are purple with red pulp, and the figs of Marseilles—yellow-white with white pulp—are simply too good to be true.

In ancient Greece, fig leaves were wrapped about fish before they were baked. Later many Mediterranean countries used them to wrap small birds.

The Phoenicians, it is said, first brought figs to France. Now the French use them with duck, the same way they use peaches, and make a medicinal drink of dried figs called *figuette*.

In Sardinia, figs are stuffed into large woodcocks or partridges, along with fresh white cheese and chopped mushrooms. Then the birds are wrapped in pork fat and fig leaves and baked over myrtle and juniper sticks. The dish is served with a purée of chestnuts, and is alleged by those who have tasted it to be divine.

The Italians, too, are great connoisseurs of figs. In Sicily, there are a great number of fig desserts: fig ice cream, *buccelato* pastry stuffed with figs, and *cucidati* fig cookies. In Calabria, *crocette* figs are half roasted, then stuffed with fennel seeds and almonds, then roasted again. *Pestringolo* is the name of an Italian fig cake, and in Apulia there is a specialty called *fichi ripieni,* in which large moist figs are stuffed with almond slivers, chopped walnuts, and candied fruits, baked, weighted, then sprinkled with liqueur and confectioners' sugar mixed with cinnamon.

In southern Italy, there's a confection of large dried figs stuffed with a toasted almond and a small amount of diced candied orange peel. The figs are baked, rolled in melted chocolate, and served when they are cool. In Portugal, it's not uncommon to be served figs with an after-dinner glass of port. Ground almonds and grated chocolate are blended and stuffed into the fruit, which are then baked and allowed to cool.

The Italians love to serve prosciutto rolled about halves of peeled ripe figs as an elegant and chic antipasto. In Malta, fresh green figs are halved, peeled, sprinkled with sugar and liqueur, baked until they've caramelized, and then served cold with thick fresh cream.

The Syrians are famous for their fig jam, and through all the Middle East, too, there's a presentation of lamb stuffed with raisins, dates, and figs.

Frittura di Fichi Ruspoli
Hot fried figs (Italy)

SERVES 4

  8 fresh firm black figs, peeled
½ cup dark rum
⅓ cup all-purpose flour
½ cup water
   Olive oil for frying

1. Soak the figs in rum for 1 hour, turning them often.

2. In a shallow bowl, slowly stir the flour into the water. Beat until smooth and creamy. Heat enough oil to the depth of ½ inch in a skillet. Dip the figs into the prepared batter, then into the hot fat. Fry until golden brown on both sides. Serve very hot.

Sauté d'Agneau aux Figues Fourrées
Sautéed lamb with stuffed figs (France)

◻

SERVES 4

1½ pounds lamb shoulder, cut into 1½-inch chunks
     Salt
     Freshly ground black pepper
3 tablespoons oil
1 garlic clove, unpeeled
2 dozen dried figs, large and supple, each stuffed with 1 shelled walnut
¼ cup lemon juice

1. Season the lamb with salt and pepper.

2. Heat the oil and gently sauté the pieces of lamb until nicely browned on all sides. Add ½ cup water, the garlic clove, stuffed figs, and half the lemon juice. Cook, covered, at the simmer until the lamb is very tender, about 1½ hours. Readjust the seasoning and stir in more lemon juice to taste. Serve very hot.

DATES

▬

Dates, strictly speaking, are not a Mediterranean fruit. They're grown in the desert, where they're the dominant food. But the desert of North Africa is very near its coast, and dates have become so important to North African cuisine that it's really impossible to leave them out.

Tunisia and Algeria have fabulous dates called *deglat noor* ("fingers of light"), so translucent you can see the pit through the light. On a long trip through the Algerian Sahara, I lived on these dates for two weeks. I bought kilos of the best I could find in the oasis of Bou-Saada, the half moist ones with a sweet nutty smoky flavor.

The Moroccans make a date and orange salad that is a good accompaniment to a spicy *tagine*. They use dates to stuff fish, and often put them into couscous.

The Tunisians stuff dates with apricot jam, walnuts, or lightly toasted pine nuts or pistachios, then dip them in syrup.

All across the Maghreb, cooks make a cake called *makroud,* a semolina-based pastry filled with chopped dates flavored with orange flower water and baked or fried in hot oil.

For the recipes that follow, you can use California dates, which can be very good, especially the *medjool* dates. But I urge you to eat them fresh and plain. I think it will be a revelation.

Jwarich
Date candies (Tunisia)

Toasted nuts and softened dates are formed into small marble-size cocoa-dusted balls. These accompany a cup of tea with a few pine nuts floating on top.

MAKES 2 DOZEN

- ½ pound dates, pitted and chopped
- 1 tablespoon clarified butter
- ¼ pound (⅔ cup) mixed whole almonds and hazelnuts
  Enough cocoa for rolling the candies, about 2 tablespoons

1. Preheat the oven to 325 degrees.

2. In a small saucepan, cook the dates with 1 tablespoon each of water and butter over low heat, crushing the mixture with a spoon until it becomes soft and glossy. Set aside to cool.

3. Blanch the almonds and remove their skins. Skin the hazelnuts. Spread the nuts out on a flat pan and toast in the oven until golden brown, about 10 minutes. Allow the nuts to cool completely.

4. Combine the nuts and dates in a food processor and process until well blended and smooth. Shape into little balls the size of marbles and roll them in cocoa. Place in paper cups and serve with tea or coffee.

Tagine bi Temar

Lamb and date tagine *(Morocco)*

SERVES 4

2 tablespoons olive oil
2½ pounds lamb shoulder, trimmed of excess fat and cut into 1½-inch chunks
Salt
¼ teaspoon turmeric
¼ teaspoon ground ginger
½ teaspoon freshly ground black pepper
¼ teaspoon finely chopped garlic
¾ cup finely chopped onion
6 fresh coriander sprigs
¾ to 1 cup pitted dates
Cayenne
¼ teaspoon ground cinnamon

1. Heat the olive oil in a large heavy casserole and lightly brown the meat on all sides. Add salt, spices, and garlic. Toss with the meat and cook over low heat for 5 to 10 minutes. Add the onion, coriander sprigs, and 2 cups water. Bring to the boil and simmer, covered, for 1½ hours (adding more water if necessary), or until the meat is very tender.

2. Preheat the oven to highest setting.

3. Spread the meat in one layer in an ovenproof serving dish. Place the dates in between the meat. Remove the coriander sprigs from the cooking liquid. Correct the seasoning, adding cayenne to taste. The sauce must be spicy. Pour the sauce over the meat and sprinkle with ground cinnamon. Set on the highest shelf of the oven and bake, uncovered, until the dates become crusty—about 15 minutes. Serve hot.

Salata Letchine

Date and orange salad (Morocco)

SERVES 4 TO 6

- 1 head romaine lettuce
- 3 navel or temple oranges
- 2 tablespoons lemon juice
- 2 tablespoons sugar
- Pinch of salt
- Ground cinnamon
- 2 tablespoons orange juice
- 1 tablespoon orange flower water
- 3/4 cup chopped dates
- 1/4 cup chopped blanched toasted almonds

1. Wash the lettuce after discarding the coarse outer leaves. Separate the tender leaves one by one. Drain, pat dry, shred, and place in a salad bowl. Keep chilled.

2. Peel the oranges and separate into sections. Mix the lemon juice, sugar, salt, 1/2 teaspoon cinnamon, orange juice, and orange flower water in a small mixing bowl.

3. Just before serving, pour most of the dressing over the lettuce and toss. Arrange the orange sections overlapping around the edges. Top with the dates and the almonds. Dribble over the remaining dressing and dust with a little cinnamon. Serve at once.

PEACHES

═══

Marmelade de Pêches
Peach jam (France)

◻

This recipe, from Elizabeth David's *French Provincial Cooking,* is wonderful, and my absolutely favorite preserve. This is not an adaptation. I give her recipe exactly as she wrote it herself.

When I do it I use 15 pounds of peaches, which is just right for my 5½-quart preserving pan.

"Immerse the fruit in boiling water for a minute and then gently skin them. Extract the stones by pressing firmly with your finger on the stalk end. Cut the peaches in halves. Weigh them. For each pound measure ¾ pound of preserving or loaf sugar [granulated sugar] and ⅛ pint [5 tablespoons] of water. Put sugar and water into a preserving pan and bring to the boil. Put in the peaches, and when the sugar has once more come to the boil turn the flame low, and leave them very gently cooking, only just moving, for ¼ hour. Remove from the fire and leave until the next day, when the jam is to be boiled as before, very gently, for ½ hour. If the syrup sets when poured on a plate, the jam is cooked. If it is still too thin, remove the fruit, pack it carefully in jars, and continue cooking the syrup until it does set. Skim it when cool, pour it over the fruit, to fill the jars; tie down when cold. A dozen average size peaches will make sufficient preserve to fill two 1-pound jars.

"This method makes a rather extravagant but very delicious preserve. Unfortunately it tends to form a skin of mold within a very short time, but this does not affect the rest of the jam, some of which I have kept for well over a year, even in a damp house."

Vin de Pêches

White wine flavored with peaches (France)

I once read a recipe in a cookbook for peach wine that called for 120 peach leaves. Thinking that most people probably don't have a peach tree, but nevertheless deserved to drink peach wine, I devised this recipe, which requires no peach leaves, and only four good fresh Georgia peaches.

I suppose the converse of peach-flavored wine is wine-flavored peach. It's very Mediterranean to dip a piece of fresh peach into a little wine left in the glass.

MAKES 1 QUART

> 4 yellow peaches
> 3 cups good dry white wine
> 2 cinnamon sticks
> 2 cloves
> ½ cup sugar
> ½ cup *eau de vie*, brandy, or vodka

1. Drop the peaches one by one into boiling water for a few seconds; remove the peel and put them in a clean jar. Cover with all the wine. Add the spices, cover the jar, and set in a dark cool place to macerate for 4 days.

2. Strain the wine into an enameled saucepan. Add the sugar. Stir over low heat until the sugar is dissolved. Cool. Stir in the *eau de vie*. Pack in a clean 1-quart bottle and plug tightly. Store in a dark cool place. Chill before serving. The peaches can be stewed for compote.

Pesche Ripiene

Stuffed peaches (Italy)

This recipe calls for yellow peaches, which appear in the market later than the white ones. If they're not ripe when you buy them, you can ripen them at home by storing them wrapped in plastic in a dark place.

(continued)

To facilitate peeling, lower peaches into boiling water for an instant. If the peaches are really ripe, you may be able to peel them simply by rubbing them with the side of a knife.

SERVES 8

8 firm ripe yellow peaches, peeled, halved, and stoned
½ cup shelled walnuts
6 macaroons or 6 whole *amaretti di Saronno*
¼ cup heavy cream
1 egg yolk
2 tablespoons Cognac
1 tablespoon sugar

1. Deepen the hollow in each peach half. Place the peaches hollow side up in a buttered 12-inch baking dish.

2. Preheat the oven to 350 degrees.

3. In an electric blender or food processor, grind the walnuts and the macaroons until crumbly. Combine with cream, egg yolk, Cognac, and sugar. Stuff each hollow with some of the filling. Any excess can be placed between the peach halves. Set in the oven to bake for 20 minutes. Serve warm.

Sangría

Wine punch (Spain)

SERVES 10 TO 12

    1 bottle (about 3¾ cups) red wine
    1 cup fresh orange juice
    1 cup fresh grapefruit juice
    ¼ cup sugar
    2 cups mixed sliced fresh fruit: peaches, apples, melon, strawberries, and
        oranges
    1 quart soda water

Put wine, fruit juices, sugar, and mixed fruit in a large jug or pitcher. Stir until well combined. Chill 2 hours. Dilute with soda water just before serving. Serve over ice, if desired.

GRAPES

There are vineyards in every country bordering the Mediterranean, producing vast quantities of grapes for the innumerable wines that are so necessary to Mediterranean life. From late August to October, beautiful grapes flood the markets, to be eaten raw, used in cooking, for pressing to make wines, or for making an unfermented grape drink called *must*.

In France, they call it *mout de raisin;* in Turkey *sira*. To make it, wash, stem, crush, and sieve ripe white grapes. Allow the juice to stand 24 hours in a glass jug in a cool place, then siphon off the clear juice from the sediment, sieve it through several layers of cheesecloth, and drink within a week, before it ferments.

On the Ionian Islands of Greece, *must* is mixed with boiling cream of wheat, cinnamon, and fresh green grapes to make a custard called *mustalevria*. It's then decorated with nuts and sesame seeds and either eaten fresh or put up in jars.

Granita d'Uva Nera
alla Simonetta
Simonetta's black grape ice (Italy)

This is a recipe refined by my friend Simonetta Ponzone, who worked out the addition of ruby port wine by sniffing every bottle in her immense cabinet of liqueurs after tasting a black grape purée and deciding it needed "a little something."

SERVES 6

> 1 pound black grapes
> 1 cup sugar
> 1/2 cup water
> Juice of 2 lemons
> 1/4 cup ruby port wine
> Small bowl of whipped cream

1. The day before you plan to serve, purée the grapes in a blender and push through a sieve to remove skins and pips.

2. Combine sugar and water in a saucepan and cook, stirring, over medium heat, until the sugar is dissolved. Boil the syrup for 5 minutes. Pour into a mixing bowl and allow to cool; then stir in the grape purée and the lemon juice. Whisk until well blended. Pour into a 6-cup ice cream mold and set in the freezer compartment until the mixture is mushy but set around the rim of the mold. Use an electric beater and beat until smooth. Return to the freezer and freeze overnight.

3. Remove from the freezer, beat again, add the port wine, and refreeze until firm. Turn out onto a serving dish and serve with whipped cream.

Kalawi bil Rimmane

Fresh lamb kidneys with pomegranate sauce (Lebanon)

Kidneys and liver benefit from sweet and sour flavorings. This *mezze* is served hot and can also be a simple lunch dish.

SERVES 8 AS PART OF A MIDDLE EASTERN *MEZZE*

- 1 pound (8) fresh lamb kidneys
- 1 tablespoon vinegar in 2 cups water
- 1 tablespoon olive oil
- ½ tablespoon butter
- 1 teaspoon crushed garlic
-    Salt
-    Freshly ground black pepper
- ½ teaspoon Aleppo pepper
-    Pinch of cinnamon
- 1 teaspoon pomegranate molasses
- ⅓ cup water
- 1 tablespoon chopped parsley
- 2 teaspoons fresh pomegranate seeds (optional)

1. To clean the kidneys, remove the membrane; with a sharp knife, cut the kidneys lengthwise and remove the inner cores. Detach the deeper sections of fat with a pair of small scissors. Soak in acidic water for about 1 hour.

2. About 5 minutes before serving, heat the oil and butter in a large nonstick skillet. Add the kidneys and garlic and sauté very gently until kidneys turn light brown on each side, about 30 seconds a side. Push the kidneys to one side of the skillet. Add spices, pomegranate molasses, and water to the other side of the skillet; tilt and boil briskly for juices to combine. Fold the kidneys into the juices and finish cooking while basting kidneys with the syrupy sauce, about 2 minutes. Serve with a sprinkling of chopped parsley and a few pomegranate seeds.

Variation

Substitute chicken livers for the lamb kidneys. Pierce chicken livers with a fork before frying to keep them from bursting and spattering. You can also use calf's liver.

RAISINS

Raisins are used in Moroccan couscous, and all through Greece and the Middle East in vegetable stuffings, pilafs, and stuffed chickens, kids, and lamb. In Corsica, eels are cooked with raisins, and in the Tunisian town of Sfax, raisins, onions, and *ras el hanout* (a spice mixture of black pepper, roses, long pepper, cinnamon, and cloves) are made into a sauce for salted fish. There is also an interesting Roman dish called *coda all vaccinara*—oxtail stewed with tomatoes, herbs, raisins, pine nuts, and grated cheese.

Canard aux Raisins
Duckling with raisins (France)

This dish is normally made with raisins, but when green grapes are in season the Languedociennes use them instead.

SERVES 3 TO 4

1 4½-pound duckling, ready to cook, with neck and giblets
Salt
Freshly ground black pepper
½ cup chopped carrots
½ cup chopped onion
1 celery rib, chopped
2 thick slices of bacon, diced
1 bay leaf
1 thyme sprig
2 to 3 parsley sprigs
1 tablespoon sugar
¼ pound yellow raisins, soaked in water or Cognac for 30 minutes
½ cup dry white wine
1 cup rich chicken stock
1 lemon

1. Preheat the oven to 350 degrees.

2. Prick the duckling all over with the tines of a fork, rub the skin with salt and pepper, and truss the bird. Spread the neck, giblets, vegetables, bacon, and herbs in the roasting pan. Place the duckling on top and roast in the oven for 1½ hours, or until tender, turning the duck at 20-minute intervals, basting with the pan juices.

3. In a heavy saucepan, cook the sugar with the raisins over low heat, stirring constantly, until golden brown. Set aside.

4. Remove the duck, cover, and keep warm. Pour off all the fat and set the pan over high heat. Pour in the wine and reduce, scraping up all the bits clinging to the pan. Add the stock, bring to the boil, and simmer a few minutes to allow the sauce to reduce slightly. Strain the sauce, pressing down hard on giblets, bacon, and vegetables to extract all their juices. Add the strained sauce to the raisins and reheat, stirring, to blend flavors. Add lemon juice to taste and readjust the seasoning.

5. Carve the duck and arrange on a heated serving dish. Spoon over the raisin sauce and serve at once.

MAIL-ORDER SOURCES

Aleppo pepper
Adriana's Bazaar, Dean & DeLuca, Kalustyan, and Shallah's Importing Co.

Bulgur in all grades
Dean & DeLuca, Kalustyan, and Shallah's Importing Co.

Cascabel peppers
Mo-Hotta Mo-Betta

Couscous
Dean & DeLuca, Kalustyan, and Shallah's Importing Co.

Dried rosebuds
Aphrodisia

Green wheat (frik, freekeh, or freekeh)
Dean & DeLuca, Kalustyan, and Shallah's Importing Co.

Lentils (very small brown lentils)
Italian: Balducci's
Spanish *pardena:* Phipps Ranch

Mediterranean oregano
G. B. Ratto & Co. and The Spice House

Mint leaves (dried)
Dean & DeLuca, Kalustyan, Shallah's Importing Co, and The Spice House

Near East Pepper
Dean & DeLuca

Olives
Peloponnese, and Dean & DeLuca

Paprika (sweet and hot)
Dean & DeLuca, Kalustyan, Paprikas Weiss, G. B. Ratto & Co., Shallah's Importing Co., and The Spice House

Pomegranate molasses (Cortas brand only)
Adriana's Bazaar, Dean & DeLuca, Kalustyan, and Shallah's Importing Co.

Pomegranate molasses
Dean & DeLuca, Kalustyan, and Shallah's Importing Co.

Semolina (coarse and fine grain)
Shallah's Importing Co.

Sumac
Adriana's Bazaar, and Shallah's Importing Co.

Tabil
Adriana's Bazaar and The Spice House

Za'atar; za'atar and sumac blends
Plain *za'atar:* Shallah's Importing Co.
Israeli *za'atar* blend: Adriana's Bazaar
Jordanian and Syrian blends: Kalustyan, and Shallah's Importing Co.

ADDRESSES

Adriana's Bazaar
317 West 107th Street
New York, NY 10025
212-316-0820

Aphrodisia
282 Bleecker Street
New York, NY 10014
212-989-6440

Balducci's
42–25 12th St.
Long Island City, NY 11101
800-225-362

Dean & DeLuca
560 Broadway
New York, NY 10012
800-221-7714

Kalustyan
123 Lexington Avenue
New York, NY 10016
212-685-3451

Mo-Hotta, Mo-Betta
P.O. Box 4136
San Luis Obispo, CA 93403
800-462-3220

Paprikas Weiss
1572 Second Avenue
New York, NY 10028
212-288-6117

Peloponnese
2227 Poplar Street
Oakland, CA 94607
510-547-7356

Phipps Ranch
P.O. Box 349
Pescadero, CA 94060
415-879-0787

G. B. Ratto & Co.
821 Washington Street
Oakland, CA 94607
800-228-3515 (California);
    800-324-3483 (rest of United States)

Shallah's Middle Eastern Importing Co.
290 White Street
Danbury, CT 06810
203-743-4181

The Spice House Ltd.
1031 N. Old World Third Street
Milwaukee, WI 53203
414-272-0977

Sultan's Delight
59–88th Street
Brooklyn, NY 11209
718-745-2121
718-745-2563 (fax)

BIBLIOGRAPHY

Arab Information Office. A *Collection of Arab Recipes*. Washington, D.C.: 1972.

Bernaudeau, A. *La Cuisine tunisienne d'ommok Sannafa*. Tunis: Imprimerie Saliba, 1937.

Boni, Ada. *Italian Regional Cooking*. New York: E. P. Dutton, 1969.

Courtine, Robert J. La *Vrai Cuisine française*. Paris: 1953.

David, Elizabeth. *A Book of Mediterranean Food*. Baltimore: Penguin Books, 1966.

———. *French Country Cooking*. Baltimore: Penguin Books, 1944.

———. *French Provincial Cooking*. Baltimore: Penguin Books, 1969.

———. *Italian Food*. Baltimore: Penguin Books, 1969.

Davidson, Alan. *Mediterranean Seafood*. Baltimore: Penguin Books, 1972.

Dumay, Raymond. *Guide du gastronome en Espagne*. Paris: 1970.

Eren, Neset. *The Art of Turkish Cooking*. Garden City: Doubleday, 1969.

Escudier, Jean-Noël and Peta Fuller. *The Wonderful Food of Provence*. Boston: Houghton Mifflin, 1968.

Ferhi, Youcef. *Grandes Recettes de la cuisine algerienne*. Paris: 1957.

Francesconi, Jeanne Carola. *La cucina napoletana*. Naples: 1965.

Giobbi, Edward. *Italian Family Cooking*. New York: Random House, 1971.

Gosetti della Salda, Anna. *Le ricette regionali Italiane*. Milan: 1967.

Herrera, Ana Maria. *Manual de cocina*. Madrid: 1960.

Kaak, Zeineb. *La Soufra ou l'art de préparer la veritable cuisine tunisienne*. Tunis: Société tunisienne de diffusion, 1976.

Karsenty, Irene and Lucienne. *Le Livre de la cuisine pied noir*. Paris: 1969.

Khawam, Rene R. *La Cuisine arabe*. Paris: 1970.

Kouki, Mohammed. *Poissons Mediterranées*. Tunis: n.d.

———. *Cuisine et patisserie tunisiennes*. Tunis: Actuel Editions, 1987.

Landry, Robert. *Les Soleils de la cuisine*. Paris: 1967.

Markovic, Spasenija-Pata. *Yugoslav Cookbook*. Belgrade: 1966.

Montagné, Prosper. *Larousse gastronomique*. Translated by Nina Freud, et al. New York: Crown, 1961.

Passmore, Jackie. *The Encyclopedia of Asian Food and Cooking*. New York: Hearst Books, 1991.

Pepe, Antonietta. *Le ricette della mia cucina pugliese*. Florence: Edizioni del Riccio. 1991.

Perl, Lila. *Rice, Spice and Bitter Oranges*. New York: World Publishing, 1967.

Pomiane, Edouard de. *Cooking with Pomiane*. Translated by P. Benton. London: 1962.

Rayess, George. *The Art of Lebanese Cooking*. Beirut: Librairie du Liban, 1966.

Roden, Claudia. *A Book of Middle Eastern Food*. New York: Alfred A. Knopf, 1974.

Root, Waverley. *The Food of France*. New York: Alfred A. Knopf, 1958

———. *The Food of Italy*. New York: Atheneum, 1971.

Ruspoli, Mario. *Petit Bréviaire de la cuisine*. Paris: 1975.

Tarhan Bookstore. *Turkish Delights*. Ankara: 1958.

Wolfert, Paula. *Couscous and Other Good Food from Morocco*. New York: Harper & Row, 1973.

———, ed. *International Home Dining*. New York: CBS, 1971.

Women of St. Paul's Greek Orthodox Church, The. *The Art of Greek Cooking*. Garden City: Doubleday, 1961.

Zeitoun, Edmond. *250 Recettes classiques de cuisine tunisienne*. Paris: Jacques Grancher, 1977.

INDEX TO RECIPES BY
COUNTRY AND COURSE

ITALY

HORS D'OEUVRES

Fava puré e cicorielle (Mashed fava beans with potatoes and chicory—Apulia), 137–138

Fiori di zucca ripiene (Stuffed squash blossoms—Tuscany), 112–113

Frittura di ricotta Pasqualina (Easter ricotta cheese fritters—Tuscany), 250

Insalata Caprese (Tomato, mozzarella, and basil salad—Campania), 84

Insalata di olive verdi (Green olive salad—Apulia), 39

Melanzane alla campagnola (Country-style grilled eggplant—Apulia), 68

Melanzane ripiene (Stuffed eggplant—Apulia), 71

Mozzarella in carroza (Cheese sandwiches), 244

Olive ripiene (Fried stuffed olives—southern Italy), 44

Peperoni arrostiti (Grilled red peppers—southern Italy), 99

Peperoni arrotolati (Yellow pepper "roll-mops" stuffed with pine nuts, golden raisins, and anchovies—Apulia), 99

Pomodori ripiene alla calabrese (Stuffed tomatoes in the style of Calabria), 82

Spinaci con parmigiana (Spinach with Parmesan cheese), 246

"Tiella" di patate e cozze (Apulian casserole of potatoes, rice, and mussels), 179–181

SAUCES

Burro rosso (Red butter sauce—Piedmont), 142

Pesto (Ligurian basil sauce from Nervi), 187–188

BEANS AND PASTA

Acqua cotta di maremma (Tuscan vegetable soup with olive oil and sage), 220

Fagioli con caviale (White beans with caviar—Rome), 117

Fagioli con tonno (White beans with tuna—Tuscany), 118

Orecchiette con patate e rucola ("Little ears" pasta with potatoes and arugula—Apulia), 143

Panzarotti (Fried stuffed ravioli with tomato-cheese sauce—Naples), 140–141

Pasta con mollica di pane (Pasta with bread crumbs—Sicily), 147

Pasta e ceci (Pasta and chick-peas—Tuscany), 120–121

Spaghetti alla puttanesca (Spaghetti with olive sauce—Naples), 48–49

FISH, POULTRY, AND MEAT

Totani arrosto (Roast squid with garlic, tomato, and rosemary), 21–22

Pollo tonnato (Poached chicken with tuna fish sauce), 28–29

Anitra con lenticchie (Braised duck with lentils), 133–134

Palombacci alla perugina (Wood pigeons or squabs with polenta—Perugia), 55–56

Fegato di vitello con foglie di lauro (Calf's liver with laurel leaves), 190–191

Costata di manzo alla romana (Rib steaks in the style of Rome), 216–217

DESSERTS

Frittura di fichi Ruspoli (Hot fried figs—Tuscany), 283

Granita d'uva nera alla Simonetta (Simonetta's black grape ice), 292

Pesche ripiene (Stuffed peaches—Liguria), 289–290

Soufflé dolce di amaretti (Almond macaroon soufflé), 263

SPAIN AND PORTUGAL

HORS D'OEUVRES

Gambas al ajillo (Shrimp in garlic sauce), 13

EGYPT, ISRAEL, LEBANON, AND SYRIA

HORS D'OEUVRES

Baba ghanoush (Eggplant dip with sesame seed paste), 73

Fattoush (Lebanese parsley and bread salad), 228

Hummus bi taheeni (Puréed chick peas with sesame seed paste), 119

Kalawi bil rimmane (Lamb kidneys with pomegranate sauce—Lebanon), 293

Labni (Fresh cheese made from yogurt), 231

Muhammara (Aleppo-style red pepper and walnut dip), 95

Mavres Elies ke faki (Lentil and black olive dip—Greek community in Cairo), 130–131

Salatit michoteta (Middle Eastern cheese salad), 245

Tabbouleh (Lebanese parsley and bulgur salad), 170

FISH, POULTRY, AND MEAT

Farareej mashwi (Broiled chicken with oil, lemon, and garlic sauce—Egypt), 27

Laban oummo (Lamb cooked in its mother's milk—Lebanon), 239

Oaf sum sum (Fried chicken with sesame seeds—Israel), 221–222

Oaf tapuzim (Chicken with oranges—Israel), 277–278

Samak bi taheeni (Fish fillets baked in sesame seed sauce—Lebanon), 132

Shish barak bi laban (Lebanese lamb dumplings and *kibbe* in yogurt sauce), 235–236

LENTILS, CHICK-PEAS, AND VEGETABLES

Adas be sabanekh (Lentils with spinach and lemon—Lebanon), 132

Fatayer bi sabanekh (Spinach and sumac triangles), 224–225

Mnazzalleh (Middle Eastern eggplant, tomatoes, and chick-peas), 90–91

INDEX